MIND AS HEALER,
MIND AS SLAYER

KENNETH R. PELLETIER

MIND AS HEALER, MIND AS SLAYER

A HOLISTIC APPROACH TO PREVENTING STRESS DISORDERS

FOREWORD BY O. CARL SIMONTON AND
STEPHANIE MATTHEWS SIMONTON

A DELTA BOOK

A DELTA BOOK

Published by
Dell Publishing Co., Inc.
1 Dag Hammarskjold Plaza
New York, New York 10017

Grateful acknowledgment is made to the following for permission to use previously published material.

American Cancer Society: excerpt from 1959 address by Dr. Eugene Pendergrass. Reprinted by permission.

American Journal of Clinical Hypnosis: Reprinted by permission from "Autogenic Training" by B. Gorton, Vol. I, No. 3 (January 1959), pp. 31–44. Copyright © 1959 The American Society of Clinical Hypnosis.

Baywood Publishing Company, Inc.: excerpts from "Neurological Substrates of Consciousness: Implications for Psychosomatic Medicine" by Kenneth R. Pelletier. First published in *Journal of Altered States of Consciousness*, Vol. 2, No. 1, 1975. Copyright © 1975 Baywood Publishing Company, Inc.

Pergamon Press, Inc.: social readjustment rating scale first published in *Journal of Psychosomatic Research* 11 (1967), pp. 213–218. Copyright © 1967 Pergamon Press, Inc.

Prentice-Hall, Inc.: excerpts from *Psychological Stress* by M. H. E. Appley and R. Trumbull.

Shasta Abbey: excerpts from *Zen Meditation*, copyright © 1974 by the Zen Mission Society, reprinted with the permission of Shasta Abbey, Mt. Shasta, California.

Drawings by John Ash

An excerpt from this book first appeared in *Psychology Today*

Copyright © 1977 by Kenneth R. Pelletier

Delta ® TM 755118 Dell Publishing Co., Inc.

1) ISBN: 0-385-28646-5 (previously ISBN: 0-440-55592-2)

Published by arrangement with Delacorte Press/Seymour Lawrence

Printed in the United States of America

15   14   13

Mind as Healer, Mind as Slayer
is published by arrangement with
Robert Briggs Associates, San Francisco

Acknowledgments

During the writing of this book, my life and the lives of the people close to me changed a great deal. There are many friends who helped with their encouragement and patience, and I feel great gratitude toward them. Among those people, I wish most of all to thank Joan Lynn Schleicher for persevering in her love and wisdom and remaining my best friend and companion through these many lifetimes; to Arthur M. Young and Ruth Forbes Young, who have been inspirations for living a full life; to Elizabeth Anne Berryhill, who showed me a realm of love and light where a child's heart can remain forever open; to Arthur E. Gladman, M.D., who has taught me so much of the science and art of healing; to O. Carl Simonton, M.D., and Stephanie Matthews-Simonton for our conversations and sharing in the search to alleviate human suffering; and to Robert Briggs, who believed in this book and made it possible to fulfill.

Throughout the last few years, many of my friends and colleagues have sensed and shared the emergence of an age in which the exploration of human consciousness in all its aspects would be restored to full significance. For this invaluable exchange of insights and friendship, I would like to thank David Bresler, Ph.D.; Joseph Campbell; Fritjof Capra, Ph.D.; Stanislav Grof, M.D.; Joan Halifax-Grof, Ph.D.; Gay Gaer Luce, Ph.D.; Jacob Needleman, Ph.D.; Irving Oyle, D.O.; Erik Peper, Ph.D.; Theodore Roszak; C. Norman Shealy, M.D.; Tarthang Tulku, Rinpoche; and R. James Yandell, M.D., Ph.D. Jack Schwarz of the Aletheia Foundation provided great personal guidance and his foundation supported some of the research cited in this book.

As this book was prepared there were physicians and psychologists who gave freely of their time and expertise, and I wish to thank Alyce Green; Elmer E. Green, Ph.D.; Joe Kamiya, Ph.D.; Tod H. Mikuriya, M.D.; Mark J. Rosenberg, M.D.; Martin L. Rossman, M.D.; Norman S. Tresser, M.D.; and Charles L. Yeager, M.D., Ph.D. Finally, the research and preparation of the manuscript were greatly enhanced by Celia Zaentz, who gave so much time and support, and by Anne Breckenridge and Peter Dreyer, who aided in editing. All of these friends and colleagues contributed a great deal and made this book possible. Together we have engaged in a quest to find a deeper meaning to our lives and to practice patience and compassion by acknowledging the highest potential within each individual. For all of us and all of you—may we experience a fulfilling journey.

KENNETH R. PELLETIER

Berkeley, California
April 1976

Contents

Foreword

Over the years, research concerning the relationship between the psyche and the body has produced a vast literature of books, articles, and monographs. Some have elaborated theoretical constructs to explain the psyche's effect on the body; others have dwelt upon the untapped powers of the mind that can be harnessed to aid the body's healing processes. Yet rarely are these two phenomena combined in such a way as to explain their delicate interplay. Only by examining both the psychological factors that predispose one to illness and the mental powers that become available within a person through various means such as biofeedback, meditation, etc., does one begin to understand their complex relationship. In *Mind as Healer, Mind as Slayer*, the author has confronted both issues, as the title suggests, as well as providing extensive coverage of the new stress-reduction techniques.

The introductory chapter is an excellent overview of the role of consciousness and of the mind/body interaction, with a humanistic emphasis on promoting health rather than eliminating disease.

Mind as Healer, Mind as Slayer is broad in scope, and

Part II integrates the vast stress literature into a cohesive and comprehensible psychophysiological model that crosses academic disciplines to explain the body's response to stress. Neuroanatomical, neurophysiological, and immunological research pertinent to the mind/body relationship is reviewed.

In Part III, specific stresses are identified and the author elaborates their role in precipitating illness. Again with the breadth of a multidisciplinary view, he examines stress in our culture from a sociological and anthropological point of view. The role of personality in illness is approached with a delicate balance and humility that comes only from an appreciation of the importance, but as yet unanswered nature, of this question. Specific diseases of our culture are explored, particularly heart disease, malignancy, and high blood pressure.

One of the complaints leveled against books informing the general populace of the effect and importance of stress on an individual's health is that they warn people of the dangers in their life-style without providing adequate solutions. Part IV of *Mind as Healer, Mind as Slayer* provides comprehensive descriptions of the various techniques of stress reduction.

The chapter on meditation covers basic techniques, concepts and misconceptions, and the application of meditation to medicine, as well as the research that has been done in this area. The chapter on autogenic training and visualization presents these processes in very complete and understandable terms. The author shows how autogenic training, visualization, and psychotherapy can be used in conjunction with standard medical treatment of physical diseases, using current work in cancer therapy as a model. Biofeedback is covered next, in an excellent section that describes both the technology and the art involved, with enough case histories to clarify the process for both patients and practitioners.

The author concludes this book most appropriately with

a chapter on holistic medicine, in which he both defines and develops the philosophical considerations underlying the recent explosion of the "New Medicine." Examples of existing holistic programs and a discussion of model design and implementation are woven together in this most pertinent concluding chapter. The bibliography is extensive and comprehensive. Having worked in the past at putting together such a bibliography, we appreciate the amount of work required.

Mind as Healer, Mind as Slayer is written with a sophistication and simplicity that allows it to span the gap between health-care professionals and laymen alike, in their search to understand the meaning of disease in our society. In the course of our own experience in dealing with the emotions and psyche to alter the course of malignancy, our most difficult challenge has been to understand the delicate interplay that occurs between the mind, body, and spirit of a human being. In addition, unless one is fortunate enough to encounter a patient who has a sophisticated education of the research done in the late 1960s and 1970s when the mind/body relationship again raised its head in the scientific realm, those of us who attempt to deliver holistic health care face another difficult task: How do we communicate what we understand about the mind/body/spirit relationship to our patients? It is our belief that this book contains enough information not only to help a health professional change the way he approaches his work, but to help every reader change the course of his life.

O. CARL SIMONTON, M.D.
STEPHANIE MATTHEWS-SIMONTON

Cancer Counseling
and Research Center
Fort Worth, Texas

PART ONE

INTRODUCTION

The Prevention of Stress-related Illness

I

"Stress" is a term used very loosely today. Though it is something we are all aware of, it is very difficult to define. Hans Selye, the great pioneer in psychosomatic medicine, used two definitions, a simple one—"the rate of wear and tear within the body"—and an abstract medical definition which will be explained in detail in Chapter 2: "the state manifested by a specific syndrome which consists of all the nonspecifically induced changes within a biologic system" (Selye, 1956). Stress is an integral element in the biological scheme of any living organism. All living things are designed with innate stress-alarm reactions which enable them to cope effectively with their environments. Without stress, there would be very little constructive activity or positive change. Two of the most basic characteristics of life, self-preservation and procreation, could not be realized without the innate stress mechanisms of all living organisms. Life without the challenges which induce stress responses would be no life at all. Yet for people living in sophisticated, post-industrial Western cultures, the degree of stress has become excessive and deleterious. Modern man has developed a social and economic structure and a sense of time urgency which subject him to more and greater stresses than have been experienced at any other time in human history, and the effect is often devastating. Most individuals feel that they have no choice but to accept these levels of stress as a fixed component of their Western heritage. Many regard highly competitive society, with its pressure to accomplish more and more in less and less time, as an inescapable life matrix to which they must adapt.

Stress affects both sexes and all ages, and is not confined to the stereotypical harried executive. People in late adolescence or their twenties may be accumulating the effects of stress, effects which may not be overtly manifested until their forties or fifties. Stress disorders are based upon the slow, developmental accumulation of psychological and physical stress responses throughout the life of the individual. Some people are vaguely aware that their personal stress is taking a heavy toll. Others are sure it is, and they have the medical bills to prove it.

Many of the major environmental triggers of stress are readily apparent. Some of the more general stressors include air and noise pollution, overcrowding in urban living situations, deadline pressures on the job, the constant sense of competition in both work and domestic life. These affect nearly everyone. Negative events such as financial difficulties, a death in the family, a violation of the law, and a foreclosure on a loan are also immediately recognizable as severe stressors. Stress may also derive from a particular individual's relationship with a difficult boss, a problem child, a friend, lover or mate. All these factors are relatively easy to identify. However, there is a host of other stressors which affect people equally strongly but which may not be evident on a conscious level. Many of these are reactions to stress which become stressors in their own right. Among these are a sense of free-floating anxiety, inexplicable variations in sleeping or eating patterns, muscle tension or spasms, and numerous other disturbing symptoms.

Not all stress arises in negative circumstances, although

this is a prevalent misconception. Recent experiments demonstrate that events which most people consider positive or pleasurable can be as stress-inducing as those that are considered negative (Holmes and Rahe, 1967). Positive occurrences such as a marriage, a promotion, a desired pregnancy, an outstanding personal achievement, and even a simple vacation can be definite stressors. These events require a person to adapt or change, taxing his physical and mental adaptive mechanisms as much as negative stressors do. Change and rapid adaptation are the common elements in both positive and negative stressors. This great variety of stress triggers in modern life is considered in detail in Chapter 3. Any alteration in an individual's life requires him to adjust, and when these adjustments must be made too frequently in a brief period of time, tension and stress are the results.

It is important to make a vital distinction between injurious and non-injurious stress responses. Obviously, not all stress can or should be avoided. A normal adaptive stress reaction occurs when the source of stress is identifiable and clear. When this particular challenge is met, an individual returns to a level of normal functioning relatively quickly. However, when the source of stress is ambiguous, undefined, or prolonged, or when several sources exist simultaneously, the individual does not return to a normal mental and physiological baseline as rapidly. He or she continues to manifest a potentially damaging stress reaction. This concept is fundamental to the understanding of psychosomatic disorders.

To help clarify this concept, think back to an incident in which your life was actually in danger, such as a car accident or a bad fall. Remember the sense of psychophysiological excitation during this stress reaction. When the danger had passed, you probably "heaved a sigh of relief" as you began to breathe normally and sensed the trembling and exhilaration in your body. That was a normal stress-alarm reaction followed by a relaxation rebound before you return to your normal level of functioning. Now compare that reaction and those sensations to the way you feel at the end of a stressful day. Psychologically they may seem very different, but the neurophysiological pattern is virtually identical. Following a stressful day, your entire physiology is likely to be functioning as though your life were in danger. But since there is actually no immediate threat to your life, there is little opportunity to identify and recover from any particular source of stress. Most of our daily threats are ambiguous, and this prevents a sufficient recovery from the stress-alarm reaction which they induce. This prolonged, unabated stress from which the individual has no respite is primarily responsible for the development of stress-related disorders.

Psychosocial stress in our culture has become a dangerously cumulative phenomenon, unremitting in its effects. One tragic consequence of this is that stress-related psychological and physiological disorders have become the number one social and health problem in the last decade. Stress-induced disorders have long since replaced epidemics of infectious disease as the major medical problem of the post-industrial nations. During recent years, four disorders have become especially prominent in the United States, Western Europe, and Japan. Described as the afflictions of civilization, they are cardiovascular disorders, cancer, arthritis, and respiratory diseases (including bronchitis and emphysema). These four disorders are most prevalent in the sophisticated, developed areas of the world. Diet, environmental contamination, and especially the increased psychosocial stress of post-industrial societies are considered major contributing factors in their development. Since these diseases afflict mainly older people, prolonged life expectancy makes it increasingly urgent that researchers and clinicians find the means of preventing or alleviating them. The fact that these disorders occur more frequently in countries where certain modes of behavior and attitudes are prevalent provides some initial clues, which are thoroughly explored in Chapters 4 and 5.

Most standard medical textbooks attribute anywhere from 50 to 80 percent of all disease to psychosomatic or stress-related origins. Even the most conservative sources classify the following illnesses as psychosomatic: peptic ulcer, mucous colitis, ulcerative colitis, bronchial asthma, atopic dermatitis, urticaria and angioneurotic edema, hay fever, arthritis, Raynaud's disease, hypertension, hyperthyroidism, amenorrhea, enuresis, paroxysmal tachycardia, migraine headache, impotence, general sexual dysfunctions, sleep-onset insomnia, alcoholism, and the whole range of neurotic and psychotic disorders. Professional training is not required to realize how prevalent many of these are among the general population. For instance, an estimated 20 to 25 million people are afflicted with hypertension or high blood pressure in the United States. The effects of hypertension are potentially lethal, since it frequently leads to arteriosclerosis, congestive heart failure, or stroke. At present, the standard form of therapy for hypertension is the prolonged use of hypotensive drugs to reduce blood pressure. Yet, of all those who suffer from hypertension, a disease so dangerous that it is often called "the silent killer," only half have been diagnosed. Of these, only half are being treated, and of those being treated, only half are being treated effectively. Thus, only one-eighth of the hypertensive population of the United States is receiving adequate care (*Hypertension Handbook*, 1974). Another awesome statistic is that 30 million Americans suffer from sleep-onset insomnia. These are the known insomniacs, and practitioners can only estimate how many others there must be who have not sought treatment. Among your friends, how many can you count who have suffered or are suffering from migraine, hypertension, asthma, hay fever, arthritis, peptic ulcer, nervous tension, or alcoholism? If you can answer "None," you have a rare group of friends indeed.

In a society and economic structure with an unprecedented level of inherent stress, it is essential that we develop the means of moderating the effects of stress on our physical and mental well-being. Models of behavior admired in our society contribute to a high level of stress with their emphasis upon ambition, drive, extreme goal orientation, financial success, and the appearance of being constantly busy. However, many people seem to be acknowledging their disillusionment with this model of behavior. More and more individuals in Western societies are looking for other approaches to happiness and contentment. Current interest in countercultural values, anti-consumerism and anti-technology, Eastern religions and meditative techniques, the widespread human-potential and self-exploration movements, and a renewed search for spiritual growth seem to indicate that people are seeking new values to help them cope with the pressures of modern living.

Prevention of disease has become a necessary consideration as medical care becomes increasingly maldistributed, costly, and often disorganized. In *Scientific American* (April 1970), Sidney Garfield, founder of the Kaiser Permanente hospitals, noted four categories of patients: 1) those who go to the doctor and think they are well, and the doctor agrees; 2) those who think they are well but are ill; 3) those who think they are ill, and are; and 4) the "worried well," who are concerned about their health and essentially are seeking reassurance about their health, which is usually excellent. This last group comprises 30 to 50 percent of all patients entering a doctor's office. Since that seminal article, clinicians and medical administrators have raised some critical issues regarding health care in the United States. A recent article summarized these issues as follows:

Does medical care make people sick? That is, does the existence of a dominant care-giving system, particularly in the absence of a non-stigmatizing alternative, encourage all who need some kind of help to "get sick." As NIMH psychologist Ed Kelty puts it, "we've taught people to speak the language of pain," and we have to behave accordingly.

Can you teach people to be well when they're not medically sick anyway? By focusing on what's really ailing patients, and teaching stress management and coping skills, is it possible to provide immediate relief and prevent future medical and emotional problems?

Can finding out who needs what help to build a well-being maintenance system to replace the present disease-oriented medical care system? [*Behavior Today*, June 30, 1975]

Recent research and clinical practice have shown that it is possible to reorient health care toward preventive stress reduction, toward true health maintenance rather than pathology correction. The implications of this for the Health Maintenance Organizations such as Kaiser-Permanente are vast, since prepaid group medical plans can be overburdened by the worried well. A research project is currently underway at Kaiser-Permanente in Santa Clara, California, based upon a plan by Robert Harrington, Chief of Psychiatry. Harrington's project includes a medical and psychological work-up which is oriented toward stress detection. Patients are enrolled in a continuing-education program designed to change their health behavior in a positive direction. Included in this program are college courses focused on such problem areas as critical life stages, effective interpersonal communication, and stress reduction. Educating individuals to recognize and alleviate excessive stress is fundamental to such a system, and the means to do this are beginning to emerge.

For most people, making a radical change in life style is simply not feasible. To eliminate the major sources of stress in one's life might involve a change of job, spouse, friends, environment, philosophy, and goals. Not many people are sufficiently bold, free enough of commitments to others, or willing to forfeit the security of a place in the system. The most common response to stress is to ignore its effect on our minds and bodies, to seek respite in alcohol, tranquilizers, and other socially acceptable drugs such as marijuana, or to alleviate the more serious symptoms with the help of medication—but these are not solutions. As the groundswell of the post-war baby-boom population grows older and reaches the illness-prone ages, the already overtaxed health-care systems are becoming prohibitively expensive and critically short of staff and facilities. With the increasing incidence of stress-related physiological and psychological disorders, it is essential that the healing professions find methods not only of alleviating but of preventing stress diseases before they occur. These methods cannot be ones which require the individual to drop out. They must be incorporated into the existing social and vocational structures as well as into the basic framework of contemporary life styles. It is a primary thesis of this book that this is possible.

Since the Middle Ages, man has been divided into the separate aspects of body, mind, and spirit. Medicine was administered by "bleeders" and "bile examiners" and concerned itself with man's physical welfare. Mind was tended by occult sciences such as magic and alchemy, and the spirit was the province of orthodox religions. Western civilization has historically tended to emphasize the individual parts of man rather than seeing him as an integrated whole. This split is still very evident in the present structure of the healing professions. Physicians are dedicated to the treatment of the body; psychiatrists and psychologists are concerned with healing the mind; and yet a third group, the clergy, is attendant on the soul or spiritual healing. While other societies have created healing rituals which involve the whole person, as well as the whole family and social group, Western healing processes and rituals are characterized by their specialization. Throughout the history of the healing professions two clear polarities are evident. On the one hand, there is a philosophical and clinical orientation which essentially dismisses all psychological factors and considers both disease and health maintenance to be based on purely physical considerations. In contrast and reaction to this is an equally extreme point of view which maintains that all physical illness is the end product of some psychological shortcoming on the part of the individual. Illness ranging from the common cold to terminal disease might indicate a divine judgment inflicted on a person because of misdeeds. This latter concept harkens back to classical Calvinism, which held that any form of physical disease indicated a fall from a state of grace. A slightly more sophisticated version of this Calvinistic approach is evident in many of the contemporary growth movements, which regard pathology as the result of a shortcoming or lack of consciousness or self-awareness on the part of the afflicted individual. Unfortunately, this attitude can become the basis of a social game of "weller than thou" in which insight becomes the latest status symbol. One common misconception in both of these orientations is their separation of mind and body as totally discrete entities.

Neither of these views is sufficient to explain the psychogenesis of disease. If the prevention of pathology is the ultimate goal, then health practitioners and laymen need to begin to consider the whole person. An individual needs to be considered physically, psychologically, and spiritually, with the intent of gaining as much understanding as possible about his relationship with his total environment. This environment includes his family, peers, job situation, living situation, his concept of himself and his role in society, as well as his childhood background, which has formed a significant part of his present character. Fortunately, within the healing professions today a new focus is emerging which is characterized by such a *holistic approach* to the individual. Holistic medicine recognizes the inextricable interaction between the person and his psychosocial environment. Mind and body function as an integrated unit, and health exists when they are in harmony, while illness results when stress and conflict disrupt this process. These approaches are essentially humanistic and reestablish an emphasis upon the patient rather than upon medical technology. Modern medicine has tended to view man as a machine with interchangeable parts, and has developed sophisticated procedures for repairing, removing, or artificially constructing these parts. These are significant achievements, but in the process the healing professions have lost sight of man as a dynamic, integrated, and complex system with marked capacity for self-healing. Consideration of the whole person emphasizes the healing process, the maintenance of health, and the prevention of illness rather than the treatment of established disorders. This concept of holistic, preventive health care is one of the most important innovations in modern medical research and its clinical applications. It is very important to note, however, that this approach is not critical of or antagonistic to contemporary allopathic medicine. There are many instances in which traditional healing practices are a necessity and the advantages of medical technology are unquestionable. Holistic medicine attempts to integrate these advances in biomedical research into a humanistic approach to the individual.

At this point it is important to examine the term "psychosomatic," since it is used throughout this book and has many connotations, depending on the context in which it is used. In traditional medicine, the term "psychosomatic" refers to a disorder which persists in the absence of clearly diagnosed organic pathology. Despite the apparent absence of organic pathology, the symptoms and the individual's complaints of distress continue unabated. In cases such as this, it is quite common for many practitioners to assume that the disorder is nonexistent, imaginary, hypochondriacal, or, in short, has no real basis. These disorders are termed "psychosomatic," which has become synonymous with "imaginary." However, in the context of a holistic model of health care, and in this book, the term "psychosomatic" has quite a different meaning. Here it is used to convey the concept of a fundamental interaction between mind and body which is involved in all diseases and all processes affecting health maintenance. Nikolas Tinbergen, recipient of the 1973 Nobel Prize for Physiology and Medicine, states this concept most succinctly: "The more that is being discovered about psychosomatic diseases, and in general about the extremely complex two-way traffic between the brain and the rest of the body, the more obvious it has become that too rigid a distinction between mind and body is of only limited use to medical science, in fact can be a hindrance to its advance" (Tinbergen, 1974). Several major medical researchers of this century, such as Claude Bernard, Harold G. Wolff, Ivan Pavlov, Walter B. Cannon, Hans Selye, A.T.W. Simeons, and Tinbergen, have created a substantial foundation for a more comprehensive understanding of the relationship between mind and body. One immediate implication is that all disorders are psychosomatic, in the sense that both mind and body are involved in their etiology. Any disorder is created out of a complex interaction of social factors, physical and psychological stress, the personality of the person subjected to these influences, and the inability of the person to adapt adequately to pressures. Once illness is viewed as a complex interaction of these factors, then it is possible to view symptoms as an early indication of excessive strain upon the mind/body system. For the most part, the healing professions have not incorporated such a holistic approach in clinical settings. Practitioners are still trained to specialize, at the expense of understanding the importance of considering the whole psychosocial constitution of an individual as it relates to his disease. Specialization is still the predominant model, despite substantial evidence that mind/body interaction is an essential component in the comprehension of the genesis, aggravation, and duration of virtually all disease. Psychosomatic considerations may be found to apply even to those diseases which are traditionally classified as non-psychosomatic, such as the infectious disorders.

Another important concept which is seen differently by traditional medicine and a holistic, preventive approach is that of "placebo." Placebo is usually defined as "an inactive substance or preparation given to satisfy the patient's symbolic need for drug therapy and used in control studies to determine the efficacy of medicinal substances. Also, a procedure with no intrinsic therapeutic value, performed for such purposes" (*Dorland's Illustrated Medical Dictionary*, 1974). "Placebo" has come to connote any aspect of the healing process which cannot be attributed to a physical or pharmacological effect. Included in this category are the patient's volition, doctor-patient interaction, lifestyle changes, and a host of other variables which are essential features of a holistic model. Disdain for "placebo effects" is not justified even in traditional medicine, since the existence of curative placebo effects is well substantiated in the treatment of a wide variety of diseases ranging from hay fever to rheumatoid arthritis (Beecher, 1955). Writing in the *Journal of the American Medical Association*, Herbert Benson and Mark D. Epstein of Harvard Medical School noted, "Patient and physician attitudes that create a sound doctor-patient relationship contribute to the production of the placebo effect. The placebo effect in most instances enhances the well-being of the patient, and this is an essential aspect of medicine. . . . More emphasis on the potency of the placebo and its positive effects is needed" (Benson and Epstein, 1975). Other types of placebo effects can be seen when the patient becomes an active participant in the healing process. As long as "placebo" remains a pejorative term, clinicians and researchers will continue to ignore the subtle and complex factors which enhance healing. Serious consideration of placebo effects would require the coordinated efforts of researchers in such divergent areas as anthropology and molecular biology. A holistic model of health care would do a great deal to further such research.

Development of a model of holistic health care would offer the opportunity for increased cooperation among many disciplines, in order to sort out the environmental, social, psychological, and biological factors in the genesis of disease and in the maintenance of health. As Tinbergen has stated, ". . . more attention to the body as a whole and to the unity of body and mind could substantially enrich the field of medical research . . . and ultimately help us understand what psychosocial stress is doing to us. It is stress in the widest sense, the inadequacy of our adjustability, that will become perhaps the most important disruptive influence in our society" (Tinbergen, 1974). The precise process by which excessive stress induces illness is quite clearly defined in some of the most prevalent stress diseases, but it is not well understood in the case of many others. It is evident that consciously or unconsciously perceived stressors alter neurophysiological activity, endocrine and immunological balance, blood supply and pressure, respiration rate and pattern, and digestive processes. These factors are well documented in books such as Hans Selye's *Stress of Life*, Walter B. Cannon's *Wisdom of the Body*, and A.T.W. Simeons's *Man's Presumptuous Brain*. Often the physiological changes resulting from stress are subtle, and individuals are not aware of these fluctuations much of the time. Whether these stress reactions are recognized or not, they significantly affect a person's resistance to disease, and create damage in their own right.

In its most basic outlines, the psychogenesis of a disorder can be described as follows: An individual is confronted with a stressful situation which is extremely difficult for him (or her) to resolve. This situation becomes overwhelming, and he sees no respite from it. As a result, he makes an unconscious choice which allows him a means of coping with this irresolvable situation. One means of resolution is to develop a psychosomatic disorder, such as a migraine headache, which affects him so severely that he is incapacitated and released from the responsibilities which weigh so heavily upon him. These symptoms allow an individual to remove himself from an untenable situation when he cannot extricate himself by any other means. Anthropologist Gregory Bateson has termed such a predicament a "double-bind situation," in which an individual must choose between two equally unacceptable alternatives while being prevented from expressing his dilemma (Bateson, 1972). His symptom frees him from the necessity of dealing with the more complex and unmanageable stress situation. Now he is ill, and his peers and family modify their expectations and demands upon him accordingly. His illness postpones or perhaps even prevents a confrontation with the underlying problem. Once this course of action is taken and proves successful, there is a tendency on the part of the person to reinitiate the same pattern of behavior in response to future stressors. Unfortunately, the decision leading to the development of disease in response to stress is usually made at an unconscious level, and these patterns may continue far beyond the point at which they are an effective means of dealing with stress.

Inevitably the issue of an individual's role in developing illness leads to the concept of *responsibility*. Discussion of this concept ranges from total dismissal to the esoteric considerations of psychoanalytic jargon. Most often the concept of responsibility is denied, on the naive assumption that no one really wants to become ill. In the vast literature concerning psychological factors in disease onset, the concept of responsibility is frequently overlooked or misinterpreted. In the context of psychosomatic disorders, responsibility denotes that an individual makes a choice concerning how to react under stress. This choice may be positive or negative, but even an expedient positive choice may become dysfunctional when automatically repeated over time. According to this hypothesis, disorders may be the result of the person's attempt to create a healthy response to crisis and stress. Unfortunately, the attempt to find this solution may result in a process which locks a person into a pattern which can be labeled psychotic behavior or disease (Pelletier and Garfield, 1976). When these unconsciously acquired, dysfunctional ways of relating to a stress situation are prolonged, they may lead to increased stress overload rather than stress alleviation. At that point they can create the preconditions for the development of more severe psychosomatic disorders.

This pattern is illustrated by the case of a young physician who was admitted to a psychosomatic-medicine clinic with the presenting symptoms of extreme muscular tension in the neck, back, and buttocks. Pain from this tension had become so great that the patient was unable to sit down on anything other than a very soft cushion. After a period of therapy involving clinical biofeedback, it became evident that during the process of breathing the physician would thrust his shoulders forward just prior to exhalation and thrust them back immediately before inhalation. This bellows motion created a great deal of unnecessary tension in his back muscles, which radiated upward into the neck muscles and downward into the buttocks and quadriceps. In the course of therapy the patient became aware of his unusual manner of breathing, and remembered that at age fourteen he had been punched in the stomach by his father and tried to recover his breath by flexing his shoulders in this bellowslike fashion. Under the circumstances, the maneuver worked very well. However, after the incident and into adulthood, every time the young man was under stress he would automatically shift into the bellows breathing pattern, and the results were deleterious. This manner of breathing no longer produced the desired end of helping him catch his breath and ultimately relax; the effect was just the opposite. This behavior contributed to his anxiety by increasing the tension in the muscles of his back, and what was once a perfectly functional response had become chronically dysfunctional. In effect, an expedient positive choice became an increasingly negative behavior, leading to extreme tension. In therapy the young physician came to realize his responsibility, and in a relatively short period of time was able to rectify the dysfunctional way of breathing by substituting a normal respiration pattern. Detecting and rectifying dysfunctional patterns is an integral aspect of holistic medicine.

Since cases like this one are quite common, any comprehensive therapy for the alleviation of psychosomatic disorders must detect these unconscious dysfunctional systems and provide the patient with alternative modes of behavior. In the case of the physician with severe muscle tension, this dysfunction was relatively easy to diagnose. Unfortunately, the manner in which pathological stress responses manifest themselves is not always so clearly defined or easily corrected. More often than not, stress affects an individual through his autonomic responses and disrupts neurophysiological reactions, endocrine functions, and involuntary musculature.

Attempts to link specific stresses with specific disorders in a linear fashion are likely to be counterproductive. Psychosomatic disorders involve a complex interaction of mind, body, and environment and require a systems or holistic approach. A psychosomatic disorder such as cardiovascular disease, asthma, or arthritis cannot be understood in a simplistic cause and effect manner. Many psychotherapeutic disciplines rely entirely upon insight as a means of rectifying a problem. But merely providing an individual with insight concerning the genesis of such disorders is not necessarily sufficient to enable him to alleviate them. Even after the patient is made aware of the sources of stress in his life and the behavior patterns which lie at the root of the problem, there is still a process to go through in order to shed the dysfunctional mode of behavior and learn a new one. What is very rarely explained to psychosomatic patients is the connection between behavior, attitudes, and the autonomic neurophysiological functions. People need to understand and sense this connection before they can learn specific skills to help them alleviate stress. Once they can come to recognize when they are under extreme stress and to sensitize themselves to its effects on subtle functions of their bodies, they can develop effective methods of stress reduction. Practicing stress-reduction techniques such as meditation and biofeedback is a great step forward in the prevention of psychosomatic disease. Teaching people meditative skills which they can apply to their stress situations and readily integrate into their daily schedules is one of the greatest challenges in the field of holistic preventive medicine.

One of the real limitations of the healing professions today in dealing with psychosomatic disorders is that there is much more information available concerning pathology and disease than there is on health and health maintenance. Most research and clinical efforts focus on the correction of existing pathology. Usually the medical model of disease is that of infection or trauma, in which there is a single cause for a diagnosed disorder. However, if a disorder results from several nonspecific stressors, then researchers need to consider what Hans Selye has termed a "general adaptation syndrome" (Selye, 1956). This syndrome involves a variety of psychological, neurological, and endocrinological factors, and is detailed in the next chapter. Despite advances in diagnosis and in the identification and etiology of organic diseases, very little progress has been made in the area of health maintenance. Research energies have been uniformly directed toward pathology and remediation. This is a dangerously shortsighted approach at a point in our history when many of the infectious diseases which plagued humanity for centuries are now nearly under control. Ironically, the more insidious diseases resulting from an overload of social and environmental stress are increasing in Western societies and exacting a huge toll in human life each year. Attempts to curb the incidence of psychosomatic disease through traditional medical methods are likely to be ineffective, since their alleviation requires the adoption of a new paradigm of mind/body interaction that is oriented toward health.

Present therapeutic interventions in psychosomatic disorders are far from encouraging. Treatment of the hypertensive patients usually involves one or a combination of drugs to regulate blood pressure. Unfortunately, the side effects of these drugs can be more disturbing than the disorders themselves. Their cost and the necessity of continued pharmacological dependence for extended periods of time make chemotherapy a rather unsatisfactory way of dealing with such a prevalent problem. For the common disorder of simple nervous tension, an alarming number of tranquilizers and barbiturates are prescribed each year. A recent review of tranquilizer use was conducted with 400 pharmacies in the United States. Results indicated that 144 million new prescriptions were written each year for psychotropic drugs, including antidepressants and minor and major tranquilizers. Over half of these prescriptions were for diazepam (Valium) and chlordiazepoxide (Librium). If this rate of increase is sustained, according to psychiatrist Barry Blackwell, "We can predict that with the arrival of the millennium, in 2000 the whole of America will be taking tranquilizers" (Blackwell, 1975). Millions of Americans are virtually on drug maintenance for the alleviation of nervous tension and spend a great part of their waking activity in a sedated state. Tranquilizers are of major concern, since "a review of psychotropic drug use reveals that minor tranquilizers are the drugs most often prescribed in general medical practice" (Blackwell, 1975). These drugs are used mainly for regulating symptoms of anxiety or depression or accompanying physical disorders. Despite this pattern, a national survey of popular attitudes toward tranquilizers indicated that most Americans believed they were effective, but many felt reluctant to take them, for reasons related to maintaining independence from medications (Mannheimer et al., 1973). According to Blackwell, these patterns suggest overuse in the prescribing practices of physicians, since patient attitudes reflect a conservative attitude toward the use of minor tranquilizers. In addition, Blackwell hypothesizes that the observed efficacy of these medications may be due to the interaction between patient and physician during discussions about the effects of the psychotropic agents. Patients seen in general practice with minor emotional difficulties display a response to a placebo of around 50 percent in various drug studies, compared to an active drug response of about 75 percent (Wheatley, 1972). Both research evidence and patient attitudes indicate that chemotherapy with psychotropic agents needs to be evaluated to discover to what extent psychosocial influences are responsible for the observed effects. Other means of alleviating stress-induced anxiety may provide an alternative which restores rather than impairs the individual's sense of personal efficacy. Prevention of stress-induced anxiety would be a first step in alleviating overuse of psychotropic agents by laymen and physicians.

Despite the present shortcomings of our health-care system, there is a sufficient body of information available to form the basis of an effective model of preventive health care. This information can be conveyed to individuals to help them maintain health and minimize the probability of developing a serious psychosomatic disorder. Preventive medicine needs to be based upon education of both practitioner and layman. Although much of what will be covered in this book relates to the correction of existing pathology, the main goal is to present and develop a number of practical methods designed to help the individual maintain a state of health and abort the onset of psychogenic disease. Rising costs and overburdened facilities make this a critical time for the country's health-care system. Education in preventive health-care techniques is not only a logical approach to the situation but an urgent necessity.

Educating people in preventive health care is not a simple undertaking. For many individuals it entails major reevaluation of attitudes, and changes in habits which are simply taken for granted. Most people believe that they are thoroughly knowledgeable about four of life's basic functions:

eating, breathing, sexual activity, and relaxation. It is assumed that these functions are automatic and that any deviation from the familiar norms is incorrect or pathological. Working with stress disorders, it becomes immediately evident that this is inaccurate, and that serious dysfunctions frequently occur in people's eating, breathing, sexual, and relaxation habits, many of them resulting from unconscious choices. As one example, many people suffer from gastro-intestinal ailments, such as problems of elimination or stomach disorders. Dysfunctional eating behavior is partially the result of stress and its effects on the digestive processes, since inadequate digestion may result from blood shifting away from the stomach under stressful conditions. Stress-induced high hydrochloric-acid levels in the stomach produce severe indigestion and may eventually lead to ulcers. Chronic diarrhea may result from the natural tendency to eliminate under stress. There is also a marked tendency for individuals to regard such perfectly normal stress reactions as abnormal, which aggravates rather than alleviates the stress. Such reactions are an essential aspect in the genesis of psychosomatic disorders. Neuropsychiatrist A.T.W. Simeons has written an excellent book, entitled *Man's Presumptuous Brain*, which analyzes this process of psychosomatic onset. He has noted,

> When these once normal and vitally important reactions to fear do reach his conscious awareness, he interprets them as something abnormal and regards them as afflictions . . . These now largely useless reactions, and their misinterpretation as signs of disease, produce a new—this time conscious—state of alarm: the dread of disease . . . It is in this way that the vicious cycles which cause psychosomatic disease become established [Simeons, 1961].

Details of this process are fundamental in understanding the psychogenesis of disease, and are fully explained in the next chapter.

Sexual dysfunction is also widespread in contemporary society, and it is evident from reading articles in the popular press that it has become a national preoccupation. Stress is certainly a major factor in the onset of sexual disorders, including impotence, non-orgasm, and frigidity. Breathing is another basic function which often becomes dysfunctional. Under stress, an individual's breathing becomes shallow and irregular. Since the person is not breathing deeply and regularly, the supply of oxygen which the blood obtains in the lungs is reduced. Very few people take time to improve their breathing habits by practicing deep breathing in a systematic fashion. If proper breathing is practiced regularly, it eventually becomes natural and aids in relaxation. However, many people continue to believe that they know all that is required about breathing functions under discussion. There is a great deal of dysfunctional response among the general population in one or more of these four critical areas. Learning new habits in the practice of these functions is an excellent way to start building a model of preventive health care. Unfortunately, the very fact that most people consider themselves to be knowledgeable in these areas is the reason that it is difficult to alter dysfunctional patterns.

Attitudes toward relaxation are the most naive of all. Many individuals assume that collapsing in front of the TV, working in the garden, spending a quiet afternoon with a book, and working out on the tennis court are effective means of relaxing and reducing stress. But in all these activities and the many others which are used for relaxation, a person can still maintain both the mental anxiety and the neurophysiological functioning characteristic of prolonged, unabated stress. Deep relaxation induces physiological changes which are quite marked and definitely stress-reducing. How relaxation techniques can be learned and the manner in which they work to reduce stress are discussed in Chapters 6 and 7. Meditative practices can affect all forms of the basic functions we have just mentioned, including relaxation. They often involve concentration upon a single external image, an internal sound, or upon a constant biological function, such as respiration, heart rate, or sexual activity. What is essential to each practice is that a particular activity be conducted in a regular manner with prolonged and focused attention. Meditation is not a passive process but a means of allowing an individual to enter into daily activity relatively free of neurotic distractions. For now, the main point is that meditative relaxation is not a spontaneously occurring state that prevails in the absence of stress. Meditation and relaxation require as much diligent practice as any other skill, and must be learned and practiced in order to be effective.

Another challenge in the practice of preventive medicine is the pronounced tendency for people to ignore or misinterpret physiological cues. Many individuals behave as though they are anesthetized from the neck down and seldom take the time to listen to the wisdom of the body. Stress is so unremitting for many people that they don't even recognize it any more, and this lack of sensitivity can be cumulatively dangerous. When we ignore the signs of stress, we are conditioning ourselves to support more of a stress overload rather than seeking means of alleviating it. Take the instance of a young, middle-management executive who may have had a hectic day and is not feeling sociable. On this particular day he has to remain in the city for a cocktail party for some clients of his firm. At the party he meets an important client for whom he has developed an unusual dislike. Despite this unpleasant situation, the executive must be engaging due to the social circumstances and the business relationship. While the two men exchange amenities, the executive may notice that his stomach is knotting uncomfortably. This concerns him, since a growling stomach is something of a social embarrassment, but it does not occur to him to ask why his stomach is secreting excess acid. This individual is under stress, and his body is reacting by shifting blood away from his stomach, with the resultant subjective feeling of emptiness and loss of appetite. At the time he may assume that his stomach problem is independent of the situation and due to one of a variety of more acceptable reasons. Fear of embarrassment contributes to the amount of stress the executive experiences and further aggravates the problem. Unfortunately, too many individuals function in precisely this manner for many hours each day from early adolescence through adulthood. Until they begin to understand the language of their own body, they will not be able to protect themselves from excessive stress and the onset of psychosomatic disorders. Identifying stressors and sensitizing ourselves to crucial bodily cues are important means to the initiation of preventive health care. To be successful, this approach necessitates some major changes in the attitudes and behavior of those who adopt it. In Chapter 3 there are guidelines concerning these signs of stress and practices designed to sensitize the individual to cues which indicate psychosocial stress. Profound discontinuities and splits between mind and body are clearly evidenced in psychosomatic disorders, but are not an inevitable state of being. Integrating mind and body is a more formidable and yet fulfilling task.

To accomplish this without guidance would be difficult, but a number of new therapies described in Part Four apply a holistic model of treatment to stress disorders. Some of the techniques, such as meditation, are ancient. Others, such as biofeedback, are quite new, with great potential for alleviating psychosomatic disease. Meditative techniques, including autogenic training, progressive relaxation, various types of classical meditation, yoga, and clinical biofeedback, are teaching people to adjust to stress on a number of different levels. Primarily, they instruct individuals in deep relaxation, which can be invaluable in the tumultuous, continually stressing circumstances which surround most people. As noted earlier, meditative relaxation does not necessarily occur spontaneously and needs to be learned. Its neurophysiological characteristics and effects are vastly different from what is achieved by means of alcohol or tranquilizers. Patients with problems ranging from cardiovascular disorders to ulcers and allergies are advised constantly by their physicians to relax, but they are seldom instructed in how to relax. Few individuals realize that meditative relaxation involves effort and practice. Our national understanding of the concept of meditative relaxation is quite confused at the moment, and it is hoped that this book will clarify some of this confusion.

Perhaps the most important accomplishment of the meditative therapies such as autogenic training, progressive relaxation, and especially clinical biofeedback is that they teach people to exercise control over their autonomic or involuntary physiological functions. Autonomic control, or voluntary control of the involuntary nervous system, was considered to be categorically impossible only a decade ago. Establishing voluntary regulation of a biological function involves the use of internal, psychological states. According to psychophysiologist Elmer E. Green: "In actuality there is no such thing as training in brain wave control, there is training only in the elicitation of certain subjective states . . . what are detected and manipulated (in some as yet unknown way) are subjective feelings, focus of attention, and thought processes" (Green, Green, and Walters, 1970). Through these processes, patients learn each day to regulate heart rate, blood pressure, brain-wave activity, skin temperature, involuntary-muscle contractions, and numerous other autonomic functions. Based upon recent research in neurology and psychophysiology, the clinical application of these methods has emerged as a potent means of alleviating a wide range of psychosomatic disorders.

Since all the research and popular literature uses the term "control," in such references as "the voluntary control of autonomic functions," it is important to clarify the definition of "control" as it is used here. A more accurate description for what occurs in these systems might be "the harmonious integration of voluntary and autonomic processes," since the regulation of autonomic functions is established only by surrendering all efforts to control them. This paradoxical situation is most analogous to passive concentration, passive volition, or the Zen Buddhist concept of *mushin* or the no-mind, and "control" is a most inappropriate description of the actual phenomenological experiences. Western man seems to be suffering from a split between his psychological and physiological processes, which he assumes can be remedied by the mind's assuming control over the body. Unfortunately, the very cause of the split is a profound distrust of unconscious or autonomic processes, and this distrust cannot be alleviated by means of control. It is a mistaken assumption that Western man must control the unconscious; what is needed is a more harmonious integration of these functions. Harvard University psychiatrist Andrew Weil recognizes this difficulty: "The problem is not to learn to control the autonomic nervous system; the problem is simply to open the channels between the conscious and the unconscious minds" (Weil, 1973). This issue is more tangible than theoretical, since all of the meditative relaxation procedures support the observation that control needs to be relinquished during autonomic regulation. Therefore, the definition of "control" denotes an act of allowing communications between psychological and physiological processes in order for a more harmonious integration to occur. In that way, an individual can learn to make more subtle discriminations in his psychophysiological reactions and begin to act accordingly.

Quite often, voluntary regulation of internal states enables patients to alleviate the symptoms of their psychogenic disorder through their own efforts, without external intervention in the form of medication or surgery. While voluntary control of internal states has only just begun to be applied to the prevention and treatment of disease, even at this time it is a potentially revolutionary force in the future of preventive health care. It has been demonstrated to be an inducement for many patients to reevaluate their life styles and attitudes. Techniques of self-regulation have the effect of returning to the individual a sense of efficacy and control over his own life and health. Loss of this feeling of efficacy can be one of the most insidious effects of excessive stress. When physical disorders begin to afflict the individual, he frequently feels helpless and hopeless, with no options for rectifying his life. In his unconscious mind he may associate his physical disorder with his psychological and emotional state, but he is not able to initiate actions to interrupt the downward spiral of psychosomatic disorders. Stress has weakened his psychological resistance, and perhaps his immunological response as well. Once he regains a sense of his own volition he can avoid being incapacitated. He begins to realize that this self-regulation extends to all areas of his life and that he can channel his life style in a more positive direction.

This concept of individual volition is essential to holistic medicine. Much of human behavior can be accounted for by genetic endowment, physical factors, unconscious choices, and environmental conditions, but a simplistic reduction of all human behavior so as to exclude volition does not seem valid according to empirical and phenomenological observation. Because of the recognized importance of volition, an increased emphasis is now being placed upon the patient as an active and responsible participant in the healing process rather than a passive victim of either the disease or the treatment. One of the key questions in the new therapies and in the prevention and alleviation of psychosomatic disorders is to what extent the treatment is capable of mobilizing an individual patient's volition. Throughout the history of healing, practitioners have puzzled about the seemingly inexplicable recovery of morbidly ill patients and the sudden morbidity of patients who should have fully recovered. Among the subtle but potent influences are unspoken changes in the patient's psychological outlook, through which he exercises a volitional control over the progress of his disease and over health maintenance. Just

as psychogenic factors play a considerable part in the etiology and duration of illness, so they may profoundly influence healing and sometimes swing the balance between
life and death. Arnold A. Hutschnecker's book *The Will to
Live* and the visualization methods of radiologist O. Carl
Simonton with cancer patients underscores the vital part
that an individual's will can play in the course of any disease. Even in the course of a terminal illness, individuals
will have unanticipated periods of spontaneous recovery
when they deeply desire to live. Often their desire is to
experience a significant life event, such as the birth of a
grandchild.

Our medical vocabulary contains a whole range of terms
to describe the unexpected results of spontaneous remission
from severe illness. Patients may emerge from illness with
increased rather than impaired functioning, but the cause
of these inexplicable cures is little understood. Whatever
else may contribute to such healing, it seems certain that
one critical area to explore is the relationship between the
psychological predisposition of the individual to recover
and its effect upon his actual recovery. Evidenced in all of
these instances is one common factor—the capacity of the
mind to play a vital part in healing or slaying the individual.

The stress-reduction techniques explored in Part Four
all involve the mobilization of an individual's volition. In
certain instances this volition takes an active form, such
as in making changes in behavior patterns, modifying attitudes toward social and environmental conditions, or de-
ciding to adhere to the practice of meditative techniques.
In other situations volition acts passively, as in the subtle
autonomic learning processes taught in biofeedback, in
which too active a striving on the part of the individual may
actually inhibit his progress. One of the most important
benefits of clinical biofeedback practice is that once the
patient realizes he can control autonomic functions, his
will to combat his disease and work to maintain a state of
health seems to become revitalized. Gaining control over

one specific involuntary function can encourage a person to exercise self-direction in other areas of his life which relate to his health and psychological outlook. It is important to note that these adjustments and changes can be accomplished within the framework of the individual's social and job commitments and do not necessarily require a total upheaval or revolution in life style.

The importance of recognizing and altering destructive behavior as a means of maintaining health is gaining greater acceptance within the healing professions. Recent research reveals a clear relationship between certain kinds of behavior and a predisposition on the part of individuals manifesting that behavior to develop a particular psychogenic disease. There is an extensive body of research indicating that there are specific personality types which predispose an individual to develop a particular type of psychosomatic disorder. Among the most comprehensive research to date on this problem is that of Meyer Friedman and Ray Rosenman, who are cardiologists at Mount Zion Hospital in San Francisco. After working with numerous cardiovascular patients, they recognized a well-defined behavior pattern among their patients. One clue which helped integrate the components of this pattern was a fortuitous observation on the part of a quizzical upholsterer. Called into the doctors' offices to reupholster the chairs where the patients sat, the craftsman remarked that the seats were worn out only on the edges, as if the patients had literally been sitting on the edge of their seats. Friedman and Rosenman took a cue from this observation and formulated a consistent pattern of personality traits among their patients. Typical heart patients were likely to sit on the edge of their seats and were noted to be impatient, aggressive, extremely goal-oriented, ambitious, restless, and always under time pressure even when supposedly "relaxing." Friedman and Rosenman termed this pattern "Type A" behavior, and reported their research in *Type A Behavior and Your Heart* (1974). In subsequent work, they designed a lengthy interview to determine more of the characteristics of Type A behavior. Personal interviews with the patients clearly supported their initial theory of a correlation between Type A behavior and heart disease. More relaxed individuals were termed Type B, and did not show up in the doctors' offices nearly as often as their Type A counterparts.

There are other personality types which seem to predispose people to particular diseases. These are described in Chapter 4. One profile is the carcinogenic personality, who is very likely to develop cancer when subjected to extreme stress. Another is the migraine-personality characteristic of individuals who develop migraine headaches, tension headaches, or both. Numerous other less-well-developed personality profiles seem to have a correlation with specific disorders. In contrast to these personality types are individuals who are medically ill but actively deny that fact. According to a recent article:

> Researchers have found that high medical utilization is closely associated with psychosocial stress. Whether there is a cause-effect relationship, it's a safe bet that the traditional medical model . . . hasn't responded to psychological and social needs. Researchers have also made some discoveries about another type of person, the medically sick man or woman who doesn't feel sick. They have the following characteristics: an anticipation of the future; caution about making changes when under stress; and an ability to maintain personal satisfaction despite life changes [*Behavior Today*, June 30, 1975].

It appears that such individuals may be ill with any number of disorders but are adept at denial in dealing with stress and its attendant disruptive influence on health. Psychogenic factors in the onset or denial of psychosomatic disorders cannot be fully evaluated or understood until further research is conducted concerning personality and its role in health and illness.

Given the identification of these personality traits, which have been known in standard psychological literature for over thirty years, the central problem still remains: How can these psychosomatic disorders be prevented? It is one matter to identify the psychosocial factors in illness, but quite another to formulate effective means by which these disorders can be alleviated or prevented altogether. Despite the extensive literature linking psychological and physical factors in disease, the methods of altering these influences remain virtually unexplored. Some recent innovations in holistic medicine are promising.

One of the most important approaches is the regulation of the autonomic nervous system by clinical biofeedback to correct malfunctions in muscle activity, blood pressure, heart rate, and the electrical activity of the brain. Research by Elmer E. Green and myself with adept meditators such as Jack Schwarz and Swami Rama indicates that individuals can also learn to regulate such bodily functions as pain and bleeding. These and many other new methodologies provide the means of creating a new medicine based on health maintenance.

At the same time that researchers and clinicians strive toward stress alleviation, it is of utmost importance to remember that not all stress can or should be eliminated. An elevated level of neurophysiological activity during exercise or transient crisis is not synonymous with chronic unabated stress. Individual development requires a variety of stimulation, and a sedentary, carefree life style does not mean health. Periods of illness, stress, or crisis in a person's life can be times of profound personal transformation. Such occurrences offer an individual and those about him the opportunity for major life changes. In a very real sense, a breakdown can be a breakthrough (Laing, 1969; Perry,

1962). Both physical and psychological illness are potentially regenerative rather than inherently degenerative. In his early writings, C. G. Jung noted that primitive people interpreted illness not as a weakness of the conscious mind but rather an inordinate strength of the unconscious mind in the process of transforming an individual from one stage of life to another. Symptoms may be an indication of an individual's attempt to undergo a profound self-healing process which may be disrupted rather than enhanced by chemotherapy. Reduction of the excessive and potentially lethal aspects of this transition is a desirable goal, but does not mean reducing the individual to a state of complacent lethargy.

Perhaps the most essential feature of holistic systems of healing is the profound alteration required in an individual's belief system. Once an individual adopts the concept that he is an active and responsible participant in the process of self-healing, he is no longer the passive victim of a disease or the passive recipient of a cure. In modern sciences, ranging from the neurophysiology of consciousness to quantum physics, it has become evident that the structure of personal belief systems concerning the nature of the self and the universe governs experience (Musès and Young, 1972). Inherent in any system of belief is a self-fulfilling prophecy: what is expected ís observed, and what is observed confirms the expectations. Any experience occurring outside this cultural, social, and individual matrix is dismissed (Kiev, 1969). One immediate implication of this principle is that when an individual alters his belief system, he becomes aware of vast new realms of possibility. Paradigms are subject to change, and the pressing need for a more comprehensive interpretation of man and his universe is all around us: in the sorcery of Carlos Castaneda's Don Juan, in the metaphysical implications of quantum physics and consciousness research, and in the applications of meditation and biofeedback in the healing professions.

Among the most fundamental challenges to the present

mechanistic belief system is the concept that consciousness is primary to matter. Science describes an evolutionary progression from inorganic matter to non-conscious entities, such as plants and lower animals, and finally to consciousness in animals and man. Consciousness is said to arise spontaneously when animals achieve a certain complexity of brain structure. This is reminiscent of the medieval theories of spontaneous combustion due to "phlogiston," prior to the discovery of the role of oxygen in combustion. Physical matter is considered to be primary, and consciousness is viewed as an epiphenomenon which arises spontaneously at a certain stage of biological evolution. At best this position is an assumption, and at worst it may be a misconception which impedes innovation.

In all meditative systems, consciousness is regarded as primary. The potential of visualization, hypnosis, dreams, and meditative practices to heal physical disorders requires such a perspective. From a purely materialistic, mechanistic stance, these phenomena are given little credence, since the minute quanta of energy involved are not considered capable of having an effect upon a large system such as the body (Young, 1976). Again, this is a misconception, since engineering and cybernetics have demonstrated that small amounts of energy can be amplified until they have an extensive effect, just as triggering a photoelectric cell can open a large sliding door. According to current neurological theory, the brain is a perfect example of such an amplifier (Eccles, 1970). A minute event such as a thought, image, or emotion can have an overwhelming effect upon the body. It is important to note that these perspectives elicited by a holistic orientation are tentative hypotheses. They must be considered and evaluated to determine if they can yield better results in understanding and alleviating illness and in promoting psychological and physical well-being.

It is far too easy to replace one set of beliefs with others equally as restrictive. It would be totally unfounded to advocate the elimination of surgical procedures and medications and to insist upon a rigid adherence to introspection and organic food. There are countless instances in which traditional healing practices are a necessity. Surgical intervention in circumstances ranging from traumatic injury to appendicitis is indispensable, and chemotherapies for diabetic control have controlled these disorders to a marked degree. However, while medication for high-blood-pressure control may alleviate symptoms or prevent organ damage, it carries side effects, and does not affect underlying problems of stress in the cardiovascular system. In fact, the time when hypertension is first diagnosed may be the time to initiate an examination of a person's life style in order to prevent more severe symptoms or the necessity of a lifelong reliance upon increasingly larger dosages of medication. It is increasingly unlikely that a pharmacological panacea will resolve the fundamental issue of illness and health. Both the benefits and limitations of surgical and chemotherapeutic intervention should be acknowledged.

In all of the literature on stress and stress-related diseases, there is little information concerning methods of avoiding or reducing stress in order to prevent illness. Most research focuses on establishing the psychophysiological link between stress and disease. Researchers and clinicians now need to investigate the means of reducing stress rather than concentrate most of the effort on the disorder that is the end result. This is not a simple task, since stress itself is difficult to identify and individuals are conditioned to ignore its sources and effects. Many people tend to suppress their feelings of stress because the current norm of social behavior is to tolerate extraordinarily high levels of stress. There is a martyrlike quality in this attitude which is not constructive. Extensive programs are needed to reeducate individuals in health maintenance. Individuals must become not only responsible for health maintenance but also active participants in the therapeutic process, aiding the efforts of the doctor when they are ill. Each person should learn to identify the major stressors in his or her life, to know when stress has reached a dangerous level of duration or intensity, how it is affecting him or her physiologically, and, above all, what methods to use to alleviate stress. All this is a radical departure from the present system, under which health care is the province of the professionals until the individual has already developed a severe psychosomatic illness.

Throughout this book, emphasis is upon biofeedback and meditative techniques as primary means of preventing psychosomatic disorders. It is of utmost importance to bear in mind that health maintenance involves many other factors. Genetics, nutrition, familial and environmental factors are all critically important, but are beyond the scope of this book. Primarily, the focus here is upon the neurophysiology of stress and effective means of alleviating destructive levels of stress reactivity. Even if this approach to the psychogenesis of disease serves only to clarify the shortcomings of our present research and clinical practice, it will have served its purpose. There is a great deal more to be discovered concerning the etiology of psychosomatic disorders, and even more to be explored in the area of intervention techniques. As soon as clinicians and laymen expand their attitudes about health maintenance and laymen begin to play an active role in their own healing processes, preventive medicine becomes a reality. In a holistic approach, integrating techniques ranging from ancient meditative systems to twentieth-century biomedical technology, lies a new medicine with an emphasis upon the ability of all individuals to maintain a healing balance within themselves and a harmony with their environment.

PART TWO

THE NATURE OF STRESS

The Psychophysiology
of Stress

2

For centuries, the nature of mind/body interaction has fascinated physicians and philosophers. Inquiry concerning how psychological processes affect health and disease dates back to antiquity, although it has always been controversial. Even today, the precise manner in which a psychological response translates into a physiological one is little understood. As a result, traditional medical practitioners have tended to limit their attention to the purely physical manifestations of disease and to avoid or discount the role of stress and emotions in physical pathology.

There are many theories concerning the nature of stress and stress-related disorders. This chapter considers the psychological, neurophysiological, and biochemical aspects of the stress response, starting with certain basic assumptions. First of all, every individual operates at a level of tolerable non-pathogenic stress, which actually contributes to heightened functioning and performance. This healthy equilibrium can be upset by a wide variety of psychological, physical, and environmental stressors. The resulting imbalance creates a dysfunction in one or more psychological or physiological systems, which then move toward a state of hyper-, occasionally hypo-activation. When this hyper-activity is prolonged, the affected individual becomes more vulnerable to negative life events such as job loss, personal injury, or other traumatic occurrences. Such triggers can precipitate a potentially deleterious level of neurophysiological stress into symptoms signaling the onset of a psychosomatic disorder.

In the pages which follow, we will trace this developmental process from minor, essential stress reactivity to chronic, debilitating pathology. However, the intent is not to dwell on degenerative or psychosomatic disorders. The very fact that stress disorders are developmental and occur only after a relatively long period of time is cause for optimism. If a pathological pattern can be detected early enough, it becomes possible to rectify the pattern and prevent the degenerative progress toward disease. This definition of the process leading to psychosomatic disorders is a necessary first step toward the ultimate goal of formulating the means of prevention.

PSYCHOSOMATIC MEDICINE

Even in the face of great resistance, the view that a patient's psychological state affects his health has persisted and gained credibility. In the nineteenth century, the eminent London physician Daniel Hack Tuke compiled an exhaustive volume titled *Illustrations of the Influence of the Mind upon the Body*, in which he concluded:

> We have seen that the influence of the mind on the body is no transient power; that in health it may exalt sensory functions, or suspend them altogether; excite the nervous system so as to cause the various forms of convulsive action of the voluntary muscles, or repress it so as to render them powerless; may stimulate or paralyze the muscles of organic life, and the processes of Nutrition and Secretion—causing even death; in disease it may restore the functions which it

takes away in health, reinnervating the sensory and motor nerves, exciting healthy vascularity and nervous power, and assisting the vis midicatrix Naturae to throw off disease action or absorb morbid deposits [Tuke, 1884].

Fortunately for the future of medicine, this doctor was not alone in his point of view. Throughout the years, many other practitioners and researchers have adhered to a belief in the importance of psychological factors in disease and have founded the field of psychosomatic medicine. It is an area in which there are still more questions than answers, but as researchers continue to seek out more evidence of the role of emotions in health and illness, it is rapidly becoming one of the most productive lines of inquiry in modern medicine.

Initially, it was through the observations of astute clinicians that the interaction between stress and psychosomatic disorders became apparent. Repeatedly they noted that certain psychological conditions seemed to be associated with specific organic disorders or with the increased severity of the disorders. However, this evidence remained purely impressionistic, no matter how compelling it was. Although a psychological characteristic or event may coincide with the onset or advance of a disorder, it is difficult to prove that it has any effect on the disease process. In fact, the psychological event may simply occur in conjunction with the disease or even be caused by it. Among the many other factors in the physical makeup of the patient and in his life situation, there may be another contributing element which the observer has failed to detect. To establish with certainty that a psychological predisposition or any other single factor is the basis of a disorder, a researcher would have to account for all possible factors in the disease process. The difficulty of establishing an unequivocal cause-and-effect relationship between psychological events and disease makes this a particularly thorny issue in psychosomatic research.

A concept taken from cybernetics provides a more helpful means of understanding the development of psychosomatic disease. This is the concept of the "feedback loop," in which one event triggers another event, which in turn triggers another, and in which any of these can be seen as either cause or effect depending on an arbitrary break in the loop. A feedback-loop system tends to be stable and self-regulatory, but a disruption in the system can be amplified through its effects on other components of the system. Such a system has considerable explanatory power in psychosomatic health or illness. According to Stanford University psychologist Phillip G. Zimbardo, this feedback loop is self-perpetuating and self-amplifying: "Noncognitive feedback becomes an auxiliary input to a closed-loop system which results in spiralling intensity whose terminal state cannot be predicted from knowledge of the initial boundary conditions" (Zimbardo, *Cognitive Control*, 1969). In psychosomatic disorders a subtle change in an individual's mental or physical function can be amplified by other physical or mental factors. Causation is not relevant in such a system, other than as purely philosophical speculation. Systems are only arbitrarily reducible to cause-and-effect relationships, and such reductionism has proven counterproductive in psychosomatic research and clinical practice. In approaching psychosomatic illness or health, it is assumed that a subtle mental or physical factor may have been the precipitating event, but after that event has occurred the entire system is affected and must be treated as a whole to restore equilibrium and health.

One example of how this progression occurs is migraine headache. Migraine may be triggered by a dietary imbalance, psychological stress, various other factors, or an interaction among them. Which comes first becomes academic, since the precipitating incident is rapidly amplified into more severe symptoms. As soon as the individual becomes aware of the pain signifying migraine onset, he experiences increased tension in anticipation of the attack and of its devastating effect on his ability to perform. His increased tension aggravates the pain, which in turn leads to more tension, and so on until the migraine episode becomes severe. Frequently there will be an increase in muscle tension, which can add a tension headache to the migraine.

If such a system produces disorders when moving in a negative direction, then it holds the possibility of inducing health and psychological well-being as it moves in a positive direction. If a negative change can be detected before it begins to do serious damage, then the individual can intervene in the process. He can introduce positive change into the system through the use of stress-reduction techniques. The effects of these are amplified and can terminate the degenerative process. For most people, psychological changes are easier to detect and work on than subtle biochemical or physiological ones. By reestablishing equilibrium, an individual can then move toward a state of heightened rather than impaired functioning.

There are two important points to keep in mind in approaching psychosomatic disorders. One is that stress reactivity, including various physiological changes such as a rise in blood pressure, is perfectly normal. A second observation is that individuals tend to misunderstand these normal physiological reactions. Writing in 1960, neuropsychiatrist A. T. W. Simeons proposed a communications model of psychosomatic disease. Drawing evidence from neurology, paleontology, and anthropology, Simeons asserts that the higher center of the brain, the cortex, has evolved to the point where it now asserts excessive control over the lower centers, the subcortical or diencephalic processes. Simeons points out that modern man is increasingly subject to moral precepts which have no biological basis and that these moral sanctions are purely cortical, i.e., consciously formulated, and have arisen solely out of the cultural environment which man has created. Man has imposed conscious censorship over his more biologically based reactions to stress. This censorship is viewed as a process of misinterpreted communications between cortical and subcortical brain functions rather than an inherent irremedial conflict between conscious and unconscious processes. Briefly, the basic observations of Simeons is as follows:

> Modern man's cortex, having censored the diencephalic reactions at the level of consciousness, is unable to interpret the bodily preparations for flight correctly. His cortex cannot understand that his primitive diencephalon still reacts in the old way to threats which the cortex no longer accepts as such. When these once normal and vitally important reactions to fear do not reach his conscious awareness, he interprets them as something abnormal and regards them as afflictions. He speaks of indigestion when apprehensiveness kills his appetite, and insomnia when fright keeps him awake at night ... The increased heartbeat becomes palpitation, the sudden elimination of waste matter he calls diarrhea, the clenching of his back muscles he calls lumbago, and so forth. It is man's civilization which prevents him from realizing that such bodily reactions may be merely the normal results of diencephalic alarm and the mobilization of those marvelous flight mechanisms to which he owes his existence as a species [Simeons, 1961].

These normal subcortical reactions are interpreted in the cortex as signs of disease which increases the individual's anxiety. In essence, this cycle is the means by which psychosomatic disease becomes established. While the basic instincts of sex, hunger, sleep, and fear are diencephalic, the wide range of human emotions, such as pity, shame, hope and guilt, is considered to be "cortical elaboration" of the more basic instincts.

Most individuals misinterpret or ignore the essential vital signs of normal stress reactivity, and it is this process which can be more destructive than stress itself. Such overreactions are the basis of "slamming doors" or "kicking the cat" after a difficult day at the office. This channeling and focusing of a general state of neurophysiological arousal is the basis of a theory of emotions propounded by Stanley Schacter of Columbia University. Schacter notes:

> Given a state of physiological arousal for which an individual has no immediate explanation, he will "label" this state and describe his feelings in terms of cognitions available to him . . . one might anticipate that precisely the same state of physiological arousal could be labeled "joy" or "fury" or any of a great number of emotional labels, depending on the cognitive aspects of the situation [Schacter, 1964].

Emphasis in Schacter's theory is upon an individual's behavior in a social situation and is not concerned specifically with psychosomatic disease, but it is based upon much the same evidence cited by Simeons. The major point here is that an individual's physiology is ill suited to cope with the extended duration of stress and anxiety common in contemporary society—from which no *physical* escape takes place. While the subcortex reacts to stress by preparing for fight or flight, the individual consciously restrains himself. Immobility is interpreted by the subcortex as insufficient preparation for fight or flight, and the individual experiences mounting tension in a highly destructive cycle. Understanding this cycle is one of the key components in working with psychosomatic disorders.

Social, environmental, and physiological stressors affect a person's capacity to adapt. Each potential source of stress in his life situation becomes an actualized stressor only at the point where it affects his psychological state and is perceived to be stressful. News releases concerning thousands of casualties from a flood are not inherently stressful unless one's close friend or relative is among that number. If the perceived threat is severe, then the reaction involves a complex neurophysiological response. When this stress reaction is chronic or prolonged, it can weaken the body's defenses and either precipitate or predispose the individual to develop psychosomatic disease. In order to define the nature of this stress response and the complex interaction of psychological and physical factors in health and disease, the next sections cover rather technical but extremely important information.

BRAIN FUNCTION AND STRESS

To understand how chronic or prolonged stress can create physical damage, there are two main areas of current medical knowledge that must be examined. First, by what mechanisms do the brain and the neuroendocrine system translate perceived psychological stress into physiological response? Second, what is the exact nature of the response, and how does it affect the body's defenses against disease when it is prolonged? The latter question, along with the most widely accepted models of the psychophysiology of stress, are discussed later in this chapter. For the moment we will focus on how the brain and neuroendocrine system relay the "stress message" throughout the body and marshal the body's innate resources to meet the challenge. Understanding of these processes provides a background for self-education in health maintenance, and encourages increased sensitivity to one's own internal functioning.

Basically, the brain (see Figure 1) is divided into two major components: the *cerebral cortex*, or upper part of the brain, and the *subcortex*, or lower part. Subcortical areas of the brain are concerned with vital bodily functions and comprise the basic control center for the autonomic or involuntary nervous system, which is principally responsible for the physiological activation which occurs during a stress response. In the subcortex, which begins at the brain stem, are located three major structures: 1) the *cerebellum*, which serves as a coordinating center for the timing and integration of bodily movements; 2) the *medulla*

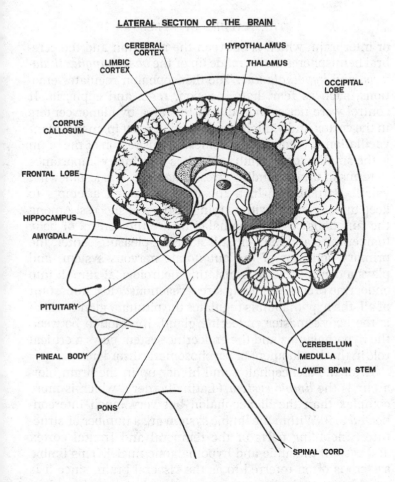

LATERAL SECTION OF THE BRAIN

CEREBRAL CORTEX
LIMBIC CORTEX
HYPOTHALAMUS
THALAMUS
OCCIPITAL LOBE
CORPUS CALLOSUM
FRONTAL LOBE
HIPPOCAMPUS
AMYGDALA
PITUITARY
PINEAL BODY
PONS
CEREBELLUM
MEDULLA
LOWER BRAIN STEM
SPINAL CORD

oblongata, which contains the centers regulating such basic processes as heartbeat, respiration rate, and blood-vessel diameters; and 3) the *pons,* which plays a role in sleep-cycle regulation. The medulla oblongata is the main connection between the brain and the spinal column. It lies between the pons above and the spinal cord below and is directly continuous with the cord.

Moving up the brain stem, the next major component of the subcortex is the diencephalon (Greek: between brain), or interbrain, which is between the midbrain and the cerebral hemispheres and is made up of the *basal ganglia, thalamus*, and *hypothalamus*. The diencephalon regulates emotions, such as fear, hate, passion, rage, and euphoria. If control were not exercised over this area by higher centers in the cortex, individuals would tend to react in an incessant vacillation of emotional extremes. In this region of the brain is the small hypothalamus, which is of primary importance in terms of understanding stress reactivity. It is a somewhat volatile structure, which the cerebral cortex attempts to keep under control, with varying degrees of success. Among the functions of the hypothalamus are the control of body temperature and hunger. It is a strong pleasure center, the primary activator of the autonomic nervous system, and plays a central role in translating neurological stimuli into endocrine processes during stress reactions. Most important of all, the hypothalamus regulates the pituitary gland, which is the body's master endocrine gland. Interaction between the hypothalamus and the endocrine system plays a critical role in the development of psychosomatic disorders.

After the diencephalon and higher up in the brain hierarchy is the *limbic system* (Latin: border), which is more complex than the diencephalon but very much interconnected to it. Within the limbic system are a number of structures, including parts of the temporal and frontal cortex and certain thalamic and hypothalamic nuclei. This limbic system is often referred to as the visceral brain, since it is an old part of the brain in terms of evolution and involves the regulation of basic biological or visceral functions. Primarily it is concerned with various aspects of emotion and behavior, especially with some types of outward expression of emotion. It also connects with the temporal lobes, which are the primary receptive areas for hearing. Surgical intervention into the temporal lobes indicates that they mediate sexual behavior and govern the presence or absence of emotional expression. Lesions in these areas of the brain produce "hallucinations, disordered recognition and memory, disturbance of reality, dream states, clouding of consciousness, sensory fits, and psychomotor epilepsy" (Gardner, 1968). This being the case, it is abundantly clear that there is a definite if undefined relationship between mood states and neurophysiological activity.

A part of the limbic system which is receiving increased attention is the *hippocampus*. This part of the brain is also termed the *rhinencephalon* (Greek: nose brain), since it was thought to be concerned primarily with smell. It is comprised of a primitive type of cortex, archicortex, and electrical stimulation of this area causes widespread convulsive activity in the higher cerebral hemispheres. Researchers have noted the potential of certain smells to evoke vivid imagery. Perhaps the hippocampus's extensive, primitive impact upon higher brain centers is responsible for this phenomenon. This area of the brain requires more research, since it may provide further links in the neurophysiology of consciousness. Just as surgical intervention into the brain produces alterations in psychological functioning, the feedback structure of the brain suggests that psychological factors such as extreme emotional states also affect brain structures.

At the apex of the brain hierarchy is the cerebral cortex, or gray matter, which governs all higher-order abstract functions, such as language, memory, and judgment. Most of these higher-order functions are localized in the frontal, temporal, and parietal lobes of the brain, with the intellectual activities of reading and verbalization further localized in the left frontal lobes and more holistic perceptions in the right frontal areas (Galin, 1974). From the cerebral cortex, control is exercised over the more primitive areas of the brain. One of the connections between cortical and subcortical systems in the brain is the *sensory motor cortex*. This can be visualized by imagining a band approximately one inch wide passing over the top of the head from one ear to the other. It is from here that voluntary muscular movements are initiated. Impulses for movement originate in the sensory motor cortex and travel down pathways to the base of the cortex, through the medulla to the opposite side of the brain, before descending down to the spinal column for transmission to the appropriate muscles. Electrical activity in the sensory motor cortex is of particular interest due to its role in psychomotor epilepsy. When the electrical activity in this area of the brain becomes slowed or desynchronous, an epileptic seizure may ensue. Recently, researchers in biofeedback have discovered that epileptics can learn to recognize the alteration in electrical activity which precedes an attack and then voluntarily reverse the process and prevent a seizure (Sterman, 1974). That this degree of sensitivity can be learned and used effectively is just one illustration of the value of educating people to "listen" to their bodies in order to achieve self-regulation.

Finally, there is one extremely crucial brain structure, called the *reticular activating system*, which has an important bearing on the nature of psychosomatic disorders and psychosomatic interaction. Prior to the 1950s, the prevailing conception of the brain was dualistic. Researchers tended to dichotomize between cortical and subcortical brain functions. Psychologists regarded the two areas as more or less separate entities and categorized human behavior as either cortical or subcortical in nature. Recently, a more innovative model has replaced this dualistic one. The frontal lobes of the cerebral cortex control and regulate many of the functions of the hypothalamus and brain stem through neurological channels *between* the cortex and the subcortex. These connections constitute an elaborate system of interdependent feedback loops. Information is fed into the feedback system via afferent (meaning: leading toward a center) nerve tracts. These afferent tracts conduct impulses directly to the cerebral cortex and also into the brain stem via collateral nerves which become intermingled with a network of nerves called the reticular activating system. Structurally, the reticular system is a "column of cells" occupying the central portions of the midbrain up into the thalamic area. Neurosurgeon J. D. French of UCLA has described the functions of the reticular system as follows:

> It awakens the brain to consciousness and keeps it alert; it directs the traffic of messages in the nervous system; it monitors the myriad stimuli that beat upon our senses, acceping what we need to perceive and rejecting what is irrelevant; it tempers and refines our muscular activity and bodily movements. We can go even further and say that it contributes in an important way to the highest mental processes—the focusing of attention, introspection, and doubtless all forms of reasoning [French, 1957].

The reticular system crosses a number of conventional anatomical boundaries ascribed to the brain and provides the basis for postulating a more integrated relationship between the cortical and subcortical functions. Since the subcortical areas of the brain control autonomic or involuntary nervous functions, the neurological evidence suggests a dialogue between autonomic processes and the centers of thought in the cerebral cortex. The reticular system is one of the best pieces of neurophysiological evidence for a profound interconnection between mind and body.

As French points out, the reticular system serves two basic purposes: 1) a general arousal function in which it activates the cortex to become receptive to visceral stimulation; and 2) the transmission of impulses from the cortex to the musculature and the autonomic nervous system. So the reticular system is a kind of two-way street, carrying messages perceived by the higher awareness centers to the organs and muscles and also relaying stimuli received at the muscular and organic levels up to the cerebral cortex. In this manner, a purely physical stressor can influence the higher thought centers, and a mentally or intellectually perceived stressor can generate neurophysiological responses.

Also, the reticular system appears to be totally responsible for selecting and screening stimuli from the autonomic nervous system prior to their being registered in the cortical or more conscious areas of the brain. There is a vast amount of research literature indicating that subliminally perceived stimuli such as white noise, noxious odors, or gory photographs can have the effect of producing anxiety in a person without that person's knowing why he is anxious (Shevrin, 1973). Some visceral stimuli are never received at a level that can be called conscious awareness, but they are registered subliminally, out of conscious awareness, and they do affect an individual's behavior.

The study of brain neurophysiology, and particularly recent information having to do with the integrative function of the reticular system, has much to teach us about stress and the genesis of psychosomatic disorders. It demonstrates graphically that body and mind function together and cannot be regarded as independent of each other. In the past, researchers have tended to view the nervous system and the higher centers of the brain as an aggregate of separate circuits, each performing a particular task. More recent evidence seems to indicate that the nervous system is a unified, holistic system, with the reticular system performing a primary integrative function. This new model suggests a continuum of mind/body interaction, with the reticular system mediating conscious awareness along that continuum.

Once the interconnectedness between the cortical and subcortical levels of the brain is understood, it is possible to begin to explore the nature of stress reactivity. Consider a stressful event which is initially perceived through the rational, mental faculties of the cortex. Such a stress message is transmitted via intracortical circuits to the lower subcortical areas of the brain, where it initiates a series of neurophysiological reactions.

There are two primary physiological systems which are

activated by stress. One is the autonomic or involuntary nervous system, and the other is the endocrine system. It is at this point that the role of the hypothalamus in the mid-brain becomes increasingly important. This unassuming structure seems to exert decisive control over both the autonomic and endocrine systems. As we have seen, the hypothalamus is closely connected with the brain's limbic structures, which are related to emotional behavior. Several of the limbic structures are involved in determining when the hypothalamus stimulates the endocrine glands and the autonomic nervous system. It is clearly established that there is feedback between the hypothalamus and the cerebral cortex. However, despite the certainty that such feedback exists, it is a highly complex interaction, and only partially understood. Many researchers consider the hypothalamus to be the chief center governing the affective aspect of human life (Chauchard, 1962; Gellhorn and Loofbourrow, 1963). In addition to the multitude of physiological processes the hypothalamus controls or influences, it also contributes to sleep-waking mechanisms and strongly influences cerebrocortical electrical rhythms in company with the brain stem and the reticular system. Of primary importance in terms of stress is the fact that the hypothalamus clearly seems to respond to emotional/psychological stimuli from the limbic system and to intellectually perceived stress stimuli from the cortex. Since it in turn activates the body's principal adaptive systems, the autonomic nervous and endocrine systems, it appears to be a critical link in the chain of events through which psychological stress produces a physical reaction.

To understand what happens when the hypothalamus signals "Stress!" to the body's defense mechanisms, it is necessary to elaborate on the functions of these systems. Once again, much of this is somewhat technical, but it can be of great value to anyone who wishes to understand his own body's behavior.

THE AUTONOMIC NERVOUS SYSTEM

As its name implies, the voluntary nervous system controls the striate or voluntary muscles, which are responsible for posture and all movement initiated as a result of individual volition. The autonomic system is referred to as the involuntary system, since it controls functions, such as gastrointestinal, vascular, and reproductive activities, which are usually thought to act independently of volition. According to classical neurology, conscious control or manipulation of autonomic functions is not possible. As we shall see later, however, modern biofeedback techniques have upset this theory and have demonstrated conclusively that people can learn to control autonomic functions and engage in subtle forms of self-regulation. This discovery is one of the most profound discoveries of contemporary medicine, with far-reaching implications for the future of holistic, preventive health care.

Much of the time, the autonomic system operates via visceral reflexes based on impulses from the viscera and some internal sensory receptors. When these impulses are received by the autonomic system, the appropriate responses to these impulses are transmitted by reflex back to the organs. Autonomic response to visceral reflexes mobilizes the body's resources to deal with stressors. When a person is subjected to a mental or physical stressor, the autonomic nervous system reacts "automatically," initiating a complex series of neurophysiological and biochemical changes in the body.

Two distinct but interdependent parts of the autonomic system are responsible for the regulation of these changes. One is the *sympathetic nervous system* and the other is the *parasympathetic* system. Generally, the sympathetic system tenses and constricts involuntary muscles, such as those of the blood vessels by means of the tiny muscles in their walls, and activates the endocrine system, although it does control dilation in some systems. In contrast, the parasympathetic system generally initiates dilation of the body's smooth muscles and induces a state of relaxation. Autonomic nervous activity generates many physical responses which are reflected in our everyday language. For example, the sympathetic system, with its increased levels of activation, has emotional concomitants which give rise to such expressions as "trembling with fear," "cold feet," "chills ran up and down my spine," "a racing heart." Each of these subjective states is the individual's psychological interpretation of sympathetic nervous activity. During stress, blood tends to shift away from the periphery of the body, such as the hands and feet, and the gastrointestinal tract, toward the head and trunk. Peripheral vascular constriction is the physiological counterpart of such sensations as "cold feet," "clammy hands," "chills," a "knot in the stomach." Our language is replete with such expressions, indicating a sensitivity to overt stress symptoms even though they are frequently ignored. Subjectively, the overall characteristics of excessive sympathetic-nervous-system activity are: dilated pupils; tight throat; a tense neck and upper back, with the shoulders raised up; shallow respiration; accelerated heart and pulse rate; cool, perspiring hands; a locked diaphragm; a rigid pelvis with the genitals numb and the anus tight; flexor muscles in the legs contracted and extensors inhibited. These reactions are virtually identical in man and animals as a preparation to engage in fight-or-flight activity. Each of these symptoms or signals is a clue to the individual that he or she is under stress.

Similarly, the action of the parasympathetic nervous system is also reflected in our language. Generally, the subjective feelings induced by parasympathetic activity are more pleasurable. Among the phrases we commonly use to describe them are "warm-hearted," "my heart goes out to you," "swollen with pride," "flushed with excitement." It is commonly assumed that the sympathetic and parasympathetic systems are mutually inhibitory, but this is not entirely accurate. In fact, the sympathetic system influences or innervates some functions that the parasympathetic does not. Among these are the sweat glands, muscles of the lungs, glucose level of the blood, and basal metabolism. Similarly, the parasympathetic system innervates some structures the sympathetic does not, such as the ciliary muscles of the eye. In other instances the two systems act together to produce an effect. For example, the parasympathetic system produces penis erection and the sympathetic governs ejaculation. There is one vital distinction between the two systems which is central to an understanding of stress responses. Parasympathetic nervous activity is relatively specific in its influences and selective in its activation of the organs it controls. The sympathetic system, although it too may act selectively, usually acts through a general excitation effect upon neural and glandular functions, termed "mass discharge" (Guyton, 1971). By means of this mass-discharge response, large portions of the sympathetic nervous system are stimulated simultaneously. This phenomenon is sometimes referred to as the "fight-or-flight" response, and constitutes the body's most comprehensive reaction to extreme stress. All of the stress responses can be considered as an ergotrophic response (Greek *ergos*: work) to initiate fight-or-flight activity. On the other hand, the movement toward deep relaxation is termed a trophotropic response (Greek *trophos*: nutrition), in which the person receives the nutrition of relaxation. Most recently, this trophotropic response has received increased attention as the "relaxation response" (Benson, Beary, and Carol, 1974), which is fully discussed in Chapter 6. At this point, suffice it to say that when the fight-or-flight response is prolonged, and when an individual cannot take action by fighting or fleeing to release his body from this response, the consequences can be deleterious to health.

ENDOCRINE SYSTEM

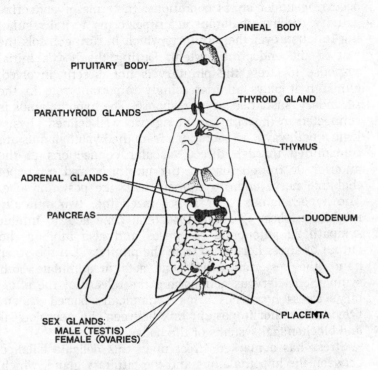

PINEAL BODY

PITUITARY BODY

THYROID GLAND

PARATHYROID GLANDS

THYMUS

ADRENAL GLANDS

PANCREAS

DUODENUM

SEX GLANDS:
MALE (TESTIS)
FEMALE (OVARIES)

PLACENTA

THE ENDOCRINE SYSTEM AND STRESS

When the sympathetic nervous system is activated in response to stress, it works in close coordination with the endocrine system (see Figure 2). Knowledge of the interaction between the central nervous system and the endocrine system is extremely important for an understanding of how a psychological event becomes translated into a physiological reaction. Glands included in the endocrine system are the pituitary, thyroid, parathyroids, islets of Langerhans, adrenals, and gonads. Endocrine-gland functions involve an extremely complex series of feedback loops. Here we will limit the discussion to those reactions occurring under stress conditions. In terms of endocrine activity, the hypothalamus again performs a vital regulating function over the pituitary, which in turn controls the rest of the endocrine system. During the body's initial response to stress the pituitary is not directly involved, although it plays an increasingly important role in the secondary, sustained stress response. The hypothalamus is connected to the pituitary along two well-defined physiological pathways: 1) secretions from the hypothalamus are transmitted through direct vascular connections to the anterior or frontal lobe of the pituitary; and 2) hypothalamic nerve endings connect with the posterior lobe. The hypothalamus itself is organized into two mutually inhibitory lobes. The anterior-lateral zone acts to inhibit sympathetic autonomic responses and also inhibits the output of stress hormones from the pituitary. On the other hand, the posterior-medial zone acts to stimulate both sympathetic nervous actions and the release of the pituitary's stress hormones. This dynamically poised system provides another important link between the neurological and biochemical systems of the body.

Stress has a marked effect upon this delicate balance between the hypothalamus and the pituitary gland, which is located at the base of the brain in the middle of the skull and is approximately the size of a small cherry. This gland is the main center for the regulation of hormones and hormone production and influences the activity of the entire endocrine system. Pituitary hormones discharge into the bloodstream and carry specific messages to the other endocrine glands. Among these substances is vasopressin, a stress-related hormone released from the posterior lobe of the pituitary. Vasopressin contracts the walls of the arteries, thereby raising blood pressure. The pituitary's anterior lobe controls the release of the adrenocorticotrophic hormone (ACTH), the thyrotrophic hormone (TTH), and the gonadotrophic hormones, which affect activity in the genital glands. These secretions serve discrete and selective functions which generally prepare the body to cope with a stressor by temporarily increasing circulation, heart action, basal-metabolism rate, and other processes. In terms of stress response, the most important of all these reactions is the action of the adrenocorticotrophic hormone, ACTH, upon the adrenal glands. At the same time that ACTH is acting on the adrenal cortex, the pituitary is also releasing TTH. This hormone causes the thyroid gland to secrete thyroxine, which affects the rate at which the body consumes fuel, as well as governing physical growth and sexual and mental development. During stress, metabolism in the tissues is intensely stimulated by thyroxine. When this happens, a person sweats easily and feels nervous and shaky; his heart beats too fast, breathing becomes rapid and unusually deep, and he tires quickly. Thyroxine and adrenalin work together closely and produce many of the same subjective effects. High levels of thyroxine apparently make the system more responsive to adrenalin. Generally, adrenalin seems to play a greater role in short-term stress, while thyroxine seems to be present in greater quantities in prolonged stress (McQuade and Aikman, 1974). Needless to say, the state of hyperactivation caused by high levels of thyroxine is not pleasant to endure for long periods of time, and may cause chronic fatigue and even insomnia. It is interesting to note that during a stress response, when the stress hormones ACTH and TTH are released into the bloodstream, the production of sex hormones and somatotrophin, which regulates body growth, actually decreases.

During stress, the initial and swiftest reaction is generated by the sympathetic and parasympathetic components of the autonomic nervous system. Together, these systems attempt to adjust various body functions to meet the stressful situation. The next step in the response, moving from neurological to endocrine reactivity, occurs when the sympathetic system stimulates the production of adrenalin by the adrenal glands. The adrenals, which are located on top of the kidneys, are only one part of the complex endocrine system, but their significance in terms of understanding the relationship between stress and psychosomatic disease is great. Though all the endocrine glands are important in maintaining resistance to disease, the adrenals and the pituitary seem to be the most responsive to information processing during stress. Their functions have been the main focus of attention by researchers in stress and psychosomatic medicine.

To understand the psychophysiological basis of stress and the genesis of psychosomatic disorders, an analysis of adrenal activity is essential. Adrenals have two functionally distinct parts: 1) the outer and larger part is the adrenal cortex; 2) the inner part is the medulla. In the initial stages of a stress response, it is the medulla which is called into action, by stress signals relayed through sympathetic nervous stimuli. In response to these stimuli, the medulla secretes adrenalin (also called epinephrine) and noradrenalin (norepinephrine). Under stress, adrenalin enters the bloodstream and is distributed throughout the body. Adrenalin release, coupled with impulses from the hypothalamus, brings the pituitary and its hormones into play. In turn, these hormones from the "master gland" influence the other endocrine glands and their hormones and thereby regulate somatic defenses and adaptation. Adrenocortical hormones play a vital role in maintaining physiological homeostasis, i.e., the body's normal state of equilibrium when it is functioning in the absence of a stress-alarm response. Although a number of hormones are involved, the secretions of the adrenal cortex can be classed into two groups, which are both stimulated by ACTH. First there are the gluco-corticoids, so called because of their ability to raise blood-sugar levels. These include the hormones cortisone and cortisol, which act to inhibit inflammation and are thus called anti-inflammatory corticoids. Second is the group called mineralo-corticoids, which increase the body's retention of sodium and chloride and decrease levels of potassium. This group includes the hormones deoxycorticosterone and aldosterone, which are called pro-inflammatory corticoids, since they promote inflammation. Knowledge of these cortical hormones is extremely important to an understanding of how stress can cause physiological damage, and is essential to understanding the arthritic disorders discussed in Chapter 5. They are associated more with long-term chronic stress than with immediate acute reactions, and they can do irreparable damage to the kidneys. These hormones also play a major role in controlling the body's immune responses. And, as we shall see later, enhanced or diminished immunological response is a primary factor in determining an individual's state of health or illness.

All of us are familiar with the feeling of a sudden flush of excitation or an "adrenalin rush." This occurs when the adrenal medulla releases its stress hormones and causes the entire body to respond with a jolt and a tremendous surge of energy. Such a reaction sometimes enables people to perform feats of physical strength that they would not normally be able to do, such as when a wife lifts an automobile to save her trapped husband. The whole system enters a state of hyperactivation in which the heart races, body temperature rises, oxygen consumption increases. There are subtle differences in the quality of this fight/flight reaction, which occur as a result of the differential secretions of the adrenals. Two secretions of the adrenal medulla, adrenalin and noradrenalin, serve different purposes, and the proportion in which they are released is controlled in a feedback loop by the hypothalamus through the sympathetic nervous system. Adrenalin acts through the liver and mobilizes glucose into the bloodstream, providing a quick source of energy for cells to metabolize in response to stress. Adrenalin also increases carbohydrate metabolism, dilates the arterials of the heart and skeletal muscles, accelerates heart rate and increases the volume of blood the heart circulates through the body, elevates body temperature, and increases oxygen consumption and carbon-dioxide production. Additionally, it acts to relax the smooth muscles of the gastrointestinal tract while producing constriction of the sphincter muscles, and it dilates the bronchial musculature. Shallow respiration and anus contraction are among the subjective components of this reaction.

In contrast, noradrenalin normally constricts the arterials and raises blood pressure, with much less influence than adrenalin on blood glucose and heart rate (Schildkraut and Kety, 1967). Both adrenalin and noradrenalin cause an increase in circulating free fatty acids. There is a discernible difference between proportions of adrenalin and noradrenalin released from one stress response to another. The reasons why adrenalin is released in one instance and noradrenalin in another are not clearly understood, but many researchers tend to regard adrenalin as the "fear hormone" and noradrenalin as the "anger hormone." In other words, a differentiation that can be clearly classified as psychological in nature seems to be the decisive factor in determining how the adrenal medulla responds.

THE IMMUNE SYSTEM AND STRESS

Potentially, one of the most negative results of excessive levels of stress is the effect on the immune response. Immune-system response constitutes man's principal defense against microorganisms. Once again, there is much uncertainty concerning the precise mechanisms by means of which psychological stress affects immunity, but there is enough evidence of a connection to warrant significant research attention. One of the most innovative researchers into the relationship of stress and immunity, particularly in terms of the role of the immune system in cancer, is George F. Solomon of the Stanford University School of Medicine. Solomon has experienced many of the difficulties confronting researchers in all areas of psychosomatic medicine. In discussing his work, he has noted, ". . . both immune responses and stress-induced physiological changes varied with the species, the genetic constitution and environmental factors, and can be manifested through multiple pathways. Both systems are multifactorial, and their interaction is doubtlessly extremely complex, tending to make the reproducibility of any effect subject to a large range of outside influences. In addition, in both systems there are stabilizing feedback loops" (Amkraut and Solomon, 1975). Nevertheless, Solomon and his colleagues have begun to develop a model of the links between the central nervous system and immunity.

Most of their research to date has focused on surgical intervention into certain areas of the hypothalamus and its effect on the thymus, which plays a central role in the immune response. Capacity to respond to an immunogen is dependent on a functioning thymus, which relies upon impulses from the hypothalamus in order to initiate immune-system activity. Both Solomon and other researchers have demonstrated that destructive lesions in a specific portion of the dorsal hypothalamus depress thymus activity and interfere with the immune response in laboratory rats. Thymus-gland activity governs the endocrine function responsible for the maturation of T-cells, which are of great importance in general surveillance and in antibody production. When parts of the dorsal hypothalamus are cut, thereby affecting thymus functioning, there is suppression of primary antibody responses and prolonged retention of antigens in the blood (Korneva and Khai, 1963). It is significant that those regions of the hypothalamus which are cut, thereby creating the preconditions for a laboratory animal to be predisposed toward disease, are precisely the same regions of the brain which are most reactive to human emotional stress. The thymus itself, through its relationship with the hypothalamus, is also stress responsive, and it plays a major part in the feedback loop regulating the endocrine system. In particular, thymus function affects the production of thyroxine by the thyroid, which speeds metabolism and increases heart rate. When hormonal levels are altered because of stress, one frequent result is often an increase in the blood of corticosteroids in the form of pro- and anti-inflammatory corticoids. When the presence of these in the system is prolonged, an imbalance may result which can seriously interfere with the effectiveness of immunological defenses.

Researchers Marvin Stein, Raul C. Schiavi, and Maria Camerino of the Mount Sinai School of Medicine in New York reported an extensive overview of the "Influence of brain and behavior on the immune system." Their article focuses primarily upon animal research concerning the effect of hypothalamic lesions on the immune processes. They cite numerous studies in which variables such as the stress of electrical shock, noise levels, and overcrowding have been determined to aggravate or enhance an animal's susceptibility to neoplastic disorders and viral infection. Based upon their research, they note that the hypothalamus appears to be the neurophysiological mechanism which mediates the psychosocial influences on immunological reactions. Summarizing their research, they conclude:

> It has been shown experimentally that psychosocial processes influence the susceptibility to some infections, to some neoplastic processes, and to some aspect of humoral and cell-mediated immune responses. These psychosocial effects may be related to hypothalamic activity. Reviewing the mechanisms that may be involved in immune responses indicates that there is no single mediating factor. Various processes may participate, including the autonomic nervous system and neuroendocrine activity [Stein, Schiavi, and Camerino, 1976].

Clearly, research needs to be conducted to determine the precise means by which psychosocial events are translated into neurological and biochemical events in order to formulate a comprehensive model of psychosomatic disorders. Central to this model is the role of stress and its effects upon the immunological system.

Immune system structure can be thought of as comprising three separate limbs: the afferent, central, and efferent. The afferent limb is the first to respond to the introduction of an antigen in the system. This primary response involves three types of immunocompetent cells: 1) the T-cells, which are thymus-derived; 2) the B-cells, or Bursal Equivalent Cells, which initiate the immune response; and 3) macrophages, which have the capacity to engulf foreign particles. The central limb of the immune system is concerned with the sequence of immunization and galvanizes defense mechanisms against the disease process. The extent of immune response to a given antigen, and possibly the nature of its interaction with immunocompetent cells, depends on the number of preexisting T- and B-cells capable of responding specifically to it. In the efferent limb, the T-cells destroy the antigen by direct contact or by secreting toxins, and the immunological response is completed. While the immune response is in general self-limiting, the feedback mechanisms involved are poorly understood. However, it is clear that these mechanisms involve both physiological and psychological factors. This appears to be particularly true in infectious diseases, autoimmune diseases, allergies, and cancer. According to Solomon:

> Stress and emotional distress may influence the function of the immunologic system. Thus, environmental and psychologic factors might in some circumstances be implicated in the pathogenesis of cancer . . . as well as of infectious and of auto-immune diseases, which seem to have an association with states of relative immunologic incompetence. There are considerable data to link personality factors, stress, and particularly, failure of psychologic defenses to the onset and

course of cancer and of infectious and auto-immune diseases [Solomon, 1969].

Immunological response functions adequately under most conditions but is susceptible to stress. It is generally believed that any individual is continuously exposed to antigens which may give rise to such diseases. Usually, the mechanisms of resistance are adequate to prevent the disease process from taking hold. Under normal conditions the body maintains a constant balance between pathogenic events and the immune defense mechanism.

According to Solomon's model, the body's "surveillance" ability is based upon the T-cells' recognizing the new surface antigens on mutant cells. This is the first line of defense against cancer. Minimal weakening of this ability could permit "sneaking through" of tumor cells. Solomon notes, "Thus, marginal suppression of either central or efferent activity by stress-associated events . . . would aid in the progress of the tumor" (Amkraut and Solomon, 1975). It has also been observed that many patients suffering from advanced cancers of various types seemed to have decreased immunity. In some cases, the injection of immunity-enhancing agents such as the tuberculin bacillus Calmette-Guerin (BCG) may reduce tumors.

Stress appears to affect chiefly the efferent and to some extent the afferent limbs of the immune system. Solomon and his colleagues theorize that macrophage activities are probably a major if not the most important target, since they play a significant role in all three limbs of the immunological system. Macrophages are cells which are ultimately responsible for ridding the organism of dead or damaged tumor cells. Stress-induced change in the immune system is generally small, and determines the course of the disease chiefly by shifting the balance between toxic factors and defense mechanisms in the disease process. These relatively small changes in immunological balance can shift the entire system and predispose an individual toward the development of a severe disorder. It is not necessary to detect large changes in the neurophysiological system of an individual in order to account for his increased susceptibility to disease. Changes may be very subtle and difficult to detect, but it is hypothesized that extreme emotional reactivity, induced by stressful life changes, is sufficient to produce dysfunctional activity in the brain, which may in turn disrupt the individual's basic immunological balance.

The immunological system is quite amenable to the standard scientific method of isolating increasingly minute elements for scrutiny. This is a productive but highly limited approach which neglects the multiplicity of factors outside of the immune system which have a clear impact upon its functions. In concluding a recent overview of his work, Solomon notes:

> While information in both immunology and endocrinology is reaching explosive proportions and new facts relevant to these studies are coming to light each day, we do not believe that the study of our problem will be greatly simplified in the near future ... We believe that the solution lies in the evolution of the matrix, which will have to be viewed and studied as one ... [this] will also tend to fix the interrelations between emotions and endocrines on the one hand, and those between endocrines and immunity on the other—subjects which are obviously very difficult to study independently. In other words, relationships that we establish in such a study will give us a three-point fix on stress, endocrines, and the immune system and will strengthen all three disciplines involved, behavioral sciences, neuroendocrinology, and immunology [Amkraut and Solomon, 1975].

Basic immunological research of Solomon and others has strengthened the hypothesis that stress induces small changes in immune mechanisms. Effective interventions may be able to regulate these minor imbalances before they become amplified beyond correction.

THE FIGHT-OR-FLIGHT RESPONSE

To recapitulate the stress model which has evolved so far, it is clear that perceived information produces changes in the central nervous system which can trigger the stress reaction. Psychological stress can initiate hypothalamic discharges and stimulate the pituitary during the secondary, sustained stress response to secrete hormones which in turn stimulate the appropriate endocrine glands. Some of these endocrine secretions are distributed through the bloodstream to the brain, where they further excite the brain or stimulate specific parts of the hypothalamus. This feedback-loop system influences the nature and intensity of the response and the individual's accuracy of perception (Gellhorn and Loofbourrow, 1963). Cortical arousal, hypothalamic activity, muscle tone, sympathetic discharge, and endocrine functions are all closely correlated and in a constant state of dynamic fluctuation. Under most circumstances these fluctuations are oriented toward maintaining homeostasis, and there is a minimum of variation. At other times, when the interaction between mind, body, and environment is disrupted by stressful stimuli, these psychophysiological fluctuations stimulate vigorous activity in the organ systems and marshal the body's defenses to meet the challenge.

If you have managed to follow and bear with the foregoing descriptions of these complex interacting systems, you already have a fairly comprehensive understanding of how the body responds to mental and physical stress. Also, it should be clear to you that if you are subjected to psychological stress, there will be attendant neurophysiological consequences.

Human stress reactivity is an essential psychophysiological process which enables individuals to respond to the multitude of challenges confronted each day. It is one of the body's most sensitive and vital survival systems. There is a basic problem, however, in the way people are designed to respond to stress. Physiologically, man is equipped with much the same systems as animals to cope with stress. But there is an added complication in human reactivity. Information perceived through the higher awareness centers also generates a physical stress response. This information is of a psychological and emotional nature, based upon the individual's perceptions of events in the environment around him. Basically, when human beings are subjected to major stress, they are roused to a fight-or-flight reaction in the same way that animals are. Herein lies the problem: an animal can deal with a threat through fight or flight, but we often cannot. Much of the stress we experience cannot be dealt with by fighting or running away, although our initial inclination may be to do one or the other. In our complex society with its highly refined codes of acceptable behavior, fighting and fleeing are often not considered appropriate reactions to stressful situations. When your boss informs you that you will not receive the raise in salary you expected, you cannot physically assault him, nor can you literally run away from the situation. Therefore, you muster all your resources to respond in a dignified manner and internalize your distress. However, your body is entering into a state of stress preparedness, despite your enforced outward calm. Messages are transmitted throughout the neuroendocrine system which cause significant changes in your biochemistry. When an animal is aroused to fight or flight, a similar biochemical reaction quickly takes place. But once the animal has taken action by fighting or fleeing, its neurophysiological stress response subsides and its body rebounds into a state of deep relaxation and ultimately back toward homeostasis. But human beings may have no socially acceptable action to take.

Since the negative psychological state persists, the physiological stress response also continues. It is under these circumstances, when a stress response is prolonged and unabated, that the biochemical changes associated with stress become potentially detrimental to health.

Our neurophysiological responses for dealing with stress have become anachronistic. Since society dictates that the standard modes of stress-release behavior are unacceptable, and since the nature of our social organization places such an unprecedented amount of stress upon each individual in the society, many of us sustain prolonged stress responses far more frequently than is conducive to health maintenance.

SELYE'S GENERAL ADAPTATION SYNDROME

Precisely what happens during a prolonged and unabated stress response that wreaks so much havoc? Much of the theory on this subject is still speculative, but, due to the work of a few researchers, a body of information is accumulating. Foremost among stress researchers is Hans Selye, an endocrinologist who is Director of the Institute on Experimental Medicine and Surgery at the University of Montreal. In 1956, Selye published *The Stress of Life*, which remains a classic in the field. His research on the adrenal glands and their relationship with the pituitary and other physiological processes laid the groundwork for a great deal of later research on stress. As we pointed out earlier, Selye defines stress as "the state manifested by a specific syndrome which consists of all the nonspecifically induced changes within a biologic system" (Selye, 1956). In other words, stress is manifested as a specific configuration of physiological processes rather than as the processes themselves. This specific series of processes he has termed the General Adaptation Syndrome (G.A.S.). Activation of the G.A.S. may result from any number of different stimuli and is therefore "non-specifically induced." Through the years, Selye has observed that diseases and their particular agents produce response syndromes specific to those diseases and agents. Each disorder produces a pattern of neurophysiological alterations which is characteristic of that particular disease. But, at the same time, the G.A.S. occurs in conjunction with these disorders and is not selective in its manifestation. Selye's work has been aimed at determining the nature of that syndrome and its consequences for health.

Selye's initial work was with laboratory rats, which were subjected to various kinds of extreme stress. He noted four consistent characteristics in the way the rats responded physiologically. There was substantial enlargement of the cortex of the adrenal glands; shrinkage or atrophy of the thymus, spleen, lymph nodes, and other lymphatic structures; an almost total disappearance of eosinophil cells (a kind of white blood cell); and bleeding ulcers in the lining of the stomach or duodenum.

Selye's stress model places heavy emphasis on the role of the pituitary hormone ACTH, which stimulates the adrenal cortex to release its corticoid hormones into the system and initiates general stress reactivity. Recently, researchers have tended to distinguish between two kinds of stress and their respective effects upon the body. First is acute stress, in which the threat is immediate and the need to respond instantaneous. Second is chronic stress, which is prolonged and unabated. Most current investigative work seems to indicate that in acute stress it is the adrenalin and noradrenalin of the adrenal medulla which are called into play. In chronic stress, the role and presence in the blood of corticoids from the adrenal cortex increase and assume more importance. Selye and others regard the kidney as an essential organ in the General Adaptation Syndrome. It regulates the chemical composition and water content of the blood and tissues by virtue of its elimination functions, and it is crucial to the maintenance of homeostasis. When there are large amounts of corticoids in the system for extended periods of time, the blood pressure is raised and the kidneys can be seriously damaged. The pro-inflammatory corticoids can produce kidney disease through raising blood pressure (Selye, 1956). In this manner, a prolonged stress reaction can ultimately lead to severe hypertension due to kidney damage, which in turn aggravates the hypertension. This is another example of a closed-loop feedback effect moving in a negative direction toward an acute psychosomatic disorder. Pro-inflammatory corticoids can also cause tears in the arterial walls, which are then repaired by cholesterol plaques, a type of scar tissue. When a buildup of cholesterol plaques occurs, the heart is subjected to increased stress. Too many plaques constitute what is commonly called "hardening of the arteries" or arteriosclerosis. When arteriosclerosis becomes advanced, it diminishes the supply of blood and oxygen to the heart and can even lead to coronary failure. In addition, it is not unusual for the cholesterol plaques to become detached from the arterial walls and travel through the arteries to the heart. When this occurs, blockage of the heart's major coronary arteries can occur, which may cause part of the heart muscle to die and can again lead to coronary failure. Normally it is the liver which monitors the amount of corticoids in the blood and which acts to reduce their levels when necessary. But during stress the liver's control mechanism is bypassed, and this permits continued high concentrations of corticoids to circulate throughout the body.

Apparently, high levels of corticoids, plus elevated levels of hydrochloric-acid secretion coupled with the action of the sympathetic nervous system, can be responsible for producing gastrointestinal ulcers. These are also characteristic of prolonged G.A.S. reactivity. As early as 1842, the British physician Thomas Curling described acute gastrointestinal ulcers in patients who had extensive skin burns. Again, in 1867 a Viennese surgeon noticed the same phenomenon in patients after major surgical interventions complicated by infection (Selye, 1974). There was no conceivable reason to associate ulcers with the patients' other disorders, but once these lesions were established as characteristic of a nonspecific stress response, their presence in patients with other problems become understandable. Research has shown that in short experiments which produced fright in dogs and monkeys, hydrochloric-acid secretion in the stomach actually decreases. Sustained stress resulted in a reversal of this reaction, and hydrochloric-acid secretion increased substantially. Again, the evidence seems to point to long-term stress as the major protagonist in terms of precipitating disorders.

Selye also includes the reduction in number of eosinophil cells as one of the major components of the G.A.S. These cells are an important part of the body's immune response, since they regulate "serologic immune reactions and allergic hypersensitivity to foreign substances" (Selye, 1956). In essence, they are the body's heroes on white horses, which engulf invading alien forces. Significantly, the numbers of these cells in the blood of cancer patients is often markedly depleted. This observation was one of the first research findings to suggest a link between prolonged stress and weakening of that part of the immunological system responsible for surveillance against cancerous cells. During chronic stress, the fact that eosinophil cells are present in fewer numbers than normal points also to lowered resistance to various types of infectious disease. The microorganisms responsible for infectious disease, which are constantly present in our systems, are normally rendered ineffectual by white blood cells. When there are less of these white cells, we are more vulnerable to microorganisms and the diseases they cause.

Selye's stress model also includes a phenomenon which he terms the Local Adaptation Syndrome (L.A.S.). Part of this syndrome involves inflammation, i.e., swelling, redness, heat, and pain. Inflammation can be caused by any number of agents, such as foreign microorganisms, when we are cut or wounded. Some other inflammatory agents are: allergens, such as dust or pollen; insect bites; the presence of waste products in overexerted muscles, which causes that familiar muscular ache. No matter where in the body the inflammation takes place or what the agent is, the process is much the same. The purpose of inflammation is to isolate the invading agent in order to prevent it from spreading and, once it is isolated, to allow the body's defenses to destroy it by action of the white blood cells and enzymes. Adrenocortical hormones play an important role in inflammation, since some of them promote inflammation while others inhibit it. The Local Adaptation Syndrome appears to link into the G.A.S., for it is the G.A.S. which mobilizes the activity of the adrenocortical hormones. In this way, a purely physical, localized stressor can bring the body's whole stress mechanism into action.

It is important that the pro- and anti-inflammatory corticoids respond appropriately. Inflammation can do serious damage to the body by causing destruction of cells and formation of scar tissue, and by diverting needed resources from other bodily processes. During prolonged stress, when there are large amounts of corticoids in the blood for extended periods, this balance can become upset and abnormal, or inappropriate inflammation can result. For example, allergies are usually characterized by an inflammation of the mucous membranes of the nose, throat, and eyes, and may represent faulty functioning resulting from an overabundance of pro-inflammatory corticoids in the system. Research in this area has offered a possible psychophysiological basis for the observation that allergic reactions are frequently stress-related. Conversely, during prolonged stress an individual might be more prone to infection than usual as a result of a surplus of anti-inflammatory corticoids in his bloodstream, which prevents an essential inflammatory process from taking place. In either instance, stress can induce an inappropriate adaptive response which may become a further source of stress rather than serving as a means of alleviation.

According to Selye, the G.A.S. passes through three phases: alarm, resistance, and exhaustion. The alarm phase is the first and most dramatic response to a stressor. At that point the body's entire stress mechanism is mobilized, and the stressor has a generalized effect on psychophysiological functioning. During the alarm stage, adrenocortical secretions rise sharply. One of the primary tasks of the G.A.S. is to delegate responsibility for dealing with a stressor to the organ or system most capable of handling it, seeking out and calling into action the most appropriate channel of defense. At this point, the resistance state is initiated. During this period, adrenocortical secretions decrease and coping with the stressor becomes the specific job of the particular systems best suited to the task. Resistance to the stressor is high during this phase, but because of the effects of the G.A.S. and the fact that resources are diverted away from other areas, general resistance to disease may be low. During the exhaustion phase, the organ system or process handling the stessor becomes worn out and breaks down. Once again, adrenocortical secretions rise, and the burden is shifted away from the worn-out system and again taken on by the nonspecific response characteristic of the alarm phase.

In effect, this entire process functions to maximize the body's ability to resist the stressor. Even after the exhaustion phase has occurred in one area, the burden may be shifted to another system equally capable of dealing with the situation. This three-phase response does not inevitably lead to psychosomatic illness, and stress reactivity should not be equated with damage or pathology. In fact, stress can be instrumental in stimulating the rejuvenation of cells and tissues. Such artificially induced stressors as bloodletting and electric and chemical shocks, and natural ones such as high fever, may actually excite the body out of an ineffectual response, promote a transference of responsibility for defense to other areas, and stimulate the production of fresh cells to assist in this defense (Selye, 1956). Prolonged stress, however, will wear out the body and lower resistance. When the body fails to adapt or overcome stress, diseases of adaptation are frequently the result. What Selye calls "diseases of adaptation" are simply ordinary diseases which develop as a consequence of the unabated G.A.S. reactivity. Such disorders cannot be attributed to stress alone, but to the fact that the body's attempt to adapt to stress may create physiological conditions which precipitate disorders or predispose an individual toward pathology. When a machine is overworked, the weakest part breaks down first. It is the same with the human body: the weakest link in the chain of vital physiological processes will succumb first. Such factors as heredity, environment, general health habits, behavioral variables, and past illnesses may all play a role in determining whether illness will occur as a result of prolonged stress. Furthermore, these factors will also predispose an individual toward the development of a specific type of disorder which precipitates out of this condition of general stress reactivity. At this point, the most important fact is that generalized, prolonged, and unabated stress places a person in a state of disequilibrium, which increases his susceptibility to a wide range of diseases and disorders.

In defining this potentially pathological state of excessive stress, Selye's research on the psychophysiology of stress is among the most comprehensive to date. It provides us with a clear, scientifically based conceptual framework for understanding the genesis of psychosomatic disease. However, there is one important area in which Selye's stress model is lacking, and this is the least-understood area of stress research. This issue concerns the precise process by which psychosocial stimuli are converted into physiological stress reactions. Previous discussions of brain function help us understand how this conversion takes place. We have seen how information perceived through the senses or through the rational-intellectual cerebrocortical centers in the brain is transmitted to lower brain centers concerned with emotional activity, and then to the hypothalamus, which initiates impulses based on this information to the body's physical stress-response systems. According to Harold G. Wolff, a stress researcher whose work dealt primarily with the relationship between psychosocial events and illness, "Stress becomes the interaction between external environment and organism, with the past experience of the organism as a major factor" (Wolff, 1953). Once this network of information processing is factored into Selye's stress formula, we should have a comprehensive picture of how psychosocial events exert their influence on physiological functioning and how unabated psychological duress can lead to a breakdown of the body's coping processes and result in psychosomatic disease.

A NEUROPHYSIOLOGICAL STRESS PROFILE

Even when we accept all the evidence that points conclusively to a relationship between stress and psychosomatic disease, we are still confronted with many unanswered questions. Stressful situations have different effects upon different people, and this is based upon a large number of variables in the person's emotional and physical makeup, past experience, and the constellation of factors defining his current life situation. In order to predict responses or even understand the derivation of a psychosomatic illness, there is much that needs to be understood about the individual in question. Only a holistic approach can help us predict and prevent psychosomatic disorders. When health professionals devote all their energy and resources to treating disease per se, they may be overlooking many vital factors. Disease may be merely the clearest symptom of a much larger matrix of problems and circumstances. If preventive health care is to become a reality, researchers and clinicians need to view health, disease, and potential vulnerability to disease in a larger context.

At the present time there are a number of opinions concerning the direction of such research and clinical practice. These are aptly summarized by stress researchers Appley and Trumbull:

1. Stress is probably best conceived as a state of the total organism under extenuating circumstances rather than as an event in the environment.

2. A great variety of different environmental conditions is capable of producing a stress state.

3. Different individuals respond to the same conditions in different ways. Some enter rapidly into a stress state, others show increased alertness and apparently improved performance, and still others appear to be "immune" to the stress-producing qualities of the environmental conditions.

4. The same individual may enter into a stress state in response to one presumably stressful condition and not another.

5. Consistent intra-individual but varied inter-individual psycho-biological response patterns occur in stress situations. The notion of a common stress reaction needs to be reassessed.

6. The behaviors resulting from operations intended to induce stress may be the same or different, depending on the context of the situation of its induction.

7. The intensity and the extent of the stress state, and the associated behaviors, may not be readily predicted from a knowledge of the stimulus conditions alone, but require an analysis of underlying motivational patterns and of the context in which the stressor is applied.

8. Temporal factors may determine the significance of a given stressor and thus the intensity and

extent of the stress state and the optimum measurement of effect [Appley and Trumbull, 1967].

Reactivity to stress varies considerably from individual to
individual and from response to response. With the myriad
factors involved, it is extremely difficult to predict circumstances under which stress will lead to a physiological or
psychological disorder.

My own clinical research has been oriented toward the
development of a *neurophysiological stress profile* for a
particular patient. As Selye, Wolff, Simeons, and other
researchers have indicated, excessive stress is likely to be
manifested in a specific physiological system. A neurophysiological stress profile is intended to detect which
system is being most adversely affected by prolonged stress
before more severe symptoms or gross pathology are
evidenced. When a patient is referred to our Psychosomatic
Medicine Center at Gladman Memorial Hospital in Berkeley,
California, he can choose this diagnostic procedure in
addition to a multiphasic examination. Most patients are
referred for specific disorders, including general tension,
migraine, back or post-operative pain, neuromuscular rehabilitation hypertension, cardiac dysfunction, stress management as an adjunct to cancer treatment, as well as the
whole range of psychological disorders. Whatever the presenting symptoms, the person is given a series of tests to
establish a neurophysiological stress profile. Along with a
life-history interview and a psychological profile, the stress
profile is an integral aspect of diagnosis and treatment.

The stress profile is based upon the person's level of
neurophysiological stress reactivity and the effectiveness
of various means of stress reduction. This profile is created
by monitoring multiple neurophysiological indices and
establishing an overall pattern of response (Pelletier and
Peper, 1974; Pelletier, 1975; Pelletier, 1976). Included in
this diagnostic are: an electroencephalograph (EEG) for
brain-wave activity; electromyograph (EMG) for muscle

activity; detection of peripheral temperature in the hands and feet; galvanic skin response (GSR) for noting emotional lability; blood pressure; electrocardiogram (ECG) for heart rate and regularity; and respiration rate as well as respiration pattern. In the course of a one-hour diagnostic session, these indices are monitored while the person engages in normal, stressful, and resting activity. All indices are recorded, and a profile is established for the person in each of these conditions. There is no need to detail this procedure except to point out that each person will tend to manifest a unique pattern or clustering of these measurements. For example, when a particular person is alert and engaged in a complex arithmetic task, the neurophysiological indices will demonstrate a moderate stress response. Then the person is asked to relax as fully as possible and the same indices are recorded again. Using just these two sets of measures for simplicity, it is possible to detect if one or more of these systems are hyper- or hyporeactive when compared to the general profile. For example, a person may exhibit increased EEG and EMG activity during the stressful conditions. Then, in the relaxation condition, only the EMG drops within a normal relaxed range. This may indicate that the individual has a predisposition to maintain psychological anxiety even when physically relaxed. When the comprehensive profile is reviewed, it becomes possible to detect each specific system in which stress reactivity is having an adverse effect. Given this information, the next step is to have the patient learn to regulate this potentially dysfunctional system through biofeedback, meditative, or autogenic techniques.

Any neurophysiological profile is extremely complex, and my research to date is more suggestive of a direction than it is a fixed procedure. However, after five years of clinical research and outcome evaluation, it appears to be quite possible to detect the effects of stress upon a particular system for a particular patient and for that person to alleviate this stress reactivity. The methods of early stress detection can be extended to include monitoring biochemical imbalances, elements in the blood indicating tissue fatigue, respiration-gas analysis, immunological reactivity, and a host of other subtle variables indicating potential areas of stress. These detection systems are an essential prerequisite if we are to evolve truly preventive health-care practices.

Stress Triggers

3

Our advanced technological society is responsible for much of the stress overload from which we suffer. General environmental and social stressors which affect all people to some degree include living and working conditions, increased mobility, and the constant influx of information from mass communications. It is possible that twentieth-century man has designed a social and economic structure which is antipathetic to his health and psychological well-being. If this is so, can an evolutionary change help us adapt in a new version of survival of the fittest? Will the social system regulate itself when it becomes evident that its psychosocial complexity is affecting its members negatively? Or will man take it upon himself to scale down the proliferation of technological progress and concentrate upon a more inner-directed quest to preserve his mental and physical equilibrium?

Whatever changes occur in Western societies in the next decades, however, it will certainly require longer than a generation for social and economic organization to alter sufficiently so that levels of stress in individual members of society will be lowered. An even greater period of time would be necessary for human beings to adapt or evolve to a point where they are physiologically and psychologically capable of tolerating high stress levels without adverse effects. Measures to reduce stress must therefore be taken by each individual.

A necessary first step is a personal appraisal of the sources of stress and their effects. If particular stressors are confronted directly, perhaps the negative consequences can be more readily avoided. When a person recognizes the stressor and knows when it is affecting him, he can utilize stress-reduction techniques to alleviate or abort pathological reactions. Each individual responds differently due to his or her circumstances, as well as physical and emotional makeup, so evaluating the stresses in our lives requires serious self-examination. As you read the discussion which follows of the multitude of stresses to which contemporary man is exposed, be honest in your attempt to analyze the influence of each upon you and upon those with whom you share your life most closely.

As you assess these influences, keep in mind a definition of what stress actually is. Stress is not simply the result of factors that cause you worry, anxiety, or strain. Actually, you are under stress every time you are required to adapt or adjust to personal, social, and environmental influences, positive or negative. Adaptation is necessary all the time, to varying degrees. It is essential to personal development, progress, and simply adjusting to the business of daily life. However, when the amount of adaptation required of you by circumstances in your life becomes excessive, then the resulting stress can become potentially damaging to your health. According to Hans Selye,

> Stress is the non-specific response of the body to any demand made upon it . . . All agents to which we are exposed produce a non-specific increase in the need to perform adaptive functions and thereby to reestablish normalcy. . . . It is immaterial whether the agent or situation we face is pleasant or unpleasant; all that

counts is the intensity of the demand for readjustment
or adaptation [Selye, 1974].

Both positive and negative changes elicit an adaptive
response. It is not just the setbacks in life that require
adaptation. For that reason, recognizing when we are
overstressed and knowing when to practice stress-reduction
techniques can be a subtle and difficult process.

SOCIAL CHANGE

An acute degree of constant change in modern life is the
most common and cumulatively taxing source of stress.
Even events which people regard as normal milestones in
their progress through life are often highly stress-inducing.
This is particularly true if a number of them occur during
a telescoped period of time. These events, such as a marriage, a pregnancy, a job change, or a geographic move,
are referred to as developmental stresses. When too many
of these stimuli occur at once or in rapid succession, the
result is too much pressure on the individual's physical and
mental adaptive mechanism and decision-making processes, and stress is the result.

Adolph Meyer, professor of psychiatry at Johns Hopkins
University, was one of the first to link life events, excessive
stress, and disease when, at the turn of the century, he
began keeping "life charts" on his patients. These sketchy
biographies demonstrated that illnesses tended to happen
at times when clusters of major events occurred in people's
lives within a fairly short period of time. Following up on
this research, Harold G. Wolff made careful notes of the
life circumstances and emotional states surrounding his
patients' illnesses. He also reported on conditions in
central India, where society was undergoing rapid changes.
There was increasing upward mobility for a number of
Indians living in this area. They were relatively affluent,
well nourished, hygienically oriented, educated, and West-
ernized. In the larger communities, their living conditions

were far superior to those of their compatriots living in villages and city ghettos where people were overworked, underfed, uneducated, and not attentive to hygiene. Yet it was among the wealthier Indians that such diseases as diarrhea, ulcerative colitis, neurocirculatory asthenia, and asthma were increasingly prevalent. They were overtaxed by the necessity of adjusting to new values and new circumstances, since they were caught between two social systems and did not find security in either one. Their reactions to this period of excessive change caused them to be tense and anxious, and to exhibit both offensive and defensive protective patterns of behavior. Based upon these observations, Wolff concluded that these people were under constant stress, and that this contributed to their high incidence of psychosomatic disease (Wolff, 1968).

Similarly, Navajo Indians taken from their homes and put onto reservations only a few miles away suffered an appalling increase in mortality from tuberculosis after they had moved (Moorman, 1950). Although the new physical environment was nearly identical to that from which they had come, and circumstances such as food, clothing and hygiene were the same or better, the social disorganization which resulted from the move overburdened the adaptive capacities of many of these Navajos, and they became ill. As still another example of this phenomenon, it is very common for ambitious Indians living in small mountain communities of Peru to move their families to the coast and seek better work and living situations in Lima. These people suffer extreme problems in adapting. They are ethnically different from the Negro, Asiatic, and European population on the coast, and their language is different. Also, the climate, type of work, eating habits, and social organization to which they are exposed are completely new to them. C. A. Seguin, who has conducted comprehensive studies on these Indians, notes that a psychosomatic maladjustment syndrome sets in shortly after the move and severely incapacitates great numbers of these people (cited in Wolff, 1968). Often there is a direct triggering event which precedes the illness and precipitates constant strain. This event might be bad news from the mountain family, trouble with employers or co-workers, breakup of love affairs, being laid off from a job, or any of a number of other such occurrences which push an already overstressed individual into developing a psychosomatic disorder.

Stress levels can rise in periods of economic instability or recession. During a recent economic recession, the medical statistics from the Department of Health, Education and Welfare's Epidemiology Center in Atlanta, Georgia, indicated a marked increase in peptic ulcers, heart attacks, impotence, weight loss, and other psychosomatic disorders. Clinicians have frequently noted that the incidence of psychosomatic disorders among patients is higher as the Dow Jones average moves downward. Loss of a job is a clear source of stress which affects the person's psychological and economic stress level. Recently, Sidney Cobb of the University of Michigan undertook a study of one hundred workers who were about to be fired from a Detroit auto-paint factory (Fier, 1975). His research began six weeks before termination and followed the workers for two years. There was a marked increase in hypertension, peptic ulcers, arthritis, and other psychosomatic disorders among the men. Furthermore, within two months of termination three wives were hospitalized with peptic ulcers, which are unusual among women.

Sources of psychosocial stress may be as obvious as economic instability, or they may be so integrated into a cultural life style as to become invisible. Stress can be induced by such socially acceptable addictions as alcohol, a self-administered tranquilizer, or coffee as a stimulant and antidepressant. According to John F. Greden, a University of Michigan psychiatrist, excessive caffeine intake from coffee breaks and soft drinks can induce behavior disturbances. Symptoms of excessive caffeine are nervousness, insomnia, headache, sweaty palms, and perhaps ulcers

(Greden, 1975). All that is required to produce such severe reactions is approximately 250 mg of caffeine, and one cup of coffee contains 100–150 mg with tea containing 65–75 mg. Based upon clinical observations, Greden indicates that excessive amounts of caffeine can induce "irregular heartbeat, flushing, and, in extremely large dosages, circulatory failure. On the gastrointestinal side . . . nausea, vomiting, diarrhea, stomach pains and even occasionally a peptic ulcer." Withdrawal from excessive caffeine may be equally unpleasant for a few days, since the person may feel irritable, lethargic, and depressed, and have a pronounced headache. Excessive caffeine intake is such an integral aspect of many people's daily activity that its effects may go totally unnoticed as a major source of neurophysiological stress. Reliance upon socially acceptable addictions such as caffeine, alcohol, sleeping medications, aspirin, and laxatives may be an indication of severe underlying stress. Ubiquitous commercials promise quick relief, rather than introspection concerning the fundamental causes. Despite such social support, these panacea methods mask or aggravate rather than alleviate stress reactivity.

When major social change occurs, there is always stress upon individual members of society. Even though such change might be an ongoing phenomenon acting subtly over the years, the individual must deal with the changes as they affect him. New freedoms that resulted from the upheavals of the sixties forced many people to confront new issues and reexamine their values. At all levels of society, people had to adapt to a changing world view. Of course, this kind of social evolution has occurred throughout human history, but communications systems now propagate these ideas and attitudes at an unprecedented rate. For example, the Women's Liberation Movement has received extensive media coverage. As a result, men and women at all levels of society are reinterpreting masculine and feminine roles and their relationships to one another.

Powerful stresses are created both within family structures and for single people as they try to understand and act out the new "liberated" roles portrayed by the media. Women may suddenly feel that they must abandon their traditional roles and compete in a new arena. This can be both exciting and profoundly disturbing to them. Either way, this involves personal stress. As women assume a more active role in society, men may begin to feel insecure as a result of the challenge to their preeminence. They may feel seriously threatened, and under stress.

Another current social orientation which creates great stress in individual members of society is the idolization of youth. For the person who has everything, youth becomes the most precious commodity. Young people fear becoming old, and the old fear being abandoned in a youth-fixated culture. In the nuclear family, individual members scatter at an early age, seeking to assert their independence rather than contributing to the strength of the family unit. One result of this can be that older people are left unsupported by the younger members of the family. Ours has become a society which casts off and ignores its senior members, leaving them to suffer an ignominious and neglected old age in nursing homes or senior-citizen communities. Of course, this is not always the case, but it occurs frequently enough to lead to an understandable fear among many people of growing old. As the post-war baby-boom children approach old age, there will be an unusually large number of old people for society to absorb. This will inevitably create stress both for society as a whole and for its individual members.

Various groups are working to change this situation, among them a California organization called SAGE (Senior Actualization and Growth Explorations). Activities of the SAGE group were initiated by Gay Gaer Luce in Berkeley, California, and are based upon meditative and self-exploration practices. After two years of work, it is clear that elderly people have a marked capacity for profound change and personal growth. Old age is the perfect time for reflection upon a full life and for engaging in innovation once the social demands of occupation, child rearing, and material acquisition have been satisfied. Much more could be said on this subject, but the point here is that the strains of living in a youth-fixated culture, with its undue emphasis upon external appearance rather than inner development, are not inevitable and, like the other sources of stress described in this chapter, can be overcome by a change of life style and personal philosophy.

Closely tied to the devaluation of elderly people is the devaluation of spiritual concerns in contemporary society. The influence of organized religion has waned drastically in the recent past. This has left people stranded in a materialistic society which has no clear belief system to relieve their anxieties about the meaning of existence and about death. We are not at all reconciled to our own mortality, and since we have no idea what is to come, this uncertainty is another major stressor in contemporary life. A strong belief system can ease the fear of death and lend a sense of direction to our passage through life. Concerns such as philosophy and religion may not appear to be as stressful as trouble at the office or a difficult marriage, but the devaluation of these concerns appears to have created a malaise which is distinctly stress-inducing. This is clearly evidenced by the search among today's young for gratification through adherence to various Eastern religions, gurus, pop psychologies—any source of values and transcendent beliefs. When belief is absent, there is a feeling of incompleteness and a spiritual vacuum which can be extremely disconcerting. Each person today experiences the increased life stress of having to consider and resolve fundamental spiritual questions in the midst of an increasingly materialistic society. There is a marked absence of a philosophy which will instill meaning into the proliferation of scientific and social facts. Facts, statistics, and data analysis are potent tools but poor guiding principles. With a renewed attention to the quality of life, there is an inevitable quest for philosophical principles. If excessive stress is to be alleviated, a profound philosophical reorientation needs to be undertaken. Values and ideals are an integral aspect of any individual's attempt to truly live rather than simply exist. In its most fundamental form, the crisis of stress and its attendant disorders is one of personal and cultural values.

THE WORK ENVIRONMENT

Job stress is one of the most universal and intense kinds of stress experience. It affects nearly everyone. Job stress can be defined as a lack of harmony between the individual and his work environment.

Such stress may derive from any number of sources, including supervisor conflict, conflict with co-workers, job dissatisfaction, responsibility overload, lack of support, unclear job expectations, and time pressure. In one recent study, it was found that emotional strain associated with job responsibility preceded heart attacks in 91 percent of a group of coronary-heart-disease patients, while among a normal control group only 20 percent reported similar strain on the job (Russek, 1965). After extensive analysis of sociological data, another study indicated that certain occupational groups, such as accountants and auditors, had higher measured job dissatisfaction and higher mortality from coronary heart disease than other occupational groups, regardless of socioeconomic status (Sales and House, 1971). Effects of time pressure and work overload are also clearly illustrated by the research of Friedman, Rosenman, and Carroll with tax accountants under the stress of deadlines. They obtained blood samples that were analyzed for serum-cholesterol level and blood-coagulation time (Friedman, Rosenman, and Carroll, 1958). Among the accountants who volunteered for the study, it was found that a marked rise in serum-cholesterol levels occurred during peak periods of job stress—for example, just prior to the April 15th deadline. Acceleration of blood-co-agulation time showed a similar response to deadline pressure. Since other factors such as diet, exercise, and weight remained relatively constant, these changes could not be attributed to anything but the increased pressure on the job. One interesting sidelight of this study occurred because one of the participants kept a daily diary and rated the degree of his stress on a scale of 1 to 100. Correlations between his own feelings of being stressed and an elevation of his serum-cholesterol levels was extremely high. This executive's ability to accurately evaluate his personal stress is a source of optimism. It is another indication that people can sensitize themselves to stress, which is the first essential step in any effort to reduce stress and avoid the negative consequences of stress overload. In another study of heart-disease patients, 64 myocardial-infarct patients were compared to 109 normal people, and it was found from their descriptions of themselves and their life situations that they differed in three principal ways: 1) excessive overtime work; 2) hostility toward others who slowed them down; and 3) dissatisfaction with their jobs (Theorell and Rahe, 1970). Among the group of control subjects, these complaints were rare, indicating that a less-pressured orientation toward work may lower the incidence of myocardial infarction.

In a study of London bus drivers and conductors, the role of job responsibility in creating excessive stress and coincident physiological changes was clearly demonstrated (Morris et al., 1966). During this five-year study it was found that the bus drivers had a significantly higher incidence of heart disease as well as substantially higher blood-lipid levels than conductors of the same age. Although the results were attributed to differences in physical activity, since the bus drivers sat a great deal and conductors continually walked and moved about, this seems a simplistic explanation. It is far more likely that the responsibility for passengers' safety and the constant need to make decisions while driving lay behind the increase in stress. This is consistent with what is known about stress and coronary heart disease. Although the information yielded by this study remains somewhat ambiguous, it does seem to indicate that a high degree of alertness, which must be maintained without relief, may be one of the factors that predisposes people toward stress-related disease.

A very dramatic example of how time and production pressure on the job can create unnecessary stress is found in a study of 12 women in the invoicing department of a large office (Levi, 1967). Normally the women were capable of producing approximately 160 invoices per hour, and they were paid a fixed monthly salary for their work. In this study, the pay schedule was changed to a piecework system on two pre-designated days. Under this system, the more quickly and accurately they worked, the more they were paid, but deductions were made for clerical errors. During the period of the test, checks were maintained on the women's physical and mental conditions by means of questionnaires filled in every two hours and urine samples which were analyzed for the stress hormones adrenalin and noradrenalin. During the piecework days, production per hour rose substantially, with the incidence of mistakes no higher than usual. However, the added stress on the women clearly took its toll. They reported greatly increased strain, sensations of discomfort, such as pains in their arms, shoulders, head, and back, and almost twice the fatigue, which left them mentally and physically exhausted and still tired when they returned to work the next day. In addition, the excretion of stress hormones into the urine was 27 percent and 40 percent higher on the two piecework-pay days. Although the rise in production might encourage employers to institute a piecework pay schedule, it is logical to predict that continued strain on employees from such a system would ultimately lead to health complications, such as nervous disorders and muscular pains, and consequently increased sick leave, low morale, and more turnover among a dissatisfied staff. This cost might not show up immediately on the company's ledgers, but in the long run it almost surely would. Personal cost to the employees in terms of health and morale would be inestimable.

Although most stress research focuses upon prolonged hyperactivity as the basis of psychosomatic disorders, it appears that unabated hypoactivity may be equally destructive. Recent research indicates that boredom can induce disorders as much as excessive activity can. Swedish psychologist Marianne Frankenhaeuser has described how stress can be produced both by work overloads and by what she calls the "stimulus underload" of monotonous work (*Behavior Today*, June 9, 1975). Further research by the Institute for Social Research in Ann Arbor, Michigan confirms this finding. Researchers studied 2,000 male workers in 23 occupations and found that the traditional sources of stress such as long hours, heavy workloads, and pressing responsibilities produced less anxiety, depression, and physical illness than less demanding jobs did (Caplan, 1975). Family doctors reported the highest degree of job stress, yet manifested lowest anxiety and fewest physical disorders. Assembly-line workers with normal working hours reported the highest levels of depression, irritation, and physical problems. Based upon these findings, the researchers noted that job satisfaction was the key factor. In order to alleviate the stress-inducing boredom of assembly work, the employees formed small groups and became involved in decision making. Some workers reported less stress in these conditions, while others reported a marked increase. Any attempt to alleviate the stress of boredom needs to consider each individual's reactions, and no simple formula appears adequate. Stress is induced when individuals are in an imbalance due to excessive reactivity or the virtual absence of reactivity. Moving toward a balanced state requires that each person become aware of these polarities and adjust accordingly.

It must be remembered in evaluating these studies on job stress that such physiological changes as temporary evaluations in serum cholesterol, increased blood-coagulation time, and higher levels of adrenalin cannot be directly linked to psychosomatic disease on a short-term basis. These temporary physiological fluctuations in response to job stress need to be studied over a long period of time if one is to obtain an accurate picture of the relationship of job stress to disease. Changes in blood pressure should also be considered as they relate to work pressure, since chronic hypertension is a major contributing factor in coronary heart disease. Work environments may be some of the best laboratories in which to examine indices of psychophysiological stress in a relatively controlled setting. Holding other factors constant, specific working conditions can be altered one at a time to determine their role in contributing to higher stress levels among large numbers of employees. Excessive strain on the job, along with concentrated periods of life change, are perhaps the most common sources of the type of stress that may eventually precipitate a psychosomatic illness.

TECHNOLOGICAL INNOVATION

Another major contributor to the high generalized level of stress of the modern world is the sheer amount of technological innovation. Technology has greatly increased the necessity for rapid and frequent adaptation. Our communications systems bombard us with information at a rate that is almost impossible to absorb. An average person is exposed to advertising every day to the point of saturation. Much of the input to which people are exposed cannot be analyzed or integrated into the person's daily activity. It is not unusual for people who consciously strive to stay abreast of the media to become anxious when they find they are overwhelmed by the amount of information they believe they should be able to absorb. Mass communications have also tended to transport people out of the boundaries of their particular social networks. Unfamiliar modes of behavior and quite different value systems are constantly presented to people via television, and they must adapt to this information.

Air travel and the rapidity with which we can move from culture to culture, environment to environment, also requires constant adaptation. This has had the positive effect of encouraging understanding and tolerance of other cultures and attitudes within the "global village." However, it also has the effect of breaking down the protective barriers between social networks and compelling individuals to evaluate and choose between divergent approaches to living. People find themselves involuntarily outside the confines of a supportive and homogeneous community which sets standards by which all members abide. Inevitably, great stress is induced by the necessity of constant reevaluation of social and moral issues when there are few social structures to dictate decisions on these issues.

Our modes of transportation and communication are also characterized by tremendous speed. Man has become the only creature on earth who spends a great deal of his time traveling from place to place at speeds far exceeding those at which he was originally designed to move. These speeds can be disconcerting or seriously stressful, as illustrated by the phenomenon of "jet lag," in which an individual becomes disoriented as a result of the speed at which he has traversed great distances. Most people think they have successfully adapted to the speeds at which they drive their automobiles. However, even long-distance driving at high speeds for extended periods of time can cause a mild form of biorhythm disorientation (Luce, *Body Time*, 1973). Temporary disturbance of biorhythms and reflexes due to air travel is even greater. This, combined with the need to adjust to abrupt changes in climate, time, and total environment, requires a substantial amount of adaptive energy and leads to stress.

Our concept of time is closely related to the extraordinary speed of contemporary modes of transportation and communication. People in post-industrial societies are constantly trying to "save time" and to find shortcuts in their daily routines. Housewives are constantly being instructed in how to decrease the amount of time they spend on household chores, by means of an armamentarium of household conveniences. This kind of "hurry sickness" (Friedman and Rosenman, 1974) or unnatural preoccupation with time means that many people tend to be thinking of what they have to do or are going to do next while engaged in an activity that should be absorbing all their attention. Time-pressured activity is highly stress-inducing. This kind of behavior has been institutionalized in our economic and job structures. Much of modern man's work revolves around the concept of the deadline, which becomes an ax hanging over the head of all those affected by it. A worker's production is valued for its quantity and production speed rather than its quality. When an individual must meet the ubiquitous deadline, there is little value placed upon accomplishing a task with deliberate patience and careful attention.

Unfortunately, the attitude toward time that is prevalent in the working world can also extend into people's domestic lives to an alarming degree. The inherently competitive nature of our economic system can have an insidious impact upon the non-vocational aspects of contemporary life. Preoccupation with time can lead to a frenetic and unnecessarily stressful rush to acquire material goods, social position, respect, and the whole array of socially sanctioned goals and values. "Deadline time" may eventually come to apply to leisure time as well. Far too many people experience guilt or disease from the non-utilitarian use of leisure time. They are plagued by feelings that they must be continually engaged in some "constructive" activity, or always "accomplishing" something. This legacy of the Puritan ethic and Utilitarianism can induce a sense of guilt during nonproductive leisure time and lead to increased stress levels rather than lowered ones. Our leisure hours offer an opportunity to alleviate the effects of stress experienced during non-leisure time. When leisure becomes a rigidly scheduled source of stress in itself, a dangerous syndrome can result. This syndrome is frequently manifested by victims of coronary heart disease. Drs. Friedman and Rosenman, in *Type A Behavior and Your Heart,* suggest a number of "exercises" designed to help people correct this kind of destructive attitude toward time. One of their more amusing suggestions is that Type A individuals force themselves to read Marcel Proust's masterpiece, *A Remembrance of Things Past.* Proust takes hundreds of pages to state what a typical Type A individual might attempt to express in a paragraph, in his impatience to rush on to something else. By the very act of allowing himself to flow with Proust's remarkable meanderings, a Type A person can enter into a new rhythm which is considerably slower and more relaxed. This is just one very small example of how behavioral changes can help free a person from much of the stress induced by technological change. In contrast to future-oriented, time-pressured behavior is the style of living in the present advocated by all meditative systems. Present time is seen as the only reality. Any single moment devoid of past ruminations and future anticipations leaves the individual free to respond spontaneously to his present situation.

THE INDIVIDUAL AND PSYCHOSOCIAL NORMS

All of the social and environmental stressors described above contribute to raising the baseline level of tension and anxiety throughout the societies in which they are operational. When rapid change occurs within a society and anxiety-inducing factors outlast the anxiety-resolving factors, the amount of stress is compounded. Due to the fluidity and multiplicity of stress factors in contemporary society, researchers have tended to rely increasingly upon relatively isolated minority groups in order to study specific stress factors. Among certain racial subcultures, it is possible to isolate a particular stress variable, since it may be more emphasized in that subculture than in the general culture at large. Looking into the research concerning isolated stress factors among subcultures can provide significant insight concerning factors which operate upon all individuals in the predominant culture. An anecdote reported by researcher L. W. Simmons about the Hopi Indians of the western United States illustrates the persistence of traditional beliefs in modern society. A father in a traditional Hopi family believes that when he treads on the tracks of a snake he will get sore ankles. To avoid this, he seeks the help of the tribal medicine man, who performs certain rites to insure that the pain never develops, or, if it has, goes away. In this particular family, the son is educated and has abandoned traditional Hopi beliefs. He has moved into the larger culture outside the Hopi group and disdains the authority and effectiveness of the medicine man. Despite this, the son does get sore ankles when he walks in the tracks of a snake. Even as he consciously tries to adapt to new values and beliefs, the old ones persist and create problems for him (Simmons, 1950). In the case of many people like this young Hopi, the authority and security of an old system are rejected before they understand and feel comfortable with new social and ethical constructs. When this occurs, the individual is left for a period of time in a sociocultural vacuum, having to make decisions and resolve problems without the guidance of traditional norms. Such a situation can produce a great deal of stress.

An individual's degree of dependence or independence from psychosocial norms can contribute strongly to the stress he or she experiences. Essentially, there are two ways in which a person can react to the psychosocial norms. He can either accept them fully and merge his own identity into that of the community in which he lives, or he can resist them and seek to achieve a sense of identity outside of and apart from this community. Sociologist Gordon E. Moss calls these two orientations the "identified" and the "autonomous" personalities (Moss, 1973). Obviously, there is a range of attitudes which fall between these two extremes. Moss assumes that, for most people, one of life's biggest challenges is to try to reduce the amount of uncertainty one encounters and to maximize one's real security in order to insure survival. An identified person will attempt to do this by associating himself closely with organizations and other established social structures. He will abide scrupulously by existing norms of behavior and take the peer group's beliefs and goals as his own. An identified person is not a risk taker, and he attaches himself to the group for its strength and its ability to endure. He feels secure in the group, insulated from the vagaries and uncertainties of a life without strong cultural reference points. The autonomous person may have the same long-range goals as his identified counterpart, but he seeks to achieve them in a wholly different way. For him, uncertainty is an unavoidable fact of life, and genuine security can be achieved only through complete independence and self-sufficiency. An autonomous person develops a moral code all his own, and his vocation will be one that is financially sound in a variety of life settings. Such a person reacts to new input from a more centered position than the identified individual and has greater tolerance for the stress of life changes. His expectations are largely ones he has formulated himself, although these will not necessarily be easier to achieve than those imposed by a group. In general, the autonomous individual will tend to be more socially and geographically mobile, counting on his own self-developed principles and expectations to shield him from the uncertainties and discontinuities he experiences as a result of this mobility. In a sense, he trains himself to develop adaptive capabilities and inner resources so as to meet challenges without having them disrupt his life or throw him off balance.

The impact of these two life orientations on stress reactivity and health is double-edged. If an identified person is able to maintain his supportive association with a larger community and enjoy the security, insulation, and low level of major social change it affords, his life stress will be low and his overall health will benefit. In contrast, the autonomous individual will incur much more stressful experience in his quest for independence and self-sufficiency. At the same time, he builds up a tolerance for change, disruption, and uncertainty. When they confront him, he can respond with a degree of equanimity and a learned adaptive capability which enable him to control his level of stress better than his identified counterpart can. The identified person, when exposed to events which threaten the viability of his group or communications network, is ill-equipped to cope. Major social change may reduce the cohesion and support potential of the group for the identified individual, leaving him to confront a new and stress-inducing social order on his own. Events of a more personal nature may change his standing in the group, robbing him of the security of his place within it. Or they may overwhelm him to such an extent that the group can be of no real assistance to him, as in the case of the death of a spouse or a major financial setback. An identified individual expects stability and relies on his cultural frame of reference to provide it. He has few resources with which to deal with instability, and he is much more likely to suffer a pathological reaction to the severe stress that results from instability and rapid change.

One striking example of the benefits to health and mental well-being of an "identified" life style is the community of Roseto, Pennsylvania (Wolff, 1968). Roseto was established in 1882 by a group of Italian immigrants from a town of the same name in Italy. Snubbed by their primarily Anglo-Saxon neighbors, the Rosetans clung together for support, and over the years they maintained an essentially homogeneous community. They adhered to many of the values of their old peasant way of life and shut out much that was alien in the new culture. Because of their mutual supportiveness, crime and poverty became almost non-existent in their little subculture, and many Rosetans prospered and became wealthy. Yet even those who gained a measure of financial success did not attempt to distinguish themselves from their less fortunate neighbors. They dressed the same, socialized freely with other Rosetans, and invested their wealth back into the community. A 1962 study indicated that, despite high intake of animal fat and widespread obesity, the Rosetans suffered an incidence of death from myocardial infarction less than half that of surrounding areas, as well as a reduced rate of coronary artery disease (Hampton et al., 1964; Stout et al., 1964). When a follow-up study was undertaken on Rosetans who had moved away to nearby New York and New Jersey, it was found that the rate of death by myocardial infarction and of coronary heart disease increased significantly. Since genetic and ethnic factors remained constant in the comparison, this research seems to indicate that the social homogeneity and identified life style of the Rosetans had much to do with their superior health. It is reasonable to postulate from this example and many others like it that in societies where a fixed social hierarchy exists and one's place in life and relationships to others both in work and outside are well defined and accepted, psychosocial stress is substantially reduced. If such stress is avoided, then the neurophysiological reactions to it are minimized and the beneficial results are demonstrated in the overall health patterns of the community.

In another study, undertaken between 1967 and 1971 in the Japanese community of the San Francisco Bay Area, a group of researchers from the University of California

School of Public Health reported similar findings (San Francisco *Chronicle*, July 29, 1975). After extensive examination of life styles in the Japanese community, it was found that those Japanese who had adopted American life styles and moved away from traditional Japanese social and family structures suffered an incidence of heart disease comparable to that among the indigenous white population (about 350 heart-related deaths per 100,000 men per year). In contrast, those who had stayed close to the Japanese community and adhered to traditional modes of behavior and social relationships had a rate of heart disease substantially lower, comparable to that in Japan itself (50 heart-related deaths per 100,000 men per year). Researchers Michael G. Marmot, S. Leonard Syme, and Warren Winkelstein, Jr., speculated that the difference may lie in the way the two cultures adjusted to competition and individual ambitions. In Japanese culture there is great social and job security provided by the individual's peer group, and particularly by the corporation for which one works. Unlike his Japanese counterpart, the typical American businessman is hard-driving and intent on competing with his peers to achieve success, and he does not have the supportive family and business background available to the Japanese.

Another study cited by Wolff (1968) focused upon a Chinese subculture and involved a group of 100 non-Communist Chinese students who had been expatriated to New York as a result of the Chinese Revolution. These students were studied in comparison with two groups of Americans, one of women and one of men, which included both the most frequently ill and the least frequently ill from an industrial population. Members of the three groups were interviewed with a protocol developed by anthropologist Ruth Benedict. Included in the protocol were wide-ranging questions encouraging the students to talk about their families, cultural backgrounds, attitudes, goals, frustrations, and illness patterns during their lives. It was found that periods of illness for all the students tended to coincide with or follow shortly after stressful periods for each individual when the respondents had experienced a high level of life change or frustration of goals. However, the group of Chinese students, whose lives had recently undergone the most extreme sort of disruption, had better overall health than the group of American women. Here again the question of individual expectation and adaptation to stress enters into consideration. In their homeland, the Chinese had been exposed to enormous social upheaval, repeated change, and destruction of old, familiar social patterns. They had come to expect such change, and had developed an accepting and adaptive attitude toward it. Events had forced them into an autonomous life outlook, with the result that they were better able to tolerate the disorientation and dislocation caused by their expatriation. Under the circumstances, their overall health indicates that they were more able than the American workers to adjust to the stress caused by life change.

Variability of individual response to stress is dependent on multiple factors, and it is extremely difficult to draw inferences from subcultural research which apply to the culture as a whole. For this reason, the identified and autonomous modes of behavior are limited in terms of what they indicate about stress reactivity. As will be shown in later chapters, there are a number of behavior patterns which are much more clearly delineated responses to life situations.

Certainly it is unrealistic to assume that the fragmentation of supportive subcultures will abate and that the preservation of such units will be an effective means of alleviating psychosomatic disorders. Subculture peer groups are essentially an external source of support and security and are subject to radical fluctuation. As an alternative, it may be possible to replace this reliance on external support with an internal reliance based upon increased self-awareness. Perhaps the chaos of external security can provide impetus for the evolution of human consciousness toward a more internal sense of solidity and well-being.

Numerous attitudes acquired during youth affect the way an individual reacts to stress. For instance, all of us suffer from performance anxiety at various times in our lives. Most people, when they are under extreme pressure to perform, cope with this natural anxiety so that it does not become debilitating. Yet consider the case of a person whose family has emphasized performance and achievement to the exclusion of all other characteristics. Such a person might well come to equate his ability to inspire love and affection with performance alone. In later life, the attitude engendered by his early upbringing might severely damage his ability to form healthy social relationships, and he may suffer a crippling level of continual stress resulting from his constant need to achieve and excel.

Acquired attitudes and expectations strongly influence an individual's perception of life events. When these attitudes and expectations become destructive or severely limited for the individual, the problem is likely to fall within the domain of the psychotherapist long before it becomes chronic and leads to physical pathology. When an acquired attitude simply becomes a source of stress, the primary option open to the person in question is the rejection of the attitude, which implies a deviation from peer-group norms. This deviation from family and peer group is, in turn, itself a well-documented and profound stressor.

Not all acquired attitudes are potentially problematic. When a young child receives positive reinforcement and encouragement from his family, teachers, and friends, fear and anxiety will play little part in his early maturation process. It is likely that such an individual will have effective personal resources to rely on in instances of psychosocial stress. Having been encouraged to express himself and play an active role within his family and among friends, he will approach later life with the belief that he can actively master or influence his environment rather than being a passive acceptor. Inevitably frustrations will occur, but the essentially positive attitude acquired in youth will persist through all but the most overwhelmingly negative circumstances. Unfortunately, this is far more of an ideal model than a realistic appraisal of how the majority of us cope with stress.

A comparison of the relationship between parent and child in Japanese and American families gives an interesting contrast illustrating how learned attitudes can alter perception of stress. In Japan, a great value is placed on filial piety. Young Japanese have a lifelong commitment to honor and obey their parents, and to remain close to the parental hearth. In the United States young people are encouraged to become independent as soon as possible and to build lives for themselves based on their own perceived needs rather than those of their family. If either a Japanese or American young person is unable to meet his family's and his culture's expectations of him, then guilt, hostility, confusion, and great personal stress can be the result (Wolff, 1968). Common to each of these examples is the factor of individual rebellion against the dominant social norm. When this departure from peer-group support is positive, an individual gains increased freedom. However, when it is unsuccessful, the person is subject to excess stress which increases his susceptibility to psychosomatic disorders.

The links between familial influence, psychosocial attitudes, and neurophysiological stress reactivity has not been adequately explored. An innovative approach to this complex interaction of variables is the research of Daniel H. Funkenstein with a group of Harvard College students (Funkenstein, 1957). In Funkenstein's experiments the students were exposed to a series of three highly stress-inducing interviews. They were subjected to intense needling by the interviewers and were asked to answer a nearly impossible series of quizlike questions which left them frustrated, with their confidence shaken. They experienced anger at the absurdity and injustice of the questions. At the same time, various physiological indices of stress reactivity were monitored in addition to their behavioral and psychological responses. Funkenstein and his co-workers designated one of the responses which occurred regularly as "Anger-in" or intropunitive. Rather than overtly expressing anger at the interviewers, the "Anger-in" respondents blamed themselves, turned their anger inward, and suppressed their hostile feelings. In the total sample of a large number of students over a two-year period, only eleven students responded to all three interviewers with "Anger-in." Of these eleven, ten were from old New England families on both their paternal and maternal sides. These students were the epitome of aristocratic graciousness and restraint, for which their backgrounds had so aptly prepared them. In their view, acquired from a strong family and cultural tradition, "Anger-in" was the only gentlemanly and acceptable response. Ironically, this acquired gentility caused them, according to the physiological indices, to suffer far more severe and prolonged physical stress reaction than did the members of the group who responded with "Anger-out."

There is considerable evidence that internalized anger induces prolonged stress reactivity, which is more damaging than the transient strain involved in the immediate expression of aggression. A simple analogy from Hans Selye's most recent book summarizes this interaction between an individual's reactive style, neurophysiological state, and expression of stress:

> . . . you are walking quietly down a city street and you meet a drunk who showers you with insults. The drunk is the indirect pathogen; what happens depends on how you react. If the drunk is harmless and you are a coronary candidate, you risk biological suicide by reacting violently. You will have killed yourself. The appropriate reaction is, therefore, syntoxic—adaptation or avoidance. On the other hand, if the

drunk is hostile and is armed with a knife and it is
clear he wants to kill you, the only proper response
is catatoxic—an attempt to repel: the drunk is a
pathogen. The body, therefore, meets invaders in the
same way you meet social pathogens, with the same
two choices—adapt or fight [Selye, 1974].

Taking neither course of action leaves the individual with
no respite from a state of physical excitation without abate-
ment. This common predisposition to repress and conceal
the effects of stress is in and of itself a major contributor
to the development of stress disorders.

Clearly, learned attitudes strongly influence the way people adapt to stress, and also determine the situations which
they find stressful and the degree to which they react. It is
equally clear that any attempt to generalize about the interaction between acquired attitudes and the perception of
stress would be premature. Every one of us has his own
totally individual, multivariate, and highly complex set of
beliefs and attitudes, and each of us responds to stress in a
totally unique way. Suffice it to say that acquired attitudes
usually derive from one's early cultural context and from
one's social education in its broadest sense. In twentieth-century society, with its unprecedented social and geographical
mobility and cross-cultural interchange, attitudes acquired
in one's early life are likely to be frequently challenged.
This should not be regarded as an inherently negative aspect of modern life. On the contrary, it may have enormously valuable implications for social and humanitarian
evolution, much in the same way as the ongoing dialectical
struggle between generations increases cultural maturity
and strength. Despite the evolutionary benefit, however,
each time an individual confronts a challenge to a held
belief or attitude, he also experiences personal stress. Although change and mobility may serve a greater social
good, they still may have a profoundly negative impact
upon individual members of society. Since it is virtually
impossible to eliminate these factors from modern life, in-

dividuals must learn to alleviate the stress they cause if the mortality rate from psychosomatic disorders is to be significantly reduced.

ASSESSING YOUR OWN LEVEL OF PSYCHOSOCIAL STRESS

One of the most outstanding contributions to the identification of events which can "trigger" a high degree of personal stress into a psychosomatic disorder is the research of Thomas H. Holmes and Richard H. Rahe of the University of Washington School of Medicine. Holmes and Rahe developed a systematized method of correlating life events with illness and tested their hypotheses with more than 5,000 patients. Previous research by Harold G. Wolff had indicated that stressful life events play an important causative role in the genesis of disease by evoking neurophysiological reactions. This link applies not only to the classical psychosomatic disorders but also to more organic pathology, such as infectious diseases and traumatic injuries. Further studies reported that respiratory illness, due to both streptococcal and nonstreptococcal infection, are about four times as likely to be preceded as followed by acute stress (Meyer and Haggerty, 1962). Drawing upon this research, Holmes and Rahe undertook a systematic investigation of the relationship between social readjustment, stress, and susceptibility to illness. They observed with many patients that life events tended to cluster or increase in intensity prior to disease onset. An excessive number of readjustments was often correlated with illness. According to their research:

> ... the occurrence of each event usually evoked, or was associated with, some adaptive or coping behavior on the part of the involved individual. Thus each item was constructed to contain life events whose advent either is indicative of, or requires a significant change

in, the ongoing life pattern of the individual. The
emphasis is on change from the existing steady state
and not on psychological meaning, emotion, or social
desirability [Holmes and Masuda, 1973].

Initially, in retrospective studies, Thomas Holmes and
his colleagues had noted a strong correlation between the
intensity of life changes and onset of severe illness. Similar
correlations were reported with minor health changes, such
as cuts, bruises, headaches, backaches, and colds, which
may not require a physician's treatment (Holmes and
Holmes, 1970). Since these correlations appeared to be
quite clear, the next logical step was to determine if these
life events could be used to predict the probability of disease onset in prospective studies.

From their retrospective research, they devised a Social
Readjustment Rating Scale (SRE), which assigned numerical values to events that are typical in people's lives.
These events included divorce, marriage, death in the family, change of job, pregnancy, large mortgage, and so on.
Many of these events are ones that are considered to be
occasions for joy and celebration, but they take their toll on
our adjustive capabilities nevertheless. Hans Selye's theory
of the nonspecific response supports this observation. According to his theory, events which are registered as pleasurable still evoke the same neurophysiological and biochemical reaction as negative stressors. Positive life events
can produce abnormally prolonged stress responses in the
same way as negative events.

To use the Holmes and Rahe chart, you should check off
events which have happened to you within the last year
and then total up the score by adding up the assigned
values of these events. Holmes and Rahe determined that a
score of 150 based on the past year would make one's
chances of developing an illness or a health change
roughly 50–50. If someone were to score over 300 points

SOCIAL READJUSTMENT RATING SCALE

Event	Value
Death of spouse	100
Divorce	73
Marital separation	65
Jail term	63
Death of close family member	63
Personal injury or illness	53
Marriage	50
Fired from work	47
Marital reconciliation	45
Retirement	45
Change in family member's health	44
Pregnancy	40
Sex difficulties	39
Addition to family	39
Business readjustment	39
Change in financial status	38
Death of close friend	37
Change to different line of work	36
Change in number of marital arguments	35
Mortgage or loan over $10,000	31
Foreclosure of mortgage or loan	30
Change in work responsibilities	29
Son or daughter leaving home	29
Trouble with in-laws	29
Outstanding personal achievement	28
Spouse begins or stops work	26
Starting or finishing school	26
Change in living conditions	25
Revision of personal habits	24
Trouble with boss	23
Change in work hours, conditions	20
Change in residence	20
Change in schools	20

Change in recreational habits	19
Change in church activities	19
Change in social activities	18
Mortgage or loan under $10,000	17
Change in sleeping habits	16
Change in number of family gatherings	15
Change in eating habits	15
Vacation	13
Christmas season	12
Minor violation of the law	11

within a year, his chances of experiencing a health change go up to almost 90 percent. As the score increases, the probability that the health change will be a serious illness increases also. Rahe's work with 2,500 officers and enlisted men aboard three Navy cruisers dramatically illustrates the validity of the Social Readjustment Rating Scale. Of the 2,500 men, the 30 percent with the highest life-change scores developed almost 90 percent more first illnesses during the first month of the cruise than the 30 percent with the lowest scores (Rahe, 1973). During the rest of the cruise, the high-scoring 30 percent consistently developed more illnesses than the lower 30 percent. This degree of predictability is quite high and demonstrates that effective predictive measures for illness susceptibility can be developed for application in preventive medicine.

Another prospective study was undertaken by Holmes and Rahe with 84 resident physicians (Holmes and Masuda, 1973). In this study, the life changes for the previous 18 months were used as the quantitative measure for predicting the onset of illness in the near future. Data concerning disease occurrence was collected eight months later. The outcome: 49 percent of the high-risk group with 300-plus life-change units reported illness; 25 percent of the medium-risk group with 200–299 life-change scores reported disorders; and only 9 percent of the low-risk group with 150–199 units reported any illness. Clearly, the SRE scale demonstrated a high degree of prospective applicability. In a subsequent study of medical students, 52 percent of the participants experienced major illnesses during a two-year risk period. Of these students, 85 percent had high life-change scores, 48 percent had moderate scores, and only 33 percent had low scores. Two additional findings were of considerable significance. A student's chances of experiencing illness during the second year was in direct proportion to the magnitude of his life-change score. Also, the data indicated that the students with major health changes also experienced more minor illnesses (Holmes and Masuda, 1973). Overall, these studies are a clear indication that it is possible to predict susceptibility to both minor and major illness. An empirical assessment of these risk factors is a major step toward the development of a holistic, preventive medicine. If the probability of illness onset can be determined, then such a scale can be used to indicate when preventive measures need to be initiated.

All of the life changes listed in the Holmes and Rahe Social Readjustment Rating Scale are common in people's lives. For the most part, these occurrences take place within a delimited time period, except for the gradual changes in social and health habits such as recreation, eating, and sleeping. Stress resulting from these changes is usually concentrated within the time during which the event happens. Generally, the response to such stressors is normal in terms of both intensity and duration. It is only when these events occur in clusters with their effect becoming cumulative that dangerously prolonged stress reactions take place.

Whenever predictive measures are employed, there is always the possibility of their becoming a self-fulfilling prophecy, as a result of which a person is influenced to become ill because he is informed that it is highly probable. This is clearly not the case with the SRE scale, since it was developed and standardized in double-blind experimental procedures to eliminate this possibility. Of course, when the scale is self-administered or used in clinical practice, then this is a potential issue again. The intent of such predictive measures is not to notify a person of the probability of becoming ill. Rather, its application should encourage preventive measures, when needed, to reduce that probability. More sensitive scales are being developed, and any predictive measures need to be used with sensitivity on the part of the patient and clinician. Psychosocial factors such as life events need to be considered in conjunction with neurophysiological indices. Holmes and Masuda (1973) have postulated that these life events enhance the probability of disease onset by lowering bodily resistance. This lowered resistance, they theorize, is due to adaptive efforts by the individual that are dysfunctional in kind and duration. Life-stress scales coupled with a neurophysiological stress profile may prove to be the fundamental tools of a holistic, preventive medicine.

At the present time, most of the constructive research in stress and psychosomatic disorders focuses around the relationship of life events to illness and on determining the precise nature of the mind/body interaction which leads to the development of disorders. It is still not known for certain whether stress overload merely predisposes a person to illness or actually precipitates it, but without doubt there is a clear causal link. Some of the most recent research is available in a book entitled *Life Stress and Illness* from a Symposium for Life Stress and illness sponsored by the Science Committee of NATO (Gunderson and Rahe, 1974). Papers presented at this symposium supported the Holmes and Rahe thesis that life change, when concentrated in short time periods, relates directly to illness patterns. The disorders investigated were primarily myocardial infarction, coronary heart disease, and depressive and schizophrenic conditions. One contribution by Rahe and Romo reports significant positive correlations between heart attacks occurring relatively early in midlife and total "upsets" from life events in the preceding year. Those patients who died from myocardial infarction had higher levels of life changes than those who survived. Also, Paykel reports in the same volume that patients who made suicide attempts reported the highest magnitude of antecedent life events. This anthology of papers was released at the same time as another book, entitled *Stressful Life Events*, by Barbara Snell Dohrenwend and Bruce P. Dohrenwend (1974). Both of these books emphasize retrospective studies but cite the need for more prospective research in developing accurate prediction.

With stress deriving from myriad psychosocial, environmental, and personal sources which often operate at subliminal levels, it is a formidable task for each person to sort out these factors in his or her life. This task is further complicated by the tendency to romanticize certain stressful modes of behavior by associating them with success and superior performance. If we are to make progress in reducing the toll taken by stress-related diseases in contemporary society, people need to recognize the connection between high stress levels and their health. Once this correlation is acknowledged, then people can develop the self-awareness needed to monitor their responses to events, and to spot the attitudes which create stress for them.

An obvious next step is to become aware of the "weak links," those systems in each person which are most vulnerable. To do this, it is necessary to consider the personality variables of a particular person and how that excessive stress is channeled through the personality toward a specific disease or organ system. This important question is the subject of Part Three.

PART THREE
STRESS AND DISEASE

Personality and Illness

4

So far we have outlined two steps in the development of psychosomatic illness. First, a baseline level of tolerable stress is escalated to a level of excessive stress. Then, when this high stress level is prolonged and unabated, it produces alterations in neurophysiological functioning which can create the preconditions for the development of a disorder. At that point, either a high concentration of life-change events in a given period of time or an acute accumulation of a single persistent or extreme source of stress can precipitate a severe psychosomatic disorder. Then at this juncture, the role of personality enters the picture. Although it is difficult to demonstrate a clear causal link between personality factors and disease, many professionals have noted that when a prolonged neurophysiological stress response is channeled through a particular personality configuration, a specific disorder will result. Personality clearly affects the way a person handles stress. Stress experiences early in life may lead to the adoption of certain methods of coping with problems. Certain psychological and behavioral defenses are then integrated into the adult personality, and determine the way the individual attempts to manage stress throughout his life.

Personality factors as they relate to illness are an exciting area of research, since the opportunities for preventive intervention are so dramatic. For the most part, people are more sensitive to their own subtle psychological states than they are to minute shifts in neurophysiological functioning. Though it is difficult for people to alter their life-long behavior patterns, behavior is clearly more amenable to voluntary change than are elevated levels of adrenal corticoids in the blood. For this reason, if behavior can be truly shown to have a direct causal relationship to disease, the potential for prevention is enormous.

During the last year, the National Institute of Mental Health released a progress report reviewing the last twenty-five years of mental-health research and assessing its implications. Throughout the report there is an evident conflict between biochemical and psychosocial approaches to mental health. Essentially, the issue is whether to allocate funds to develop more effective chemotherapy or to institute psychosocial research oriented toward pathology-inducing social and environmental factors: "Vigorous disagreement exists between biological and psychosocial investigators as to what constitutes optimal present and future distribution of resources between these two approaches to the study of mental illness" (NIMH Public Information Office, 1975). This controversy is of concern to every individual, not just to government bureaucrats. The option of choosing between a pharmacological intervention and a change of style is an important one. Though the alternatives are obviously not mutually exclusive, they involve entirely different perspectives. If personality factors are as vital as they appear to be in the development of psychosomatic illness, the search for a more effective pill should not be the main thrust of future research.

Concern over life style, personality characteristics, and stress disorders is pervasive in contemporary society. On a recent episode of the popular television series *All in the*

Family, Edith Bunker arrives home one evening with a questionnaire entitled "Your Personality May Be Killing You." The questionnaire, which is to be self-administered and self-scored, purports to be able to predict longevity on the basis of personality and behavior traits as revealed by the respondent's answers to multiple-choice questions. Before dinner the entire family answers the questions, with much prompting among them to encourage honesty. Everyone was found to be in store for a healthy long life with the exception of the cantankerous "pater familias," Archie Bunker. When he finally tallies up his score, he is shaken to discover that the test predicts that he will not live past the age of fifty-six. After the family permits a reappraisal of Archie's answers and engages in some dubious mathematics in the scoring process, peace and tranquility are temporarily restored. This is hardly the means of instituting a health-maintenance life style, but the show did suggest to viewers both the applications and limitations of assessing personality and stress disorders.

That such a subject should occupy the writers of one of televisions most successful series indicates the extent to which the idea of a relationship between personality and health has already influenced the public consciousness. Certainly the idea is not new, but it has gained impetus and credibility recently, largely as a result of the work of Drs. Friedman and Rosenman and others on the correlation of behavior patterns and cardiovascular disease, described in the book *Type A Behavior and Your Heart* (1974). Evidence is accumulating that specific personality configurations may be associated with heart disease, cancer, and arthritis, as well as ulcerative colitis, asthma, migraine, and other disorders generally designated as psychosomatic or stress-induced. As more research information indicates a connection between personality and illness, the value of a holistic, preventive approach to health care becomes increasingly apparent. If personality traits and certain modes of responding to life's vicissitudes can be clearly defined and shown conclusively to be destructive to health, it may be possible to teach people how to modify or avoid this destructive behavior well before it leads to physiological symptoms. Many doctors are already giving advice on behavior modifications to cardiovascular patients, since it is in heart disease that the most convincing research has been done on the causal role of personality. At the same time, the behavior patterns typical of victims of other major diseases, most notably cancer, are beginning to receive greater research attention, with some revealing results. It will indeed be interesting to see how far this kind of investigation contributes to the preventive medicine of the future. Judging from present trends, it is possible to envision a time when personality and behavior characteristics will be one of the first factors that health practitioners attempt to evaluate in assessing their patients' state of health or susceptibility to illness.

Where can researchers and clinicians begin to seek information that will help us to understand the nature of dysfunctional behavior? Attempts to define potentially destructive behavior patterns are difficult. We all know when we are irritable, tense, and overwrought, but our normal tendency is to attribtue these states to outside factors rather than to our own psychological predisposition. Also, some individual methods of adjusting to the stresses of daily life create more rather than less stress. Most of the time these individuals believe they are "mastering" their environments, coping with situations at maximum efficiency, and actively overcoming difficulties, when in fact their aggressive-defensive behavior pattern causes continual psychological and neurophysiological strain. In contrast to this active mode of dealing with problems is behavior in which the individual becomes completely passive and internalizes his stress. Such an individual may allow events to run their course without making any attempt to control situations at all, while resentment and frustration build to levels verging on neurosis. Both of these types are extreme and may result in dangerously prolonged stress. When such patterns are rigid, neither of these personality types ever has a chance to alleviate the accumulating tensions and to recover from a prolonged neurophysiological stress response. These examples are cited to point up how behavior patterns which might appear outwardly functional can give rise to clearly dysfunctional levels of sustained stress. Very few people exhibit these behavior patterns consistently, although all of us may slip into them from time to time to cope with particular situations. The understanding of personality and behavior is critical in stress mastery and stress reduction. If people are aware when their behavior is increasing personal stress, then they can be encouraged to modify it.

Efforts of researchers to define "dysfunctional" behavior as it relates to disease have focused on analyzing behavior and personality types among groups of patients suffering from specific diseases. Although such research is in a fledgling state, it appears that specific personality configurations are associated with specific diseases. By examining someone's psychological orientation and behavior, it is often possible to predict what disease he will be susceptible to if psychological and physiological defenses fail for any reason or because of prolonged stress. Why a particular personality type will be susceptible to one disease rather than another is as yet an unresolved issue. However, as research proceeds it is becoming clear that a particular personality type tends to get heart disease, another is predisposed to cancer, and yet another to arthritis. As these behavior and personality types become more well defined, it will probably become easier for practitioners to recognize these early predispositions with patients before any symptoms appear. Then, the possibilities for corrective intervention through voluntary behavior modification and life-style reorientation will increase enormously.

Biofeedback technology is already able to provide us with a means of mirroring the connections between a person's psychological and physiological activity. The neurophysiological profile mentioned earlier is one means of demonstrating to the patient the effects of his personality upon his entire physiology. By monitoring such functions as brain-wave activity, heart rate and regularity, involuntary muscle tension, blood pressure, peripheral circulation, and the like, it is relatively easy to detect when a particular function is hyper- or hypoactive. Each individual's unique profile of "normal" functioning can then be compared to a generalized profile in order to yield more information about the particular person's neurophysiological state (Pelletier, 1976). Brain-wave activity, for instance, is used as a primary index of neurophysiological activation. When a brain-wave pattern is predominantly beta (high-frequency, low-amplitude pattern of thirteen cycles per second and above), the person is in a state of normal waking consciousness. If the beta activity is extremely high, it is possible that the person is in a state of hyperactivation. Other physiological indices will reflect this state as well. In order to move from an aroused, beta dominant state to a relaxed state, most individuals merely have to close their eyes and relax. When the individual is in an unstressed state, slower wave-length activity will be visible in his brain-wave output. Most often, alpha brain waves (which form a low-frequency, high-amplitude pattern of between eight and thirteen cycles per second) become predominant. It is already possible to recognize when one function is out of line with the individual's particular pattern or with a generalized pattern. For instance, if someone is in a low-activation alpha state, he may manifest a high degree of involuntary muscle tension, contrary to what is normal in alpha. When this occurs, it is possible for the clinician to detect that the muscular system is the one in which tension and stress are manifest and potentially damaging. Likewise, it may be indicated that the individual's peripheral skin temperature, in the fingertips and toes, is inordinately low when compared to all the other parameters characteristic of alpha. From this can be inferred that the person manifests his stress in the vascular system, with unusually chronic constriction in the peripheral blood vessels. Such a person may be predisposed toward certain vascular disorders, such as Raynaud's disease and migraine headache.

If we can develop profiles of personality and behavior in order to be able to recognize what is dysfunctional or potentially pathogenic, then we will have the option to intervene and change these dysfunctional modes in addition to working directly with neurophysiological feedback. Most importantly, biofeedback instruments provide an immediate and objective source of information to the patient and clinician concerning the patient's mind/body interaction. The physiological effects of certain personality characteristics such as anger can be demonstrated to the patient, and their psychosomatic disorders explained.

At present, most of the research in personality and illness is centered around determining the characteristic patterns among people who have already contracted a particular disorder. Some of the personality characteristics typical of people with particular disorders may sound remarkably like your own. You should not be alarmed by this, since it does not inevitably follow that you will incur the diseases associated with these characteristics. These personality profiles are merely useful guidelines, to make people aware of what potentially hazardous behavior patterns might be. Self-assessment is seldom accurate, and analysis of behavior patterns should always rely on the interpretation of a skilled clinician. Personality profiles are only one element of diagnosis, and they are inconclusive in and of themselves. It is common among graduate students in any clinical area to imagine themselves stricken by each disorder that they are studying. With further training, they realize that diagnostic assessment is complex and indicative of a direction, rather than being definitive. Anyone approaching the subject area of personality and disease requires a comparable note of caution.

TYPE A BEHAVIOR
AND CARDIOVASCULAR DISORDERS

To date, the most comprehensive work in the area of personality and cardiovascular disorders is that of Friedman, Rosenman, and their colleagues in the formulation of Type A and Type B behavior as they relate to coronary heart disease (Friedman and Rosenman, 1974). One of the early clues indicating that a consistent pattern of behavior might exist among coronary patients came to these two cardiologists from the upholsterer who noticed that their patients' chairs were worn only on the front edges, as if people had been sitting in tense expectation. Another clue came to Friedman and Rosenman during a study on the role of dietary cholesterol in coronary heart disease with a group of volunteers from the San Francisco Junior League and their husbands. In the study, women suffered significantly less heart disease than their male counterparts. Dietary and cholesterol factors, the great bête noir of early coronary research, could not have made this difference, since the eating habits of the husbands and wives were exactly the same. Female hormonal differences were not likely factors, since white women in other countries had as high an incidence of heart disease as men, and black women in the United States were slightly more susceptible than black men. If sex hormones were to be implicated, then the hormones of the Junior League women had to be biochemically different from those of other women. Finally, one of the Junior League wives proclaimed that she could tell the doctors what was causing the husbands' heart attacks. She said it was stress that they incurred in their jobs. At that point, the research on the Type A behavior pattern began in earnest.

Over years of observation, using questionnaires and personal interviews to assist them, Friedman and Rosenman developed a detailed profile of the Type A personality and his less-stressed Type B counterpart. They attribute the inordinate degree of Type A behavior in the United States to a legacy of the Puritan ethic and the evolution of our economic system, since both encourage competition, achievement, and the acquisition of material wealth. Contemporary society has institutionalized and glorified these traits. In fact, typical Type A behavior is generally regarded with some reverence, since the Type A man has the desirable traits of drive, ambition, and the urge to get ahead with material success. All of this would be well and good were it not for the fact that the constellation of these Type A characteristics is an extremely stressful mode of behavior.

Friedman and Rosenman suggest that there are two traits which, if they occur together, automatically make up a Type A personality. These are excessive competitive drive and a chronic, continual sense of time urgency, accompanied by the feeling of always having to meet deadlines. Along with these two characteristics, Type A individuals show an easily aroused hostility. This hostility is usually well rationalized, and for the most part it is kept under control and externalized only during brief and random outbursts at unexpected times, when it may appear to others unwarranted. Contained and properly channeled aggression is a fundamental aspect of competitive ambition. When that drive is selective and appropriate, achievement and efficiency can result on a psychosocial level. Human neurophysiology adjusts easily to short-term activation in order to achieve a specific goal. However, when this aggression is generalized and the effects are diffuse on both a psychosocial and neurophysiological level, then the prolonged stress may produce both behavioral and physical disorders.

Predictably, the Type A man is fiercely impatient. If

someone is holding him up or taking too long to do a job, he becomes agitated and cannot restrain himself from interfering to get matters moving more quickly. On one of the personal interview tests devised by Friedman and Rosenman, the interviewer is asked to stutter deliberately, a phenomenon which is guaranteed to drive a Type A person to distraction. After several stuttered phrases, the interviewers can always spot Type A's, because they interrupt to finish the question before the interviewer is halfway through. This kind of "hurry sickness," as Friedman and Rosenman call it, pervades the whole life style of the Type A individual and extends even into his leisure time. He will always feel the need to be accomplishing something, to be engaged in some activity he considers constructive, so as not to waste a single minute of precious time. Time literally becomes the Type A individual's enemy, since he is always trying to beat it by setting unrealistic deadlines. He may create undue time pressure for himself in tasks ranging from getting out a report, cleaning out the attic, beating the commuter traffic home at night, to swimming his daily exercise laps in the pool. His competition with the clock is unrelieved, and although the Type A person may win minor skirmishes, time pressures inevitably leave the Type A man frustrated, nervous, hostile, and even more firmly determined to step up his efforts to accomplish more in less time.

Closely related to the Type A person's preoccupation with time is his tendency always to judge accomplishments in terms of numbers. If he's a lawyer, he'll tell you how many cases he won last year; if a surgeon, how many operations he performed; if in industry, what his production volume was; and, of course, he's bound to mention that perennial yardstick of dollars earned. However, contrary to what might be expected, the Type A person is not so concerned with what money can buy as he is simply with the numbers game that money represents. For him, money is merely a way to gauge his achievements, and he may have little or no idea of how to put his income to work to improve the overall quality of his life. Time, productivity, and money all become merely standards against which to measure himself. Since the Type A individual has no idea when enough is enough, or when his methods of self-measurement have become an end in themselves, the struggle is a never-ending exercise in futility. There is no time for genuine leisure and his sense of time urgency robs him of the ability to enjoy many of life's greatest pleasures: quiet contemplation; noncompetitive social interactions; a peaceful, unstructured day in the country; spontaneous sexual activity; books, music, art, and a whole catalogue of delights which he excludes because they are irrelevant to his continual struggle to achieve.

Typically, the Type A person will be aggressive and extroverted. He may have a very strong "social" personality and dominate conversations and gatherings wherever he is. This trait, although it may be very attractive when accompanied by wit and grace, is often tiresome for those around the Type A man, since he frequently tends to lead conversation back to his own interests and may exhibit little patience for discussion of topics which are unfamiliar to him or in which he is not interested. In their numerous interviews with Type A's, Friedman and Rosenman have noted that a typical Type A's outgoing personality conceals a deep-seated insecurity about his own worth. This insecurity may stem from the fact that his long-range life goals may be ill defined or unformulated due to his constant preoccupation with more immediate measures of his success. He is hopelessly myopic, concentrating always on today's achievements and spending little or no energy considering the far more important question, "What is it all for?"

Clearly, when someone is continuously engaged in an immediate struggle to overcome time, accumulate income, and best competitors on both business and social levels, great stress is the result. When an individual's security rests solely on the quantity of achievements, that security is under constant threat. Friedman and Rosenman have noted that the Type A man's well-concealed insecurity reflects itself in the way he relates to other people. Although few people want to be disliked, a Type A person will usually sacrifice the esteem of his peers or those who work under him for the respect and regard of his superiors. Admiration of those above him on the ladder is a gauge of status, and since one of the ways a Type A appeases his insecurity is by upgrading his status, his relationships with people other than those whose approbation he seeks may suffer. His contained aggressiveness and hostility will probably be reserved for underlings and intimate friends, although a Type A person will bristle noticeably when he encounters another equally ambitious, aggressive Type A individual.

Type A behavior is extremely complex and certainly in need of more extensive research before it can become a definitive tool for the prediction and prevention of cardiovascular disease. At the annual meeting of the American Psychosomatic Society on March 31, 1974, in Philadelphia, a variation upon the Type A pattern was suggested. Jenkins, Zyzanski, and Rosenman offered a new description of the coronary-prone personality as that of an individual who is basically noncompetitive with his peers. This is in contrast to the original description of an individual with a profound inclination and eagerness to compete and a persistent desire for recognition and advancement. This revised profile characterizes a coronary candidate as an essentially phlegmatic individual, with low self-esteem. This latter observation is extensively examined in a book entitled *Exercise Testing and Exercise Training in Coronary Heart Disease* (New York: Academic Press, 1973). Ironically enough, both of these observations concerning the Type A behavior might well be correct. A phlegmatic personality may well engage in a self-destructive compensation. In other words, an individual who is basically lazy and reluctant to achieve, with low self-esteem, may compensate for these inherent qualities by being overtly extremely gregarious, outgoing, hard-working, and achievement-oriented. This driving orientation in an individual who is not of that inclination creates a profound stress and split in psychological functioning. As a result, to be competitive and striving may be more destructive for that individual than for the person who is truly competitive and striving. Such an individual is not only engaged in stressful Type A behavior but is also struggling against his own inherent predisposition. These "phlegmatic" Type A's are almost certainly under even greater stress than their natural Type A counterparts, and the consequences for their health may be still more serious. Of course, all of these speculations will need further evaluation and testing before a definitive statement can be made concerning the nature of a Type A personality.

For the sake of clarity, but also because they believe it is valid, Friedman and Rosenman have divided people into two groups. They acknowledge freely that there is a wide range of variation possible along the spectrum, and there are many instances when Type A traits may be exhibited by an essentially Type B person and vice versa. But basically they believe that people tend to fall into one category or the other in varying degrees.

For the purposes of this chapter, it is the Type A pattern that is of greater interest, since it has been demonstrated to predispose people to cardiovascular disease. However, it is valuable to briefly examine the traits characteristic of Type B's for several reasons: first, to dispel the common misconception that a noncompetitive Type B will be less effective in his job and will be passed over for the "success" the Type A man so avidly seeks, and second, because by examining the Type B approach to life it is possible to derive some useful information concerning how to modify Type A behavior. Although the focus of most research is upon the pathogenic personality, understanding the Type

B approach to life is a step toward developing a profile of a positive personality style conducive to health maintenance. It is important to remember that Friedman and Rosenman have found no special pattern to the occupational involvements of the two types. Type B individuals are just as likely to be surgeons, accountants, bank presidents, and advertising executives as are Type A personalities. Similarly, there are many Type A's in job positions not generally regarded as high-powered or demanding. Furthermore, a Type B may be just as ambitious and have just as much "drive" as a Type A, but "the character of this drive is such that it seems to steady him, give confidence and security to him, rather than to goad, irritate, and infuriate, as with the Type A man" (Friedman and Rosenman, 1974).

Usually, the Type B will be free of the frantic sense of time urgency so typical of Type A's, except perhaps at certain times on the job when it is truly warranted. Time pressure will certainly never be a factor in his leisure time, since the Type B generally values his leisure for being just that—a time when he can relax without guilt. If he is ambitious, the Type B's ambition will probably be based on goals that have been well thought out. He does not feel the need to be measuring himself constantly against his peers or in terms of the number of his achievements. His sense of self-worth comes from knowing and working toward life goals which usually transcend mere material and social success. Also, he understands both his strengths and his weaknesses and tends to accept his deficiencies philosophically. In contrast to this, a Type A is never sure about his values and therefore seeks continual confirmation of his worth. Because the Type B works for personal satisfaction rather than to beat out the competition, he is not compulsively competitive like a Type A and is free of the hostility which so often accompanies a strong competitive drive. Type B individuals frequently allow themselves time for quiet contemplation in a self-styled meditation. When confronted with a problem or a task, a Type B considers alternatives, weighs all sides of the issue, and takes the time to think through an effective course of action. Interestingly, this method of coping seems to contribute to more creative output among Type B's than among Type A's. With the Type A's eagerness to get things done as fast as possible, he may respond to challenges in a rote fashion. Ultimately this may cause him to make errors in judgment, and since he never takes the time to consider new approaches to, or implications of, a situation, his creativity will be inhibited. For this reason, Type B's are frequently more successful in their vocations than Type A's. Hasty decisions, stereotyped responses to problem solving, and free-floating hostility are all an integral part of the Type A behavior pattern, which is not likely to win a Type A man the promotion when there is a Type B man around who is more thoughtful, original, equally competent, and less abrasive personally. Clearly, chronic Type A's would do well to study their Type B counterparts, since a Type B is far more likely to achieve a life style approaching genuine happiness. Furthermore, a Type B's low-stress mode of behavior is much more conducive to health maintenance. A more contemplative and considered life style based upon inner stability is at least as productive in a traditional sense as one based upon achievement and insecurity.

In their efforts to validate the Type A-B thesis, Friedman and Rosenman have gone beyond simply analyzing the personality data of heart-disease patients. They have also considered the neurophysiological profiles of classic Type A's, with some very insightful results. First of all, they noted that the serum-cholesterol levels seemed to vary directly with the intensity of the Type A behavior pattern, as with tax accountants prior to income-tax deadlines. Once the cardiologists established that serum cholesterol was affected by the Type A pattern, they proceeded to check on other indices related to coronary disease. According to their findings:

> ... we found that subjects *severely* afflicted with [Type A] behavior pattern exhibited every blood fat and hormone abnormality that the majority of coronary patients also showed. In other words, the same blood abnormalities that so many of our colleagues believe precede and possibly bring on coronary heart disease were already present in our Type A subjects. To us, the logic is irresistible: the behavior pattern itself gives rise to the abnormalities [Friedman and Rosenman, 1974].

This is one of the most unequivocal statements of personality characteristics as causal factors in organic disease. Personality attributes which are active over time affect the cardiovascular system and actively predispose an individual toward coronary disease.

Most recently, Rosenman and his colleagues reported the results of an eight-and-a-half year follow-up study of 257 male patients between the ages of 39 and 59 for predicting coronary disease. Incidence of coronary heart disease (CHD) was significantly associated with parental history, diabetes, education, smoking, blood pressure, and serum-cholesterol levels. Researchers have noted that these classical factors account for only about one half of coronary incidence in middle-aged American men. From the Rosenman study, it is clear that Type A behavior was a strong factor in CHD and that "this association could not be explained by association of behavior pattern with any single predictive risk factor or any combination of them" (Rosenman et al., 1975). Comprehensive data were obtained from the men who were employed by ten California companies. After analyzing these data, it was clear that the Type-A-behavior risk factor could not be "explained away" by the other risk factors and was clearly a contributing factor itself. Behavior patterns of Type A operate in addition to and in conjunction with the classical risk factors. Coronary risk factors are complex in their interconnection, so any attempt at a causal interpretation of these results using one single factor is not likely to be adequate. However, all together, these factors can be useful in predicting CHD and may aid in primary prevention. Intervention is still untested, and the report concludes: "It has not yet been shown whether altering facets of the behavior pattern in surviving Type A CHD patients reduces their risk of reinfarction, but research along these lines is strongly indicated." Since CHD is due to multiple factors, preventive intervention would require several simultaneous life-style changes, including diet, exercise, psychotherapy, and stress-reduction practices. These methods of prevention may prove to be a potent means of alleviating cardiovascular disorders.

Research and clinical work by Friedman and Rosenman have given a significant boost to theories connecting personality, behavior, and stress to psychosomatic disease. Although many of their colleagues initially viewed their thesis with skepticism, the thoroughness of their research over many years is convincing evidence that Type A behavior is a major risk factor in coronary heart disease. As a result, many cardiologists are now beginning to counsel patients in methods of behavior modification and attitude reorientation as part of their treatment. This is an encouraging step forward. Friedman and Rosenman offer a variety of suggestions to aid heart patients in breaking out of the Type A mold. Many of their patients have successfully done just that, especially after a first heart attack has shocked them into a reevaluation of their approach to life and health. However, few of their suggestions involve specific instructions in deep relaxation or meditative practices. It is hoped that the exercises and suggestions for behavior change presented in later chapters will add substantially to the effective methods available for rectifying the Type A risk factor in coronary disease.

PERSONALITY AND EMOTIONS IN CANCER

One of the most fascinating and highly controversial areas in current medical research is the role of personality and behavior in cancer. Emotional and psychological factors may influence neurophysiological functioning and hence depress the vital immune response, increasing susceptibility to viral infections and thereby creating conditions in which the growth of cancerous tumors and mutant cells is allowed to proceed unchecked by the body's normal defense mechanisms. Inevitably, the question arises: What specific psychological and emotional patterns precede the development of cancer? Over the last fifty years, this has been an actively investigated subject, although it is still controversial. Researchers themselves are not sure whether such a "carcinogenic personality" really exists, or, even if it does, to what extent it is responsible for the onset of cancer. However, the information that has accumulated from an ever-growing number of sources seems to point to a fairly well-defined emotional and psychological complex which appears consistently among cancer patients.

A composite profile of the cancer victim has been derived from psychological testing of people of various ages and diagnostic categories (Greene and Miller, 1958; Klopfer, 1957; LeShan, 1961). Typically, a cancer patient has suffered severe emotional disturbance in early childhood, up to the age of fifteen. Most frequently, this resulted from his (or her) relationships with parents or a breakup in the unity of the family. Due to divorce, death of either parent, chronic friction between parents, or prolonged separation of one or both parents from the child, the child experienced a great sense of loss, loneliness, anxiety, and rejection. He felt he had failed in his earliest attempts to form warm and satisfying relationships. His reaction to this may have been to overcompensate by trying constantly to please others and thus win their affection. If he continued to be frustrated in these attempts, his anger, loneliness, hopelessness, and self-hatred became more pronounced, with anxiety and depression becoming his constant companions. Later in life, cancer victims are frequently described by their friends as exceptionally fine, thoughtful, gentle, uncomplaining people, and almost "too good to be true" (LeShan and Worthington, "Personality . . . ," 1956). All of these traits appear to be an amplification of the frustrated need to win love and affection. Underneath, these individuals may still have feelings of unworthiness and self-dislike. Feelings of hostility are bottled up and suppressed rather than brought to the surface and worked through. This "too good to be true" trait can assume an almost martyrlike quality, and many cancer researchers speculate that it masks a chronic low-key depression. During adulthood, a cancer victim usually achieves love, healthy relationships, and some measure of success through marriage, a career, or parenthood. For the first time in his life, he may feel genuinely happy and optimistic. However, since this happiness is dependent upon external factors such as spouse, children, and job, it is inevitable that the emotional matrix which supports the individual will change. Change may take the form of death of a spouse, loss of a job, retirement, or children leaving the home to embark on their own lives. When this occurs, the old patterns return and engulf the individual in a sense of isolation, hopelessness, and depression. With a high degree of predictability, such individuals are found to succumb to cancer within six months to a year. When the disease is discovered, their despair deepens, and the classic "helpless-hopeless" cycle is initiated. As psychological defenses fall, the disease aggravates the preexisting state of chronic depression. This degenerative cycle is yet another example of a negative closed-loop feedback system, with the individual left totally defenseless as the disease runs its course.

Observations of early traumatic events as an important contributing factor in the development of neoplastic disease were recently underscored by researchers at the University of Kansas Medical Center. Shirley Lansky, Eileen Goggins, and Khatab Hassanein conducted a study in order to evaluate the psychological functioning of nine boys and nine girls, aged 5½ to 15, who had leukemia or solid tumor (Lansky, Goggins, and Hassanein, 1975). They studied three factors: anxiety, fantasy, and reality testing. They designed their study to "get beneath the surface of passivity to the child's inner world." In the younger age group, males showed a significantly higher anxiety level than females, thus supporting the general assumption that males have generally greater susceptibility to stress than females. However, the findings in the older age group indicated that males have a better ability to view things realistically than females. In terms of fantasy, "a significant trend emerged revealing a difference in the fantasy life of normal children who usually evince a balance of positive and negative fantasy and the fatally ill child where the balance is skewed to the side of negative fantasy." In terms of reality testing, the studies indicated that children with malignancies had great difficulty in adequately testing out reality. Many displayed a propensity for distortion and unrealistic thinking, particularly in unstructured situations.

Questions of causation clearly cannot be answered by such a study. However, it supports other research which suggests that individuals with malignant neoplastic diseases are more anxious than their counterparts. Certainly, knowledge of the presence of the disease is a contributing factor. It is not possible to know yet whether these factors predispose a child toward the development of the disease or whether the disease in fact triggers these personality changes. For our purposes here, the hypothesis is that subtle psychological changes initiate subtle neurophysiological changes which in turn create further aberrations of the psychological processes in a negative closed-loop system which ultimately predisposes the individual toward the development of severe organic pathology later in life.

The hypothesis that individuals may be psychologically predisposed to the onset of cancer is hardly new, although it is still controversial. Even the ancient physician Galen observed in 180 A.D. that melancholy women were more likely to suffer from cancer than sanguine women. Samuel J. Kowal of Boston University has investigated the attitudes of eighteenth- and nineteenth-century physicians toward cancer. According to Kowal's overview, these physicians were impressed by the frequency with which certain life situations seemed to occur prior to the development of a neoplasm or cancerous growth. A common denominator which they noted was a reaction of despair and hopelessness following such diverse occurrences as the death of a friend or relative, separation, economic, political, professional, and other frustrations. Their patients apparently lost all desire to live, and by virtue of this type of passive surrender the stage was set for the development of a malignancy (Kowal, 1955). New York surgeon Willard Parker, who operated on breast-cancer patients between the years 1830 and 1883, addressed himself to the question of whether anxiety played a role in cancer onset. His conclusion was this: "There are the strongest physiological reasons for believing that great mental depression, particularly grief, induces a predisposition to such disease as cancer, or becomes an exciting cause under circumstances where the predisposition had already been acquired" (Parker, 1885). More recently, other researchers have speculated upon the role of psychological factors in the progress of the disease once it has been contracted. One group of researchers who worked with 40 breast cancer cases stated the problem as follows:

> Modern cancer investigators believe that everyone carries the cancer potential within him, that it is

simply a matter of whether you die of something else before you die of cancer. This approach raises the interesting question of why the dormant, pre-cancerous state remains dormant in many, whereas in others it changes early and rapidly. Why, after it appears as a malignancy that can be diagnosed, does it or does it not metastasize early or late in some? And what is the nature of the body's defensive reaction to cancer? [Bacon, Rennecker, and Cutler, 1952].

In answer to these questions, the breast-cancer researchers indicated they believed that psychological factors had a great deal to do with both the onset and progress of the disease. Another group, whose main focus of interest was disease progress in a group of cancerous men, concluded that intense emotional stress may exert a profoundly stimulating effect on the growth rate of an established cancer (Blumberg, West, and Ellis, 1954). They hypothesized that we might begin to explain host resistance to cancer in terms of ability to reduce or adapt effectively to stresses which are brought on by environmental or emotional conflicts. There are numerous other theories concerning the role of emotional factors in the onset and course of cancer. It is unlikely, however, that single causative factors are involved. Predisposition to cancer and all psychosomatic disorders is based upon a developmental process involving multiple psychosocial and neurophysiological influences. This multiplicity of interacting factors is in itself a convincing argument that a holistic approach to cancer needs to be adopted.

Lawrence LeShan, former Chief of the Psychology Department at the Institute of Applied Biology in New York, has conducted some of the most extensive work concerning the carcinogenic personality. One of his studies involved a group of 250 patients with malignant disease, whose personalities were evaluated by means of the Worthington Personal History, which is a projective test designed to elicit open-ended responses. In addition, clinical interviews were given to 80 of those patients: 71 patients were seen for two or three hours, and 9 were interviewed more intensively, for a total of 1,070 hours. Based upon the information collected, LeShan concluded that certain psychological patterns were clearly characteristic of this patient population. Four factors were found to differentiate the cancer patients from a control group: 1) a lost relationship prior to the diagnosis of cancer; 2) an inability to express hostility in their own defense; 3) feelings of unworthiness and self-dislike; and 4) tension over the relationship with one or both parents. Furthermore, he observed a psychodynamic pattern based on a traumatic event in childhood which applied to 62 percent of the cancer victims and only 10 percent of the control group (LeShan and Worthington, "Some recurrent . . . ," 1956). Emotional disruption between the patient and parent during early childhood appeared to be one of the major factors in the psychodynamic predisposition to cancer later in life.

Problems in sexual adjustment appear to be another major factor in the emotional makeup of cancer patients, particularly in women who develop cancer of the cervix or breast. In one study, the personality profiles of 100 women with cancer of the cervix were compared to those of another group of women with cancer at other sites. According to the researchers:

> Prominent in this study was a dislike of sexual intercourse, amounting to an actual aversion to it, in a high proportion of the patients. The failure to achieve orgasmic satisfaction during intercourse, the high incidence of divorce, desertion, unfaithful husbands, separation, sexual intercourse with others than the marital partner, are probable indications of poor sexual adjustment. All of these occur more frequently in patients with cancer of the cervix than in those with cancer at other sites and antedate the onset of the cancer by many years [Stephenson and Grace, 1954].

Similarly, Harold Voth, a psychiatrist at the Menninger Foundation, has indicated that women who have never nursed children are more susceptible to breast cancer than those who have. Some researchers feel that this is because the breast tissue has never performed its natural function of producing milk. However, as Voth notes: "A more sophisticated hypothesis is that early childhood experiences are such that these women do not have it in their psychological makeup to nurse." He goes on to emphasize the importance of childhood trauma in creating future problems:

> We know that the ability to handle life's vicissitudes is tied to childhood experience. Research shows that individuals who experience loss in the years before adolescence are especially pregnable to loss later. The child does not know how to mourn, or is taught to "be a good boy or girl" and not to mourn. Grief gets frozen within him. Then losses later in life reawaken painful memories and the person is confronted with a double loss [*Moneysworth*, May 26, 1975].

In effect, Voth has speculated that childhood conflicts involving emotional expression may be a predecessor of the sexual maladjustment noted in certain forms of female cancer. Inhibited emotional expression or disrupted relationships are only one factor and are not causative in and of themselves. They are simply one step in a progression involving many factors which collectively predispose an individual toward cancer. Research concerning these types of cancer suggests that, by analyzing the personality and emotional characteristics which precede them, it may even be possible to look at other individuals and to predict the site at which a future cancer will develop. Also, it may be that early psychotherapeutic intervention to correct sexually related emotional disturbances will become an important factor in our efforts to prevent these types of cancer.

Voth has also conducted research paralleling that of

LeShan with victims of other types of cancer. He has examined many patients and studied the medical records of numerous others who have had the disease over the last hundred years. Based on these records, Voth believes there is a dramatic correlation between susceptibility to cancer and a melancholy, anxious disposition, accompanied by continual low-key depression and a limited capacity to cope with life. Also, he has noted that most victims suffered a "significant emotional loss" up to five years before the onset of the disease, and this lends considerable support to LeShan's earlier observations.

Similar research has been conducted by David M. Kissen with 366 male patients between the ages of 55 and 64 in three general hospitals. Of these, 218 had lung cancer, and the other patients were assigned as a control group. Some of the controls were chosen because they had long histories of psychosomatic disorders, and others because they had experienced almost none. Male patients with lung cancer again exhibited several characteristic traits and emotional profiles. These were: 1) childhood trauma resulting from death or absence of parents, or chronic friction between them; and 2) an adult life in which the main adverse events related to work and interpersonal difficulties, particularly marital (Kissen, 1967). Duration of adult problems seemed to be significant. If the difficulties had lasted more than ten years, they seemed to have more influence than those of shorter duration. Interestingly, there was a marked similarity in the psychosocial histories of the lung-cancer patients and the psychosomatic men. However, the lung-cancer victims differed in one important respect: they typically had "poor outlets for emotional discharge." This factor was viewed as quite important, since it pointed to the fact that the specific life event may not be as important as the person's reaction to that occurrence. Personality factors determine how an individual will react, and that reaction can be healthy or pathogenic. Certain predispositions are established but are not irrevocable.

One of the most substantial studies concerning psychological factors in malignant-tumor onset is a recent study by Caroline Thomas and Karen Duszynski of the Johns Hopkins University School of Medicine. Their study is significant because it is prospective rather than retrospective, and goes a long way toward resolving whether certain psychological factors predispose individuals toward cancer or are the result of that diagnosis. Through extensive psychological testing, Thomas and Duszynski studied 1,337 Johns Hopkins medical students who graduated between 1948 and 1964. They were trying to determine if there were predictable precursors of five disease states: suicide, mental illness, malignant tumor, hypertension, and coronary heart disease. According to their findings, the suicide, mental-illness, and malignant-tumor groups showed psychological differences from their unaffected classmates starting from one to twenty-three years before the onset of disease or death. Most importantly, the group who developed malignant tumors were the most psychologically distinct. In all three groups, the "lack of closeness to parents" was the significant predictor of future disease, with the twenty male medical students in the malignant-tumor group being most distinct on this parameter. When discussing their results the researchers noted that these findings agreed with those of LeShan, Bahnson, and Kissen:

> Our finding that subjects who later developed malignant tumor perceived their relationship to their parents as one which gave evidence of a lack of closeness seems to be consistent with the hypotheses suggested in the retrospective studies cited, and is, we believe, the first piece of prospective evidence that such may actually be the case [Thomas and Duszynski, 1974].

Also, the researchers note the need for developing a more complete set of psychosomatic predictors by including physiological, biochemical, and immunological predictors with these psychological parameters. Although such research is in its infancy, it appears to be promising.

As should be evident from the foregoing, clinicians are still far from understanding if and how personality and emotional factors influence the onset and course of cancer. Although there does seem to be a pattern emerging, it is difficult to define a specific personality configuration or set of emotional stresses which correlates directly with the disease. Most often, it appears that a wide variety of emotional conditions precede cancer onset. However, several elements do tend to recur consistently, such as the "despair" syndrome noted by LeShan: a barren and hopeless state, in which the afflicted individual experiences an extreme sense of unrelatedness to everything around him. Despair engulfs him to such an extent that love cannot bridge the gap, nor can he express such emotions as anger, resentment, jealousy, and hostility in order to ease the loneliness. He sees no possibility of ever attaining any satisfaction or meaning in his life, and in spite of any effort he may make, there is no hope for the future. This particular *Weltanschauung* may have been latent or suppressed for a prolonged period of time. It crystallizes after a major traumatic event in the adult life of someone who has suffered severe emotional disruption in childhood, or in someone who perceives relationships as dangerous and potentially painful. Fairly soon after the traumatic event, cancer is likely to be diagnosed. LeShan (1961) and others have summed up their statistical and clinical research as follows: 1) there seems to be a correlation between cancer and certain types of psychological situations: 2) the most consistently reported psychological finding has been the loss of a major emotional relationship prior to the first symptoms of the tumor; 3) there appears to be some relationship between personality organization and the length of time between a traumatic event in the life of the patients and the appearance of a neoplasm; and also there may be some relationship between personality organization and the type or location of a cancer.

It is important to realize that these observations do not imply an inevitable progression of degenerative disease. Such research carries a note of optimism, for it suggests that psychosocial and personality factors can be changed in order to promote healing and a movement away from despair. Carcinogenic factors are influences and predispositions, not certainties.

Numerous clinical studies, using psychological testing with cancer patients, have supported LeShan's observations and added refinements. Results of these studies were summarized by Charles Goldfarb and his colleagues at the St. Vincent's Hospital and Medical Center of New York: "Most patients with malignancies appear to have the following characteristics: 1) maternal domination; 2) immature sexual adjustment; 3) inability to express hostility; 4) inability to accept loss of a significant object; and 5) pre-neoplastic feelings of hopelessness, helplessness, and despair" (Goldfarb, Driesen, and Cole, 1967). Using this personality profile, these researchers suggested one way of interrupting the helpless-hopeless cycle. They report the cases of three women with advanced breast cancer and concomitant depression who were treated with electroshock therapy while undergoing cancer chemotherapy. In all three cases there were positive effects upon the cancer and metastases, with one woman experiencing a complete remission for eighteen months. Goldfarb and his colleagues interpret these results to indicate that the alleviation of the depression associated with cancer may have a positive effect upon the immunological system. Linking depression and cancer in a causal manner is too simplistic, since this disorder involves a complex developmental matrix comparable to cardiovascular disorders. However, these results may at least indicate that a positive alteration in an individual's emotional state can have an effect upon the course of malignancy. If a clear profile of the susceptible personality is formulated, it will be an invaluable tool in cancer prevention, by making possible early psychotherapeutic correction and reorientation of psychological attitudes and behavior.

Even now some specialists hypothesize that an effort of conscious will can overcome the predisposition to disease. Researchers at the University of Rochester School of Medicine who have studied the psychological factors modifying host resistance to experimental infections observed, "Life situations judged stressful, such as the loss of a loved one, might be expected to predispose some to disease states and have a protective effect on others" (Friedman, Glasgow, and Adler, 1969). By this they imply that a traumatic event, such as those which typically precede cancer onset, might serve to jar the individual out of a depressed, listless state and encourage him to act positively in restructuring his life. Friedman and his colleagues have focused upon the interaction between psychosocial factors, neurophysiology, and disease onset. They have concluded that psychosocial factors do in fact play a major part in lowering host resistance to infectious diseases and cancer:

> From the experience included in this report and the many studies of other investigators reviewed elsewhere, it now appears certain that environmental factors of a psychological nature can modify resistance to a number of infectious and neoplastic diseases. Further studies that merely demonstrate this fact cannot, therefore, significantly advance our state of knowledge. . . . It also appears that no available single theory of stress can predict the effects that a particular form of stimulation will have upon host resistance and that even the direction of change and susceptibility is dependent upon the disease that the organism is experiencing [Friedman, Glasgow, and Adler, 1969].

Even when all or many of the predisposing factors that have been discussed here are present, there is the potential to rise above the predispositions and in fact not contract the disease, which is simply a probability. All of these experimental and clinical results indicate an increased propensity to contract cancer, but they do not preclude intervention. In fact, they encourage it. It is desirable to examine these factors to make individuals aware of them, and then to suggest positive means by which an individual might change his or her response to these psychosocial influences.

A phenomenon which supports this optimism is the spontaneous regression of cancer. This inevitably inspires heated debate whenever it is discussed. To date, the most comprehensive study has been conducted by Everson and Cole and reported in their classic book, *The Spontaneous Regression of Cancer*. According to their definition, "spontaneous regression of cancer is the partial or complete disappearance of a malignant tumor in the absence of all treatment or in the presence of therapy which is considered inadequate to exert a significant influence on neoplastic disease" (Everson and Cole, 1966). Out of 1,000 cases of supposed spontaneous regression, they found only 176 which they considered to be adequately documented examples. Proof of the existence of spontaneous regression is not easily obtained. In fact, many clinicians do not believe it exists. Everson and Cole attributed the 176 regressions to such physical factors as endocrine influences, unusual sensitivity to inadequate radiation or other therapy, fever and/or infection, allergic or immune reactions, interference with nutrition of the tumor, and removal of the carcinogenic agent (Everson and Cole, 1966). What they failed to consider adequately is the role of psychological factors. Had these factors been considered, it might have been noted that when the helpless-hopeless degenerative cycle is altered, there is a chance for the individual to engage in the process of self-healing.

Immunological imbalances are cited as a major factor in William Boyd's classic book, also entitled *The Spontaneous*

Regression of Cancer (1966). Boyd reviews twenty-three documented instances of spontaneous regression and notes that this phenomenon is not necessarily due to a single factor. He is also struck by the fact that good health appeared to induce an immunity to cancer, since cancer cells die when injected or implanted under the skin of healthy volunteers. His research suggests three possible causal factors in spontaneous regression: "1) the effects of therapy; 2) the influence of hormones; 3) the action of immune bodies." Again, there is no consideration of psychosocial influences as the link between stress and the disturbance of the immunological system which may precede cancer. In concluding his book, Boyd suggests that psychosocial factors may play a role in determining who, of the numerous individuals exposed to carcinogenic influences each day, will develop a malignancy. According to Boyd:

> When we consider that everyone is exposed repeatedly to numerous cancer-inducing agents and conditions, that indeed we may be said throughout life to swim through a sea of carcinogens, it seems reasonable to suppose that everyone . . . must develop one or more foci of neoplasia, just as he develops foci of tuberculosis infection. But in both cases they are held in check . . . when the clinician and experimentalist concentrate on immunity rather than on mortality . . . we may begin to think of the prevention, the control and the cure of cancer [Boyd, 1966].

Recently, other researchers have sought the links between psychosocial factors and immunity with promising results. However, to date none of the clinical or experimental evidence is conclusive. Systematic investigation of spontaneous regression requires a comprehensive approach. It is an area of inquiry with major implications for all cancer research and treatment.

The possibility for such a holistic approach to cancer

treatment was eloquently stated by Eugene Pendergrass, then President of the American Cancer Society, as long ago as 1959, in an address to the Society:

> Now, finally, I would like to leave you with a thought that is very near to my heart. Anyone who has had an extensive experience in the treatment of cancer is aware that there are great differences among patients . . . I personally have observed cancer patients who have undergone successful treatment and were living and well for years. Then an emotional stress, such as the death of a son in World War II, the infidelity of a daughter-in-law, or the burden of long unemployment, seemed to have been precipitating factors in the reactivation of their disease which resulted in death . . . There is solid evidence that the course of disease in general is affected by emotional distress . . . Thus, we as doctors may begin to emphasize treatment of the patient as a whole as well as the disease from which the patient is suffering. We may learn how to influence general body symptoms and through them modify neoplasm which resides within the body. As we go forward in this unrelenting pursuit of the truth to stamp out cancer . . . searching for new means of controlling growth, both within the cell and through systemic influences, it is my sincere hope that we can widen the quest to include the distinct possibility that within one's mind is the power capable of exerting forces which can either enhance or inhibit the progress of this disease [Pendergrass, 1959].

Psychological, emotional, and personal belief factors may play a more important role in the onset and course of malignancy than is currently acknowledged. In keeping with the observations of earlier researchers, O. Carl Simonton and Stephanie Matthews-Simonton cite the following psychological factors in cancer:

> Those predisposing factors most agreed upon as (negative) personality characteristics of the cancer pa-

tient are: 1) a great tendency to hold resentment and
a marked inability to forgive, 2) a tendency towards
self-pity, 3) a poor ability to develop and maintain
meaningful, long-term relationships, 4) a very poor
self-image [Simonton and Simonton, 1975].

According to the Simontons, these characteristics are
changeable depending upon the belief system of the patient,
his family, and the attending physician. One of the most
significant contributions of their clinical treatment of cancer patients concerns the interaction between a patient's
belief system and the course of treatment. Patients who experienced spontaneous regressions had very often undergone a process of revisualizing themselves as well and had
maintained a positive image of themselves. Based upon this
observation, the Simontons have devised a system of supportive psychotherapy as an adjunct to standard cancer
therapy. Central to their approach is the patient's ability to
confront his personal belief systems and to become an active
participant in visualizing the effects of the therapy upon his
malignancy. Details of their therapeutic approach are discussed in Chapter 7. To date, the Simontons have treated
152 patients, and they could accurately predict the outcome
of therapy based upon the presence or absence of positive
attitudes among their patients. Over an eighteen-month
period, only two of the patients did not fall into the predicted
categories. Overall, those patients with positive attitudes
had good responses while those with negative attitudes had
poor responses to comparable treatment. Results with these
patient cases are under systematic evaluation, but their
preliminary results indicate a profound link between psychological and emotional factors which can be utilized to
enable an individual to recover from malignancy.

PERSONALITY AND RHEUMATOID ARTHRITIS

Consideration of personality factors as they related to cardiovascular disease and cancer has encouraged similar re-

search into other disorders, including rheumatoid arthritis and migraine headache. Although this work is not as comprehensive as that on heart disease and cancer, it is productive to briefly note some of the traits that have been found to recur in patients suffering from these afflictions.

Rheumatoid arthritis and osteoarthritis are classified, along with such diseases as ulcerative colitis, as autoimmune diseases. Since these disorders literally involve the body's "turning on itself," researchers have wondered whether a particular form of self-destructive personality might not translate into an autoimmune, neurophysiological self-destructiveness. As with most of the research in these areas, the evidence is still too sketchy to draw any conclusions. R. H. Moos, who has studied the histories of over five thousand patients with rheumatoid arthritis, has isolated a number of personality traits in rheumatoid patients which differentiate them from control groups. According to Moos, the rheumatoid arthritics tend to be "self-sacrificing, masochistic, conforming, self-conscious, shy, inhibited, perfectionistic, and interested in sports" (Moos and Solomon, 1965). Female rheumatoid patients are nervous, tense, worried, moody, depressed, and typically had mothers whom they felt rejected them and fathers who were unduly strict. They also had difficulty expressing anger, in contrast to their healthy sisters. On the Minnesota Multiphasic Personality Inventory, or MMPI, women with pronounced rheumatoid arthritis scored higher than healthy females on the measures of inhibition of anger, anxiety, depression, compliance-subservience, conservatism, security-seeking, shyness, and introversion. Additionally, arthritics who responded poorly to therapy and whose disease progressed rapidly were noted to be more anxious and depressed, more isolated, alienated, and introverted, than those whose disease took a more benign course.

George Solomon, whose work on stress, immunity, and cancer was discussed earlier, made this observation about rheumatoid arthritis: "It seemed as if the occurrence of psychic disequilibrium in the presence of the rheumatoid factor might lead to overt rheumatoid disease, so that physically healthy persons with the rheumatoid factor, to remain so, need to be psychologically healthy as well. Thus, emotional decompensation in the predisposed individual might result in a specific physical illness" (Solomon, 1969). Physical factors in interaction with certain personality traits appear to be a necessary precondition for the onset of arthritic disorders. A classic study of ulcerative colitis by Engel produced personality data strikingly comparable to that of Moos on rheumatoid patients. Engel's colitis patients exhibited an obsessive-compulsive behavior pattern involving excessive neatness, indecision, conformity, overintellectualism, rigid morality, and anxiety (Engel, 1955). Like the patients suffering from rheumatoid disorders, they could not express hostility or anger directly and seemed immature and dependent. Colitis patients generally had mothers who were controlling and had a propensity to assume the role of martyr, much like the mothers of rheumatoid-arthritis victims. Given these similarities in personality factors, and the differences in the site of the disorders, there is a clear indication that multiple factors are involved in the determination of which specific disorder will develop.

PERSONALITY AND MIGRAINE

Migraine headache is a vascular disorder, and migraine patients exhibit many of the same characteristics seen in the Type A pattern, although with some important differences. Again, the similarity of psychological orientation among people suffering from different disorders afflicting the same general physiological systems is noteworthy. It seems to indicate that specific behavior patterns may negatively affect specific neurophysiological systems, albeit in varying ways. Migraine patients suffer from the same sense of unworthiness that haunts the Type A person, and they also try to compensate for this by assuming more of a burden than they can cope with during work and leisure time. Like the Type A personality, the migraine sufferer wants desperately to be loved and admired, since the approval of others is essential to him in order to mitigate his sense of inadequacy. The futility of such an approach to affirming self-worth often leads to frustration, irritability, poor judgment, and hostility, which occasionally bursts forth unexpectedly, much like the free-floating hostility of the Type A individual (Friedman and Rosenman, 1974).

Migraine patients can be rigid, somewhat self-righteous, and at times almost fanatical. They simply try too hard at everything they do, and defeat themselves in the process. Harold G. Wolff, whose work on stress and migraine is still considered definitive, points up an interesting paradox in the migraine syndrome. Most frequently, migraine onset occurs during leisure time. Sundays seem to be the favored day for migraine, as if the victim has bottled up all the frustrations of his work week only to be afflicted with it when he finally attempts to unwind. One primary difference between migraine patients and Type A individuals seems to be in their relations to others. Migraine sufferers will tend to be self-sacrificing in their constant need to take on more than they can handle. Coronary-prone individuals are more likely to be aggressive and egotistical in their quest to achieve and perform. They are ruthless in their efforts to master the environment and control the course of events.

Migraine may be one end result of a developmental sequence characteristic of cardiovascular disorders. There is a consistent behavioral pattern which precedes migraine onset. With patients who suffer from migraine, the initial psychological event seems to be a drawing back and withdrawing of energy from emotional involvements (Pelletier and Peper, 1976). That person literally ceases to let his emotional expression flow out toward other people, and he begins to contain his anger and resentment. When this becomes habitual, he will then report sensations of coolness in the extremities, such as clammy hands or feet and hands that become cold quite readily. If the emotional withdrawal continues, he may report sleep-onset insomnia due to cold hands or feet. These uncomfortable sensations are merely symptoms of a more basic disorder. Sleep-onset insomnia fits well at this stage, since the last place where the migraine sufferer is likely to feel expansive is while sleeping in the same bed or room with a person he resents. Also, the insomnia can be interpreted as a normal stress reaction, initiated to maintain vigilance in a situation which is perceived to be threatening. After a period of disrupted sleep patterns, the classical migraine symptoms of nausea, light sensitivity, and visual aberrations begin to appear. Through the use of psychotherapy and biofeedback, this trend can be reversed as the patients allow themselves to express their resentment and to cease their withdrawal. Chronic withdrawal of emotional energy from close relationships appears to induce a measurable decrease in peripheral body temperature, which provides a means of detecting and altering this psychosomatic disorder.

FUTURE RESEARCH

As you consider the personality types which have been described with the implications of their apparent correlation to specific diseases, please remember that this is a speculative area of inquiry, in its fledgling stages of development. At the present time, to make any definitive pronouncements about the validity of these correlations or in any way to demonstrate a definitive causal relationship between personality and illness is simply not possible. Also, it is important to remember that the purpose of examining this data is not to alarm those individuals who exhibit some of these personality patterns. These profiles are intended to increase your awareness of what form some of these possibly destructive modes of behavior may become manifest. Just because you recognize some of your own behavior in these descriptions does not mean that you are necessarily prone to the disorders they seem to accompany. Assessment of the interaction between personality factors and psychosomatic disorders requires the attention of a skilled clinician. Perhaps by simply being aware of these tendencies, you may be encouraged to reevaluate your own attitudes and psychological orientation.

As research concerning the personality factors of disorders continues, it is likely that clear correlations will be established and the development of a holistic approach to both health and illness will advance greatly. Personality and behavioral traits are critical aspects in the chain of events from excess neurophysiological stress to the specific disorder. When life events precipitate excessive stress, these personality traits and lifelong patterns of behavior are important determinants of how that stress is likely to manifest itself. One individual's susceptible area is his cardiovascular system, while another individual's personality may predispose him toward cancer. In this model, a disorder is not a static manifestation of pathology, but rather a dynamic, developmental process. Any dynamic system can be altered away from pathology toward health, and that is a source of great optimism. Adoption of particular kinds of behavior is frequently an effort at adaptation and stress management. But such efforts may err in the direction of increasing stress rather than stress reduction. Eugene Pendergrass makes this point in assessing the role of the doctor in cancer treatment:

> He must understand man's basic need and his means of adaptation in a physical, organic, and social environment. He must study the phases of adjustment and define more clearly their determinants and what constitutes meaningful stress. He must study and devise new and effective means of aiding the adaptive efforts of the patient. He must be aware that many of the signs and symptoms manifested by the sick person are the attempts at adaptation and expression rather than disease itself. Such thoughts must be kept in mind; otherwise the attempts at therapy will deprive

the patient of defenses without making more suitable ones available [Pendergrass, 1959].

Illness itself may be the ultimate defense in a desperate last-ditch effort to cope with overwhelming circumstances. Symptoms and disorders may be the momentary attempt to initiate a protective action in fighting for survival. Many people suffering from psychosomatic disorders may be unconsciously attached to the symptoms for "secondary gains," such as to obtain the love and care they receive when they are ill, or perhaps to avoid dealing with problems they have no hope of managing successfully. Issues of personality and psychosocial factors always need to be considered when serious illness occurs if it is to be treated effectively and prevented from recurring. Underlying causes of the disorder need to be sought, and if these causes are dysfunctional efforts at adaptation manifested in particular personality and behavior styles, the patient must be made aware of alternative methods of coping. Teaching people alternative methods of managing environmental and psychosocial stress is one of the fundamental aspects of holistic medicine. If destructive, dysfunctional, high-stress behavior can be recognized early and changed, this will be a major step toward establishing a true preventive medicine.

Afflictions of Civilization

5

One of the outstanding achievements of modern medical science has been its success in reducing human vulnerability to infectious disease. This success is in large part due to vaccination, which encourages the human body to develop and maintain its own defenses against the disease agent through the introduction into the body of a minute, carefully controlled, non-pathogenic amount of the agent itself. Western society is now largely free of such devastating and frequently fatal illnesses as smallpox, typhoid, cholera, and polio. However, at the same time that medicine has made such remarkable advances in controlling infectious disease, post-industrial societies have experienced a staggering increase in death and disability from diseases of a wholly different sort. For the first time in history, the major causes of death and disease are stress-related disorders.

Both chronic and acute illnesses have been linked to psychological and environmental factors. Psychosomatic disorders due to psychosocial stresses have been in evidence since at least 500 B.C., when Socrates stated "there is no illness of the body apart from the mind." And yet, despite the pervasiveness of the view that such a connection exists, the precise causal links remain obscure. They seem to involve the entire life style of the afflicted individuals. In *Man Adapting*, René Dubos noted, "Each civilization has its own kind of pestilence and can control it only by reforming itself . . . just as the great epidemics of the nineteenth century were precipitated by environmental factors which favored the activities of pathogenic microorganisms, so many of the diseases characteristic of our times have their origin in some faulty factor of the modern environment" (Dubos, 1965). Perhaps the most important of these faulty factors is excessive, free-floating stress which remains unabated and eventually induces psychological, neurophysiological, and endocrine disruption. This state, which is characterized by excessive activity of the entire mind and body or profound depression, or increased susceptibility to infection, appears to be a precursor of the major afflictions of modern civilization—cardiovascular disorders, cancer, arthritis, and respiratory disease.

Up to this point, we have established a sequence in the development of psychosomatic disorders: a neurophysiological imbalance is precipitated by stressful life events and channeled through a particular personality configuration, resulting in a specific disorder. Once the disorder has been diagnosed, the diagnosis itself can become a further source of anxiety and increase the neurophysiological disequilibrium. Although this sequence does not always lead to pathology, it does so all too frequently. To complete our study of this sequence, we will now examine several of the major psychosomatic disorders and their relationship to stress. Throughout this chapter it is important to remember that the progression toward disease can be interrupted, through early intervention, through the use of stress-reduction techniques, and through educating people about life styles more conducive to health maintenance.

None of the disorders considered in this chapter can be *definitively* classified as psychosomatic in their etiology.

However, research evidence is accumulating as to the two major physiological effects of stress: 1) disruption of a particular neurophysiological or organ system in and of itself; and 2) suppression of normal immunological functions, leading to increased susceptibility to viral or aberrant cell disorders. There is clear indication from recent research and clinical practice that one or both of these effects of stress are involved in each of the major afflictions of contemporary civilization. As we mentioned before, a conference, sponsored by NATO, was held in Beito, Norway, in 1972 to consider the connection between life stress and illness. Proceedings of that meeting are available in an excellent book entitled *Life Stress and Illness* (Gunderson and Rahe, 1974), which contains some of the most comprehensive research available on the subject. It deals with the causal nature of life stress in such disorders as schizophrenia, heart disease, depression, and the prediction of post-operative recovery, and there is particular emphasis on the fact that stressful life events in an individual's recent past can be used to predict the onset of psychological or physical disorders. In that book, two sociologists, D. L. Dodge and W. T. Martin, who have devoted their research to the interaction of germ theory and stress reactivity in the psychogenesis of disorders, state, "These diseases which are very characteristic of our times, namely the chronic diseases, are etiologically linked with excessive stress and in turn this stress is the product of specific socially structured situations inherent in the organization of modern technological societies" (Dodge and Martin, 1970). Observations such as these indicate that the liabilities incurred in modern society are manifested in the four major afflictions of civilization.

HYPERTENSION AND ARTERIOSCLEROSIS

Each year, more deaths in the United States are attributed to diseases of the cardiovascular system than to any other cause. Coronary disease has increased fivefold in the United States in the last fifty years. Something in the nature of contemporary life styles and social organization appears to be responsible. The total cost of coronary heart disease to the United States, including both direct and indirect costs, has been estimated at more than 30 billion dollars per year. Although there are numerous ways in which the cardiovascular system can be affected, two of the most common forms are high blood pressure and arteriosclerosis.

Hypertension, or high blood pressure, is one of the most insidious medical problems of our time. By conservative estimate, it affects approximately 15 percent of the adult population of the United States, with the incidence in the black population exceeding that in the non-black by somewhere between 50 percent and 100 percent. Long-range effects on the vascular system, the heart, and the kidneys can be irreversible and often fatal. High blood pressure alone is listed as the primary cause of 60,000 deaths per year. But it is the underlying cause of hundreds of thousands of other deaths from heart disease, stroke, and kidney disease. An untreated hypertensive is four times as likely to have a heart attack or a stroke as someone with normal blood pressure, and twice as likely to develop kidney disease. In addition, thousands of Americans have their eyesight impaired, suffer internal hemorrhage, or miss work because of high blood pressure. It affects all ages, and men and women are equally susceptible. There has been an alarming increase in the incidence of high blood pressure among teenagers and young people in the last few years.

To further complicate the problem, most people with high blood pressure are asymptomatic. Many individuals experience no overt symptoms from the disease and may be entirely unaware of its presence. All too frequently, blood-pressure abnormality arouses attention only during a routine physical examination. Some health organizations, such as the National Heart and Lung Association, have initiated a campaign to encourage health practitioners of all kinds—

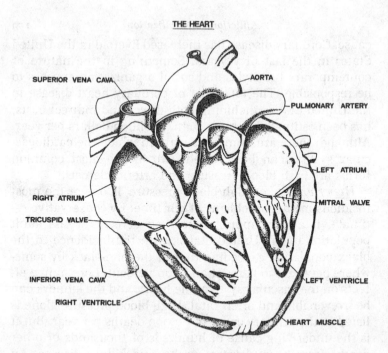

THE HEART

SUPERIOR VENA CAVA

AORTA

PULMONARY ARTERY

LEFT ATRIUM

RIGHT ATRIUM

MITRAL VALVE

TRICUSPID VALVE

INFERIOR VENA CAVA

LEFT VENTRICLE

RIGHT VENTRICLE

HEART MUSCLE

dentists, psychiatrists, gynecologists, and others who might not normally check patients' blood pressure—to begin each office visit with a blood-pressure test. Each of us can do ourselves an invaluable service by making sure to have our blood pressure checked at regular intervals. In fact, simple instructions for checking one's own blood pressure can usually be obtained from a family physician or through a local hospital. A simple check can be an important initial step toward the prevention of more severe complications.

Hypertension is a condition in which the blood vessels throughout the body are made smaller and smaller by contraction of the smooth muscles in their walls. Once it develops in a person born with normal blood pressure, it is tenacious and, unless treated, will continue throughout adulthood. Certain types of hypertension are due to glandular disorders, but the most common type is "essential hypertension," meaning that there is no discoverable organic cause. Although it is well established that anxiety, discomfort, physical activity, and other types of stress can acutely or transiently raise arterial pressure, it is difficult to isolate the causative factors in individual cases. According to *Harrison's Principles of Internal Medicine*, "a specific cause for the increase in peripheral resistance which is responsible for the elevated arterial pressure cannot be defined in approximately 90% of patients with hypertensive disease."

"Normal" blood pressure is difficult to define. Blood pressure is indicated by two readings, expressed as a fraction with the systolic pressure as the numerator and the diastolic pressure as the denominator. Both measures are recorded in millimeters of mercury or Hg/mm. Systolic pressure is the larger number and corresponds to the period of heart contraction during which blood is forced out of the heart. Diastolic pressure is the smaller number and corresponds to the dilation period of the heart, during which the ventricles are filling with blood prior to the next systolic contraction. Statistical approaches define normality on the basis of the mean pressures obtained from a large population of presumably healthy individuals. Normal blood pressure for any individual is dependent upon such variables as age, sex, and race, and requires reference to that person's peer group. As noted earlier, an estimated 15 percent of the adult population of the United States is hypertensive. This figure is based on blood pressure levels exceeding 160/95 millimeters of mercury. However, a better gauge of abnormality might be based on the demonstrated deleterious effects of blood-pressure levels exceeding certain limits. For example, if one accepts the validity of actuarial data indicating that longevity is shortened progressively in adults whose blood pressure exceeds 100/60 millimeters of mercury, then clearly the 15 percent figure could be construed to be grossly understated. Additionally, many researchers and clinicians consider any diastolic pressure in the 90–95 Hg/mm range to be dangerous. This is due to the fact that systolic pressure is relatively volatile, but diastolic pressure reflects the average pressure which the person's system must bear on an ongoing basis.

Damage due to prolonged hypertension is substantial. When there is constriction of peripheral and other vessels resulting in elevating arterial pressure, widespread vascular disease is one of the long-term effects. Since the blood volume in the system remains constant, some vessels are carrying blood under greater pressure than they would if there were no vasoconstriction and all vessels were equally involved in transporting the blood. Pressure on vessel walls is greatly increased, and if it is sustained the vessel walls can weaken and tear. When vessel walls tear, this necessitates the formation of cholesterol plaques to repair the damage. When there is an excessive number of plaques, the vessels become narrower and narrower as a result of the blockage, and this contributes to additional increase in systemic pressure and may lead to further tears. Pressure also increases due to the fact that these plaques cause the arteries to harden and become less flexible. Plaques themselves can become detached easily from the arterial walls and cause further blockage in the blood supply to the heart muscles or create a dangerous condition in which clots form easily. Elevated systemic pressure also affects the heart directly, since it must work harder to pump blood throughout the body under increased resistance. Usually, the main burden of this falls on the left ventricle (see Figure 3), which frequently becomes hypertrophic or larger and during the advanced stages of the condition can become abnormally distended. Ultimately, the function of this chamber deteriorates and the signs of heart failure begin to appear.

Although the complications of hypertension are serious, fatality usually results only after many years of progressive and continual damage from the disease. A small number of cases, variously estimated as between 1 and 5 percent of patients with essential hypertension, enter an accelerated phase which usually results in premature death. The majority of deaths from hypertension result from myocardial infarction or congestive heart failure, when a vulnerable area of the heart, generally the left ventricle, ceases to function.

Treatment of patients with systemic hypertension is directed toward lowering pressure in an attempt to halt or reverse progressive organ damage. An initial means of coping with high blood pressure is usually a simple tranquilizer medication. Through the use of tranquilizers, an individual's blood-pressure elevations do not occur as frequently and the person obtains temporary regulation. However, the behavior patterns which contribute to the high blood pressure are not eliminated by the tranquilizer, which is only alleviating the symptoms. As a result of this, the contractions of the walls of the blood vessels may begin to reoccur as previous psychosocial patterns cause the tension level to exceed the limits artificially imposed by the tranquilizer. Again the blood pressure may begin to peak more and more, at increasingly rapid intervals. A second effort of a chemotherapeutic approach would be the administration of a diuretic or "water pill" to remove a certain amount of water from the body. When the total volume which is present in the blood stream is decreased, this once again eases the signs of high blood pressure.

Most hypertension is now being regulated through the use of anti-hypertensive medications mentioned above. Since this is the case, some people may wonder why they should attempt long-term stress-reduction methods such as biofeedback or meditation. One reason for this is the specter of a lifelong dependency upon increasingly large dosages of medication. Even when chemotherapy is effective, many patients simply do not like taking constant medication or the financial burden that ensues. Another unfortunate aspect of the use of anti-hypertensive drugs is that the drugs themselves often have such unpleasant side effects that many patients give them up. Why suffer discomforts of side effects, when the disease itself causes no physical discomfort at all? Many of the major anti-hypertensive drugs can produce dizziness, dry mouth, fatigue, impaired sexual functioning including the inability to ejaculate, constipation, depression, nausea, vomiting, and severe diarrhea. Not a very appealing list of symptoms. Nevertheless, while the short-term effects of medication can be unpleasant, the long-term effects of hypertension are worse. For all these reasons, many physicians and their patients are increasingly drawn to the possibility of controlling hypertension through stress-reduction techniques such as meditation and biofeedback.

When one understands the grave dangers to health and life itself that prolonged hypertension creates, it is a shock to realize that probably fewer than one-eighth of all hypertensives in the United States are being treated effectively. There are three main reasons for this: 1) the failure of detection; 2) lack of treatment; and 3) failure of the patient to follow the treatment. To improve this disturbing situation, clinicians need to develop comprehensive programs for screening hypertensives and to educate patients to persevere in treatment and life-style alteration despite the fact that they experience no symptoms.

Arteriosclerosis is the number one killer in the United States, claiming approximately 600,000 lives each year. Basically, it is a accumulation of cholesterol deposits in the arteries, and there appear to be many causes of arteriosclerosis. Although some specialists would be reluctant to cite hypertension as a definitive cause, the inferential evidence pointing to a relationship between high blood pressure and arteriosclerosis is significant. Cardiologists Ray Rosenman and Meyer Friedman are among those who see a direct connection. These researchers maintain that the fatty deposits in the arteries are the body's attempt to heal the arteries which sustain damage in the form of small tears in their walls. Excessive pressure against the arterial walls in hypertensive patients is another cause, and may further aggravate already existing tears.

In the Framingham study conducted by the United States Government in 1968, the incidence of coronary failure in men aged 45 to 62 with blood pressures exceeding a systolic level of 160 or a diastolic of about 95 was more than five times that in men who had a blood pressure of 140/90 or less. Hypertension correlates positively with coronary failure in both men and women, with diastolic pressure being perhaps more important. On the other hand, several recent intervention studies have demonstrated convincingly that reduction of diastolic blood-pressure levels to less than 105 significantly reduces the incidence of strokes and congestive heart failure in men. In autopsies conducted on patients from a number of countries, it has been shown that histories of hypertensive disease contributed substantially to the amounts of arteriosclerosis found. In most well-developed countries, arteriosclerosis is the major single cause of premature cardiovascular deaths. According to research by A. Keys (1970), the six nations leading in death rate in white men ages 45 to 64 are South Africa, the United States, Finland, Scotland, Canada, and Australia. Furthermore, the data suggests that the people in the upper socioeconomic classes in these countries have a higher incidence than those in lower socioeconomic classes. Ironically, these high-risk individuals are the people who have adopted a Western life style, replete with a high fat diet and a lack of physical labor.

Arteries affected with arteriosclerosis gradually narrow and harden as deposits of fat slowly build up within the elastic artery walls. These layers tend to accumulate where arteries fork sharply or become damaged. After this process has continued for a period of time, the blood flow is restricted and there is extreme danger of clotting. Virtually all individuals have some degree of plaque formation as adults. As these plaques decay and die or become necrotic, they can rupture, since they are areas of inflexible scar tissue. When the rupture occurs, the circulating blood will attempt to reach it and clot. If the necrotic plaque area is quite large, a dangerously large blood clot can form.

Blood clots in arteriosclerotic arteries are the cause of most coronary heart attacks and cerebral strokes. In the kidneys these clots may cause tissue degeneration, and in the legs they may result in ulcers or gangrene. The area which is most frequently affected by the disease is the heart's left coronary artery. As this artery gradually narrows, the possibility of a clot being caught in the constricted vessel increases. If such a block occurs, the flow of blood needed to feed the ventricular muscles is shut off. Ventricular muscles are the heart muscles primarily responsible for pumping blood out of the aorta and through the body. A sudden blockage can cause starvation of the left ventricular muscles and those of the aorta, which causes them to founder in their vital functions. Starvation of these crucial heart muscles frequently produces an infarct or area of heart muscle that has died or become necrotic (Friedman and Rosenman, 1974). Depending on the size and location of the infarct, and the speed with which it is detected and treatment is administered, a patient may die quickly or survive with severe or slight impairment of the heart's pumping action. Once an infarct has occurred, the affected area is repaired with scar tissue and is no longer viable muscular tissue. If the area is relatively small, the useless dead tissue can be compensated for by other areas. This type of infarct is the usual cause of the common "heart attack" or myocardial infarction.

Arteriosclerotic blockage of coronary arteries is also responsible for congestive heart failure, which is another form of heart attack. In this case, the entire left ventricle, due to blood and oxygen starvation resulting from arterial occlusion, becomes increasingly weak in its pumping capability, and blood accumulates in the lungs. At the same time, the right ventricle pumps more blood into the lungs. Excessive blood in the lungs results in shortness of breath and may even lead to flooding of air spaces from fluid seepage through the distended veins of the lungs in the condition of pulmonary edema. Eventually, the right ventricle gives up trying to pump blood into lungs already close to bursting, and the increased back pressure causes swelling of the liver and sometimes the limbs. This situation can often be corrected by the administration of drugs to induce the left ventricle to begin pumping again, but the damage to the heart and lungs is not reversible. Arteriosclerosis is also often responsible for cerebrovascular stroke. Stroke occurs when normal circulation of blood through the brain is cut off by a clot, usually in an arteriosclerotic artery. One of the major arteries commonly affected by arteriosclerotic narrowing is the internal carotid artery, which is the main supply of blood to the brain. When this artery is blocked, the brain becomes deprived of oxygen and brain cells perish. Damage to one side of the brain usually results in loss of activity in the opposite side of the body.

There are still many unanswered questions about the genesis of arteriosclerosis. No one theory involving a single causative agent or combination of agents has received widespread acceptance. Most research implicates a number of factors whose relative importance may vary widely from case to case. Certainly hypertension is one such factor. Various studies showing the prevalence of arteriosclerosis among business executives indicate that stress may be of importance. Since arteriosclerosis is rare among undernourished populations and is quite common among people who overeat, it is generally acknowledged that diet, too, plays a major role. Since men seem to be more prone to the disease than women, both sex hormones and the greater stresses imposed on men in our society may be involved. Prior to menopause, arteriosclerosis is rare in women. But as more women enter the work force, their susceptibility to cardiovascular diseases, including arteriosclerosis, increases

(Friedman and Rosenman, 1974). Since World War II, when women in Japan became "liberated," the incidence of coronary heart disease among them quadrupled.

Hypertension and arteriosclerosis are not necessarily linked in a direct causal manner, in the sense that one always leads to the other. Both conditions are multicausative, but when one is present there is a distinct tendency for it to aggravate the physiological characteristics of the other. Narrowing of the arteries due to fatty deposits and the consequent loss of vessel elasticity would tend to elevate blood pressure. Elevated blood pressure in turn tends to increase the probability of developing arteriosclerotic symptoms. Although experimental evidence demonstrating a positive link between the two diseases has not been conclusive, most of these experiments seem to ignore the fact that a closed-loop feedback system exists between the two. One negative trigger affects another and creates a downward spiral which ultimately increases the probability of coronary failure or stroke. Once this degenerative cycle is initiated, it is difficult if not impossible to reverse its progress.

A summary of causes generally conceded to contribute to both hypertension and arteriosclerosis would include: 1) lack of exercise; 2) a diet high in calories, total fat, saturated fat, and cholesterol; 3) an occupation that is sedentary; 4) smoking; 5) sex; 6) age; 7) heredity; 8) blood factors; 9) obesity; and 10) stress. There are many ways in which these factors interact from one individual to another. Thus, while a diet with a high concentration of fatty substances almost surely contributes to arteriosclerosis, stress can speed its progress or hereditary traits slow it down.

Although it is not possible conclusively to isolate stress as a primary contributing factor to hypertension and arteriosclerosis, it most certainly does play a role, and quite probably a greater one than is now generally acknowledged. According to Friedman and Rosenman, ". . . emotional stress of any variety, because of its resistance to precise measurement, has been shamefully neglected by quantitatively oriented cardiac researchers." Stress reduction is now recommended by most doctors for patients suffering from cardiovascular disorders. Unfortunately, more than a few patients have wondered, "Well, fine, the doctor says to relax, but he doesn't offer any suggestions as to how to go about it." Relaxation and stress reduction need to be learned and practiced like any other skill. In Part Four, a series of techniques is outlined for general stress reduction. At the very least, these techniques are examples of the fact that excessive stress is not an inescapable aspect of daily activity.

MIGRAINE

Another vascular disorder which appears to have a significant relationship to emotional stress is migraine. Not all headaches are migraine, although many people believe that migraine is simply another name for any very severe headache. In spite of this rather common misconception, the name "migraine" does not necessarily have any bearing upon pain in the head or pain severity. There is no pain at all in migraine variants, and in others the pain may occur in the eyes, stomach, or cardiothoracic region. A true migraine is sometimes called a "vascular headache," since migraine headaches frequently involve the carotid artery, which carries blood from the heart up each side of the neck to the head. The lower part of each carotid artery is called the common carotid. At a point just below the ear, it splits into two branches: 1) the external carotid, which continues upward in front of the ear; and 2) the internal carotid, which disappears under the bones of the skull. Sometime before the migraine attack begins, the carotid arteries on the affected side of the head undergo a period of narrowing. This unusual behavior of the arteries may cause flushing or pallor of the skin, and is also probably responsible for some of the strange sensations experienced by migraine sufferers during the "prodrome," or pre-attack phase. During the prodrome, patients may experience light or noise sensitivity or become anxious and irritable. After this period of constriction, the arteries begin to dilate or swell. When this occurs, the arteries release certain chemicals that stimulate nearby nerve endings to induce pain. Sometimes in the early stages, pressure on the carotid artery can partially alleviate this pain. It is not certain what triggers the peculiar arterial behavior that initiates the migraine process. However, a good deal of evidence suggests that the answer may lie in the way our physiology utilizes seratonin, which is an important chemical affecting the size of blood vessels. Migraine is an extremely complex phenomenon based upon a number of contributing factors. In a comprehensive book focusing on migraine, Oliver W. Sacks notes:

> We have observed that all migraines are composed of many symptoms (and physiological alterations) proceeding in unison: at each and every moment the structure of migraine is *composite*. Thus, a common migraine is fabricated of many components surrounding the cardinal and defining symptom of headache. Migraine equivalents are composed of essentially similar components aggregated and emphasized in other ways [Sacks, 1970].

Retreating from an attempt to define these multiple variables and their combinations, researchers and clinicians have tended to focus on the course of migraine onset and the structure and shape of the pain which is usually attendant to migraine.

One of the most striking aspects of a true migraine is the "shape" of the pain. At the onset of the attack, in almost all cases, the migraine headache affects just one side of the head, as a unilateral migraine. With some patients it may later generalize and involve both sides in a bilateral migraine. This unique one-sidedness of migraine pain was noted by the physicians of ancient Greece. In fact, the name "migraine" comes from this characteristic and is a shortening of the Greek name for the syndrome, *hemikrania*, meaning "half the skull." A number of warning signals constitute the prodrome. Prodrome is another distinctive characteristic which sets the migraine apart from other types of headache. Premonitory signs of the prodrome are most often visual in nature, such as flashing lights, zigzag lines, scintillating patterns, or areas of darkness. Some migraine patients suffer from prodromes that affect other senses and even the emotions. Feelings of weakness in one or more limbs, nausea, and an ominous sense of foreboding are typical examples. Usually the prodrome occurs one or two hours before the headache itself. As actual headache pain sets in, the symptoms of the prodrome gradually lift. Headache pain normally begins in one small area of the forehead or temple and is accompanied by a throbbing or pulsating. As the area grows larger, patients often experience loss of appetite, an aversion to light, redness and swelling of the eyes, with some tear flow; nasal passages often appear swollen, and nosebleeds are fairly common. Within one or two hours from the onset, the headache reaches its overwhelming worst and then gradually subsides. A total duration of six hours is typical, but time between the prodromal phase and the attack as well as the length of the attack itself, may vary widely.

As with many psychosomatic disorders, the causes of migraine are not completely understood, but emotional factors are apparently involved. Feelings of anxiety, nervous tension, anger, or repressed rage are associated with migraine attacks in many people. Very often these feelings may be so well concealed that the patients themselves are not aware of them. Psychotherapists treating migraine patients have observed that an attack may be aborted when the individual gives vent to underlying hostility. Short-term emotional crises seem to increase the possibility of an attack as well. According to personality tests, a typical migraine sufferer is perfectionistic, ambitious, rigid, orderly, excessively competitive, and unable to delegate responsibility. Such a person often has an attitude of chronic resentment and may experience profound frustration at not being able to live up to his unrealistic ideals. Fear of failure in an immediate task and borderline panic are not uncommon precursors of a migraine. Faced with an insuperable task, such a person may experience a migraine episode.

Emotional stress and personality are not the only precipitants of migraine. Diet is apparently involved in some cases, and certain foods such as aged cheeses contain natural chemicals relating to seratonin and can trigger attacks. Some people may react to birth-control pills, alcohol, or to as many other triggering factors as there are individual patients. Each case is different, and for this reason it is a good practice for migraine sufferers to keep a diary of moods, actions, foods, feelings, tension levels, and any other personal information which might relate to migraine onset. In this way, it is often possible to detect a clear pattern which can significantly aid in treatment. Migraine attacks usually begin between the ages of 16 and 35 and lessen in frequency at around 50. Migraines associated with the menstrual cycle in women typically diminish at onset of menopause. Similarly, men may experience a decrease in the severity and frequency of attacks as they approach middle age. Although there are exceptions, migraine attacks are usually not a problem in later years.

A number of medications besides analgesics are available for the treatment of migraine headaches. All of them must be taken early, in the initial or prodromal stages, in order to provide full relief. Most of the medications contain the substance ergotamine tartrate, which acts to constrict the dilated cerebral arteries during the migraine. Caffeine is another medication given for arterial constriction, and belladonna alkaloids help to relieve the accompanying gastrointestinal spasm. However, there are side effects to these medications, including numbness, muscle pains in the extremities, weakness in the legs, and heart-rate irregularity.

On the positive side, the fact that migraine responds to medication given at the first warning signs suggests that it may be amenable to preventive measures. Indeed, migraine seems to lend itself well to a number of preventive techniques. There is considerable evidence that through the use of biofeedback, meditation, autogenic training, and other related deep-relaxation techniques, a person can learn how to alleviate or completely avoid an attack. In fact, many of the practices involving self-regulation may work more efficiently than medication in migraine treatment. Part of the elusive nature of the migraine syndrome may be due to the fact that it is symptomatic of a particular type of personality engaged in a particular life style. Migraine sufferers frequently need to realize the secondary gains or rewards which having a migraine represents for them. For one patient it is an occasion for privacy from a demanding family, and for another it is a passive means of expressing aggression toward another person. Both the psychological and physical factors need to be considered in migraine treatment. Relaxation techniques provide the means of symptom alleviation and permit the exploration of any underlying psychological conflict.

CANCER

Cancer is the second-ranking fatal disease in the United States, accounting for one out of every six deaths. Of all diseases, cancer is probably the most feared, since its causes are so little understood, its progress may not be permanently arrested in some cases, and our current options for treatment are sometimes more dreaded than the disease itself. People over 45 are most prone to cancer. In the United States, the number of cancer deaths per year for people under 45 years of age is approximately 25,000. The figure rises to 40,000 between the ages of 45 and 55 and further increases to an appalling 90,000 among individuals between 65 and 74, then makes a drastic drop down to 20,000 among people 85 and older. Cancer can and does afflict people of any age, and no organ or tissue is safe from cancer, although some physiological areas are more susceptible than others. Those organs most frequently affected are the mouth, skin, respiratory organs, blood and lymph systems, digestive organs, urinary systems, genitals, and the breasts in women. In men, the lungs and digestive tract seem to be the most vulnerable; in women, it is the breasts, digestive tract, and cervix. Cancer occurs in many forms, including Hodgkin's disease, various leukemias which are most common among children, and variants of solid tumors. This is an extremely complex disease. In our discussion we will focus on the process possibly involved in solid-tumor formation.

Cancer seems to involve a breakdown of one of the body's most vital functions, the immune response. Normally, when mutant cells, foreign antigens, viruses, and other alien substances enter the body, the immune system destroys them before they are allowed to multiply or do damage. In cancer, the body apparently fails to recognize such aberrations and mutant cancerous cells multiply without interference. The preliminary stages in the development of certain types of cancer may take years. The mutant cells may inhibit a part of the body and lie dormant for a long period of time before they suddenly activate and begin to spread to other areas or grow into a dangerous tumor at the primary site. Once a cell or group of cells has finally become cancerous, the multiplication and growth are quite swift. Unlike normal cells, which regenerate with specialized functions only when it is necessary to replace dying cells, a cancerous cell is one whose specialized function seems to be eclipsed by a primitive drive for unrestrained proliferation. Eventually this process may form a mass of malignant tissue which is identifiable as a tumor.

Malignant tumors grow in pernicious ways. They most commonly damage other cells in the vicinity by physically crowding them and absorbing an excessive share of cellular nutrients. A still greater danger is that the initial tumor may spread to other areas. When a tumor is localized, it may be treated or surgically removed quite effectively. However, the mutant cells can find their way into the blood or lymphatic system; when this occurs, they can travel to other parts of the body and the cancer can spread and ultimately become impossible to treat or control.

What is it that causes cells to mutate and become cancerous in the first place? This question has occupied hundreds of researchers in scores of laboratories on a full-time basis. In the simplest terms, a mutation involves a change in the genetic material of a normal cell. Each cell has a specific genetic code which is contained in the DNA of the cell nucleus and is passed on to succeeding cells to determine their structure and function. When the material containing the code is altered, the result is a change in the character of the cell which develops to replace the original one. Current theory supports the concept that cancerous mutations are a common phenomenon in the bodies of normal individuals. Usually the immune systems destroy them before they are able to multiply. This implies that there is danger only when the immune systems fail to eliminate the mutant cells.

A number of agents have been demonstrated to induce mutations and thus contribute to the growth of cancerous tumors if the immune system fails in its vital task. One of the earliest theories concerning the cause of cancer was put forward by Percival Pott, an eighteenth-century London physician. He related the high rate of scrotal cancer among chimney sweeps to a carcinogenic (cancer-inducing) agent in the soot. Since Pott's time, many such carcinogenic agents have been identified, including excessive exposure to radiation, certain industrial dyes, chemicals found in automobile exhausts, industrial smog, trauma, burns, and cigarette smoke. There is also evidence that heredity may predispose a person to some types of cancer. Genetic factors are apparently involved in several types, including cancer of the breast in women. The risk of developing breast cancer among the first-generation children of a breast-cancer patient is five times that of the general population.

Recently, a great deal of the effort in cancer research has focused on the role of viruses, which are the smallest and least complex organisms known. A virus can survive for years in a kind of dormant state without air or nourishment and without reproducing. Viruses are established causes of a host of common illnesses. When they are exposed to healthy cells, they become active and behave somewhat like parasites by invading the cell and moving freely within its confines. Once inside the cell walls, the virus begins to engage in reproduction. Eventually the host cell bursts and is destroyed while the viruses move on to invade neighboring cells. To date, a dozen viruses have been established as possible causes of cancer in animals, including leukemia and tumorous forms of the disease. One factor has impeded research on the role of viruses in cancer is that following the progress of viruses within a cell is quite difficult, since they are highly elusive entities. For instance, in one type of rabbit tumor, the viruses cannot be detected when they are growing most actively. They are observable only in old cells when the damage has already occurred. The reverse is true in normal viral infections, in which the viruses are most easily detected under an electron microscope as the illness reaches its peak. Some researchers speculate that by the time a cancerous tumor has developed, the virus has lost its identity by merging with the nucleic acids of the invaded cell and is therefore undetectable. To further complicate the picture, other scientists think that there may be no specific cancer-producing viruses, and that *any* virus can invade a cell and cause it to become cancerous. However, there is one significant difference between the way a virus operates in a typical viral infection and the way it behaves to produce cancer. In a normal viral infection, the virus does not invade the nucleus and performs its reproductive activities within the cell plasma. In cancer, the virus attacks the cell nucleus, which contains the critical DNA molecules, the keepers of the genetic code. Thus, the virus alters the genetic material, affecting the subsequent replication of the cell.

A major discovery occurred in June of 1974, when researchers Charles McGrath and Marvin Rich of the Michigan Cancer Foundation isolated a human virus that is implicated in breast cancer. This research was followed by the work of Robert E. Gallagher and Robert C. Gallo of the National Cancer Institute, who isolated a human virus associated with acute myelocytic leukemia (Gallagher and Gallo, 1975). This latter type of cancer accounts for less than 1 percent of human tumors, but the discovery of the virus was a major contribution to understanding the mechanism of cancer causation. The research into animal-tumor viruses has been more productive, with implications for more refined human research.

Some of these experiments have also investigated the role of stress in tumor incidence. Research has been conducted in this area by Vernon Riley of the Fred Hutchinson Research Center in Seattle, Washington. Riley subjected experimental mice to a variety of stresses, including isolation or overcrowding after being weaned from mothers known to bear a mammary-tumor virus. In a series of experiments, Riley demonstrated that mammary-tumor incidence in the offspring could be increased up to 90 percent under stress while remaining at 7 percent in a protected environment. Concerning this research, Riley noted, "The data suggests that moderate chronic or intermittent stress may predispose such mice to an increased risk of mammary carcinoma, possibly through a resultant compromise of their immunological competence or tumor surveillance system, and that adequate protection from physiological stress may reduce mammary tumor occurrence in mice" (Riley, 1975), This is an extremely important study linking research in immunology with the findings of stress researchers. While it is always difficult to generalize from animal to human research, the implications of this are highly significant. Riley's data are consistent with the hypothesis thàt stress has a role in human-cancer onset, although he does cite a number of alternative hypotheses with a purely biochemical basis. With this qualification in mind, the final statement in his research report holds intriguing implications for the study of human cancer:

> When immunological competence is compromised, even temporarily, by loss or inactivation of T cells or other vital defense elements following stress-induced corticoid hormone elevation, the host surveillance fails to destroy the transformed malignant cells during their immunologically vulnerable stage. The data further imply that once a cancer cell escapes to an organizational state beyond the limited defensive abilities of immunological surveillance, the production of a lethal tumor may then be inevitable and not reversible by natural host defenses.

Through such research, the complex interaction between stress and neurological and endocrinological factors might be more clearly mapped. Modified host resistance to viral infection following stress may provide this critical link.

What is it that breaks down the body's normal controls over the rate and types of cells that are produced? Why is it that the body, which is capable of recognizing and identifying the difference between such infinitesimally small particles as molecules of clover and rose pollen, fails to recognize the much more obvious differences between cancerous and non-cancerous cells when these differences are detectable under an ordinary microscope? These are among the major unanswered questions remaining in cancer research. It is known that prolonged stress tends to weaken the immune systems and produces increased susceptibility to viral as well as other infections. Also, it is known that during a prolonged stress reaction the number of T-lymphocytes and eosinophil cells in the blood drops off markedly. Since the function of these cells is to seek out and destroy foreign antigens, their reduction in numbers during stress may increase vulnerability to cancer. As we pointed out earlier, abnormally low levels of the number of these cells present in the blood is fairly common in cancer patients. This relationship is not necessarily causative, since the decreased cellular count may be an adjunct to, or effect of, the disease process.

The research of George F. Solomon has contributed greatly to the body of information connecting stress and cancer. He has focused on the concept of immunological balance as a key factor in the onset of both cancer and arthritis. According to Solomon:

> Resistance to cancer appears to be immunological in nature, an area of currently very active investigation. There is even speculation that cellular immunity (as contrasted to humoral immunity, which is largely responsible for resistance to infection by microorganisms) may have evolved phylogenetically as a surveillance mechanism against the neoplastic cell, which is a mutant and therefore foreign. Carcinogenic mutation, of course, can be induced by radiation, chemical carcinogens, probably viruses, or by chance processes . . . some event reducing immunologial competence at a critical time may allow a mutant cell to thrive and grow. A number of patients with cancer appear to have lowered immunological capacity, and patients with widespread diseases have less reactive lymphocytes than patients with small amounts of tumor . . . Thus, regarding stress effect on tumor immunity, the concept of "immunological balance" may be important [Solomon, 1969].

The effects of stress on the induction and growth of a variety of tumors in experimental animals have been extensively demonstrated. In both this limited human research and animal experimentation, it appears that psychophysiological events can reduce immunological competence at a critical time and may allow a mutant cell to thrive and grow.

Activity of the central nervous system may also be involved in the stress-related aspects of cancer. The development and function of each organ in the body is closely associated with nervous impulses and discharges. Coherent information traveling via the nerves to each organ system maintains an integrated and functioning set of organs. When incoherent or abnormal nervous patterns occur, it is possible that they may affect a particular organ system and induce a breakdown in normal control mechanisms. This might contribute to localized "blindness" to mutant cells and permit them to multiply undetected or without interference. Nervous-system functions are tied to information perceived by the cerebrocortical levels of the brain and to emotional activity in the hypothalamic area. Therefore, it is conceivable that emotionally induced nervous responses could create the necessary conditions for the development of cancer.

The complex relationship between hormone levels, psychological stress, and susceptibility to cancer has been touched upon by Eugene Pendergrass, former President of the American Cancer Society, who states:

> So far as I know, there is no evidence that hormones acting alone initiate the transformation of a normal cell into a neoplastic cell. However, it is known that certain hormones have a great influence on the susceptibility of experimental animals to some types of cancer and it seems not unlikely that this is also true of human beings . . . Psychologic factors sometimes have a marked influence on the behavior and rate of growth of cancer once it has occurred in the human body. It is not unreasonable to postulate that this could result from the interaction of psychological factors and hormonal levels. I want to make it clear that I am not suggesting the psychologic factors act as an initial causative agent in the occurrence of cancer. I am only suggesting that they sometimes have an influence on preexisting cancer and may have an influence on susceptibility to cancer [Pendergrass, 1959].

This observation is based upon numerous research and clinical findings citing the importance of emotional factors in host resistance. If psychosocial stress factors, acting upon the immune system, can induce cancer, then there is the further possibility that this negative process can be reversed and immunity stabilized or enhanced through stress-reduction practices. Events which trigger a negative trend toward psychosomatic disorders are not necessarily of major magnitude. Methods of altering this progression do not have to be of a large magnitude either. At early stages of the disease process, subtle but critical interventions could alter the balance from pathology to health.

ARTHRITIS

One of the major non-terminal illnesses is arthritis, which affects at least 50 million individuals in the United States, where it is the chief cause of physical disability. Approximately 17 million of these cases are severe enough to require ongoing medical attention due to chronic pain, and there are approximately a quarter of a million new patients each year. In economic terms, the estimated toll of this disorder from loss of wages and chronic medical care is close to four billion dollars per year. In terms of human suffering, of course, the toll is incalculable. The diseases which fall under the name of arthritis appear in many forms, including gout and osteoarthritis, which produces the aches and hobbled joints of old age. By far the most feared and widespread variate of this disorder is rheumatoid arthritis.

Rheumatoid arthritis usually starts in young adulthood, with the average age at onset being approximately 35, and continues into old age. It strikes three times as many women as men. The course of the disease is highly variable, and spontaneous remissions and exacerbations are characteristic, with remissions occurring more commonly in the early stages. In some individuals the disease is severely crippling, and in others it is no more than a minor irritation. According to *Harrison's Principles of Internal Medicine*, "The majority of patients will experience progressive joint damage in varying degrees over the years. Fortunately, many patients will be able to function at home or at work, but are often limited in capacity. Another group of patients, approximately 10%, will have relentless, destructive, crippling disease, leading ultimately to confinement in a wheelchair or bed. There is yet another group with mild, intermittent disease who seldom, if ever, need medical attention." Even in its less severe variants, arthritis is a disorder which can have severe psychological impact by inducing a sense of premature aging in the afflicted individual. As with the other disorders discussed in this chapter, the psychological stress factor contributes to both the onset and the progress of this disorder.

Arthritis is a combination of the Greek words meaning "joint" and "inflammation." The most frequently affected areas are the shoulders, elbows, hips, wrists, fingers, knees, ankles, and feet. There is a sequence of steps in the progress of rheumatoid arthritis. For example, in a normal finger joint the interior is lined with a synovial membrane, which secretes fluid to lubricate the joint. Rheumatoid arthritis upsets the normal functioning of the synovial cells and causes them to multiply at an unnatural rate, thereby creating swelling. Next, the synovial tissue creeps into the joint itself. In later stages of the disease, the synovial membrane packs the joint, and the unhealthy tissue eats away the cartilege covering the ends of the bones and erodes the bone until the joint is rendered useless. Eventually the joint may deteriorate so much, with scar tissue forming, that it becomes immobilized, knobby, and deformed. This is the most advanced form of the disease and is extremely painful.

Causes of rheumatoid arthritis are not clearly understood. One current theory is that the body literally turns on itself in what amounts to a breakdown of the immune system. Antibodies become directed against the self in an autoimmune response and cause tissue damage. For instance, take the case in which an infection occurs within the synovial cells of a finger joint. In keeping with a normal reaction to infection, antibodies are then mobilized to destroy the infected cells. At this point there is a malfunction, for the antibodies fail to distinguish between healthy and unhealthy cells, and they attack and destroy the healthy cells as well. As this happens, healthy cells begin to divide rapidly to replace those being destroyed by the misguided antibodies, and synovial tissue proliferates and initiates the self-destructive process described in the preceding paragraph.

Heredity seems to play a part in predisposing people to rheumatoid arthritis. There is a blood protein termed the "rheumatoid factor" which is found in at least half of rheumatoid arthritics and frequently in their close relatives. It is an inherited characteristic which increases one's vulnerability to the disease. Although the rheumatoid factor is present in patients with other illnesses, it is rare in the population at large. The rheumatoid factor appears to be made up of two antibodies, and it may be that one or both of these are involved in the non-discretionary attacks on the body's own healthy tissues during the arthritic process.

A standard treatment for severe rheumatoid arthritis is the administration of cortisone, which is a chemical synthesis of the anti-inflammatory corticoid secreted by the adrenal glands. The effect of the natural corticoid is to reduce the body's inflammatory reaction against infection. In rheumatoid arthritis, this inflammatory process proceeds unchecked and affects healthy cells. Cortisone is used to slow down this process and to prevent the body from harming itself. However, as the disease progresses, higher doses of cortisone are needed, and serious side effects may result, such as dangerously increased brittleness of the bones, deposition of fat, loss of muscular strength, ulcers, and psychosis. These side effects can be as disabling as the disease itself, and it seems incumbant upon researchers and clinicians to devise improved methods of treatment.

Stress has been demonstrated to correlate positively with arthritic attacks in theose cases in which a complete disease history has been available for a patient. Once again, the immune system is involved, and stress may play a role in inducing dysfunction of this system. The personality and behavior of the rheumatoid arthritic, as discussed in Chapter 4, are further support for the conclusion that rheumatoid arthritis and emotional stress are related. Whatever role stress plays in rheumatoid arthritis needs to be explored more fully. If such stress can be alleviated, then perhaps the increasingly large doses of cortisone can be curtailed and the side effects avoided. A combination of chemotherapy and stress alleviation may be effective against the chronic pain of arthritic disorders.

RESPIRATORY DISEASE

Over the last ten years there has been an alarming increase in respiratory diseases. Both bronchitis and emphysema were relatively rare twenty-five years ago, but now they afflict nearly 10 million people in the United States alone. Researchers are learning more about these diseases each year, but they have not yet determined the extent to which cigarette smoke, polluted air, and other factors are implicated. In any case, it appears that bronchitis and emphysema are another unwelcome byproduct of modern life.

Bronchitis and emphysema often occur together. Bronchitis is an inflammation in the lower windpipe of the throat and in the large bronchial tubes which carry air to and from the lungs. Often it is preceded by an upper-respiratory infection or a lingering common cold. Blood flow to the mucous membranes of the bronchial tubes increases to aid in overcoming the infection, and as white-blood-cell activity increases, the mucosal tissues swell. Cells in the bronchial mucosa which have been affected by the cold virus or bacteria secrete a sticky mucus which begins to clog the tubes. Mucus also interferes with the work of the bronchial cilia, which are tiny hairlike projections whose job is to filter out undesirable elements in the air before they reach the lungs. Impaired functioning of the cilia and mucus accumulation work synergistically in a degenerative spiral. As a result, the normally sterile bronchial tubes become an ideal environment for bacterial growth, adding to irritation and congestion in the tubes. Coughing, one of the unpleasant symptoms of bronchitis, is the body's reflex to expel the thick mucus from the tubes.

Another respiratory disorder, emphysema, affects the air sacs, or alveoli, of the lungs themselves and is usually the end product of chronic asthma or bronchitis. In a normal lung, clusters of minute air sacs provide a large surface for the exchange of gases which constitutes respiration. Oxygen passes through membranes into the bloodstream, while carbon dioxide enters into the air sac, to be eliminated in expiration. In a diseased lung the membranes of the individual alveoli break down and larger sacs form, cutting back drastically on membrane surface area available for this exchange to occur. Emphysema also interferes with the individual's ability to empty his lungs completely. People suffering from the disease always have partially inflated lungs filled with carbon dioxide and other respiratory wastes. Since they are not able to empty their lungs of these wastes, it is difficult for fresh oxygen to reach the sac membrances.

Some researchers maintain that emphysema may be induced by bronchial infection and constriction of the air passages leading to the alveoli. It is also possible that the reverse may be true—that the dilation and expansion of the air sacs may press upon the bronchial tubes, leading to constriction and collapse. Whatever cause-and-effect relationship exists between the two diseases, bronchitis and emphysema can have drastic effects on personal health. In severe cases, it can result in a lack of oxygen sufficient to produce brain damage. It also may create problems for the heart by inducing it to enlarge and weaken as it works harder (against the greater resistance to blood flow) to pump blood through the diseased lungs.

Asthma is another widespread respiratory ailment. Asthmatic conditions are quite common, and secondary complications from the disorder or the treatment itself—even death—are not uncommon. Contrary to popular belief, an asthmatic's main problem is not inhalation but exhalation. It is the entrapment of carbon dioxide in the lungs that leads to the asthmatic's inability to breathe. During an asthmatic attack, the muscles encircling the smallest bronchial tubes in the lungs begin to constrict. Generally this occurs as a result of emotional upset or exposure to allergenic substances in the blood or air. This tightening process constricts the neck of the air sacs and prevents air from escaping fully. When this happens, the natural reaction is fear, often bordering on panic, which only causes further spasms and tightening of the small bronchial muscles. Bronchospasm characteristic of asthmatic attacks may also be involved in other diseases of the respiratory system, including emphysema, bronchitis, and pneumonia. Such involuntary muscular spasms have always been associated with emotional stress and nervous tension mediated through the autonomic or involuntary nervous system. By practicing certain relaxation and breathing techniques, it is possible voluntarily to relax the smooth muscles involved in bronchial constriction.

Breath is life, and it is small wonder that patients suffering from serious respiratory disorders experience fear and panic. Emotional states and breathing patterns are very much interrelated. Colloquially, we use terms such as "choked with sadness" and "heave a sigh of relief" to indicate our feelings. Respiration patterns become irregular with anger, slow and deepen in relaxation, and quicken in fear or stress. The stress-reduction techniques described in Part Four can all be used to ease respiration distress. If mental and emotional states affect breathing, then the reverse can also be true. Slow, rhythmic breathing can turn an anxious mental state into one of relative tranquility and release the body from many of the other adverse effects of anxiety. Practicing proper breathing techniques is one of the most vital techniques we have at our disposal, not only as a treatment of respiratory disease, but to reduce the anxiety associated with all psychosomatic illness.

BEYOND PATHOLOGY

This chapter has considered only the most prevalent and destructive disorders which afflict contemporary Western societies. In varying degrees, all of them are stress-related. There is a vast array of other disorders generally acknowledged to be psychosomatic in origin, but to examine each of them and analyze their stress component would require volumes. The role of excessive stress in these major disorders such as cardiovascular disease and cancer is evidence enough that education in stress reduction should be a high priority in health maintenance and preventive medicine.

For most individuals, the recognition of the subtle interaction between mind and body first occurs during a period of illness. According to cancer researcher O. Carl Simonton, "In order to really grasp the concept that they [patients] can mentally influence their body's immune mechanism they eventually realize that their mind and emotions and their body act as a unit and can't be separated . . . that there was a mental and psychological participation, as well as physical one, in the development of their disease" (Simonton and Simonton, 1975). This insight opens a person's mind to the potential of self-healing. Health exists when mind and body function in harmony, and illness results when stress and conflict disrupt this process. With this one simple concept, it is possible to begin to explore the subtle means by which psychological factors can maximize individual well-being.

Reflecting back on his own career in medical research,

René Dubos has considered the issue of future directions in health care. In a lengthy interview in *Medical World News*, Dubos stated, "I do not question the importance of vaccination and antibiotics in disease control, but the field of the future is going to be the study of physiologic conditions—encompassing anything from nutrition to emotional disturbances—and how these effect susceptibility to infection" (Dubos, 1975). Research in these areas will undoubtedly continue for many years. Even now, in the absence of empirical verification, the daily toll of stress and its disorders is unequivocal.

This chapter concludes our examination of stress-related disorders, charting them from their precondition of an excessive neurophysiological imbalance, to stress triggers or precipitating life events, through a personality profile, into the particular disorder. Any such schemata must be incomplete, given the present state of laboratory and clinical research, but it can serve a valuable function even if it only highlights the gaps in present research. Once it becomes possible to detect early signals in this progression, indicating a tendency toward pathology, preventive measures involving stress reduction can be initiated. However, it is always easier to analyze a problem than formulate an effective solution, and such is the case in preventive techniques. The methods described in Part Four all require further research and refinement. Nevertheless, the moment has come in the health sciences to turn from pathology correction to preventive care and the establishment and maintenance of optimum levels of health.

METHODS OF CONTROLLING STRESS

Meditation

6

Records and phenomenological accounts of meditative practices date back over two thousand years. Only recently have there been empirical studies of the psychophysiological benefits of meditative practice. Alterations in an individual's psychophysiological state accompanying meditation seem to be opposite to those characteristics of stress reactions. From early studies of Indian yogis and Zen monks to more recent studies of meditators in the United States, a consistent neurophysiological pattern is emerging. Among the major changes which occur during meditation are a slowing of breath and heart rate, decrease in oxygen consumption, lowering or stabilization of blood pressure, and decrease in skin conductivity. Additionally, the EEG (electroencephalogram, or recording of electric currents in the brain) shows characteristic patterns of change during meditation. It is important to note that this brain-wave pattern during meditation is not the same as that during sleep. The pattern of response to external stimuli is similar to that of a person during a waking state, since meditation is not accompanied by drowsiness when practiced properly. These alterations are opposite in almost all respects to

W. B. Cannon's fight-or-flight response or the defense-alarm syndrome of arousal. From these preliminary observations and from my clinical experience with the use of biofeedback and meditation, it seems very likely that these changes are a positive antidote for preventing or alleviating prolonged stress reactivity. Incessant sympathetic arousal is a correlate of anxiety states and is implicated in a range of stress-related disorders ranging from hypertension (Sternbach, 1966) to cancer (Simonton and Simonton, 1975). Since meditation is able to produce a pattern of response characterized by inhibition of the sympathetic nervous system, it is logical to hypothesize that it may have important clinical applications in the alleviation of stress-related disorders and in staving off the adverse effects of normal daily stress.

THE NATURE OF MEDITATION

There are many forms of meditation, some of which have utilized the basic principles of the Eastern tradition to develop techniques designed for Western practitioners. Before proceeding further, it is important to define meditation and dispel the misconception that meditation is contemplation, rumination, or thinking about a concept. Meditation is an experiential exercise involving an individual's actual attention, not belief systems or other cognitive processes. Meditation is also not to be confused with prolonged, self-induced lethargy. The nervous system needs intensity and variety of external stimulation to maintain proper functioning.

In the Eastern tradition, the meditator works toward a psychological state which is termed transcendental awareness or satori. There are two basic methods by which this state is achieved: 1) *restriction or focusing of attention* on an object of meditation, such as in Chakra yoga and Rinzai Zen; or a mantra, such as in Mudra yoga, Tantra yoga, Sufism, and Transcendental Meditation; or upon a physiological process, such as internal sensations, as in Kundalini yoga practices; and 2) *opening up of attention,* in which the meditator places himself in a state of undistracted receptivity to external and internal stimuli, as in Zen meditation or Soto Zen. Underlying these two methods is the fundamental process of meditation, which is to gain *mastery over attention.* The goal of this mastery is to "develop an awareness which allows every stimulus to enter into consciousness devoid of our normal selection process, devoid of normal tuning or input selection of model building and devoid of the normal categorizing" (Naranjo and Ornstein, 1971). The meditator stops his ordinary cognitive processes so as to experience direct perception of stimuli, devoid of preconception.

Concentration is essential in all systems of meditation. The meditator learns to fix his attention firmly upon a given task for increasingly protracted periods of time. This concentration of attention overcomes the mind's usual habit of flitting from one subject to another. When the incessant activity of the mind is stilled, the meditator experiences that aspect of his being which is prior to and distinct from his thoughts and from attention itself. It is this state which has been described as transcendental awareness, cosmic consciousness, or satori.

This goal may seem deceptively simple. Once you have tried truly to quiet your mind, or to allow images to run through it without letting any particular one become distracting, you will understand why practice and perseverance are necessary if you are to be successful. Mental activity is a wayward and not easily controlled phenomenon. At first it seems to have a life of its own. When you exert will or volition and attempt to become quiet, it is very likely that you will be perversely and regularly disobeyed. Your mind jumps unbidden from one thought or concern to another despite your efforts to concentrate on eliminating such activity. With practice and experimentation to determine the best approach for you personally, you can gradually increase your ability to regulate your attention and reduce or rectify the mind's overwhelming tendency to generate incessant activity and distraction. At this point, the subtle benefits of meditation become more pronounced.

Several points need to be clarified before examining the clinical evidence for the value of meditation as a stress-reduction technique. First, although empirical testing has demonstrated that meditation is effective in reducing stress, stress itself is a multifaceted and complex phenomenon which may require many dimensions of correction. If deep-relaxation techniques such as meditation are to work most effectively, it is necessary to undertake them with the guidance of someone trained in the particular method you have chosen. Although later in this chapter techniques are described in enough detail for you to begin experimenting with them by yourself, do not underestimate the value of help and supervision from people thoroughly knowledgeable in the technique you wish to pursue. In the initial stages of meditative practice, much of the benefit will occur on the physical level. You will be aware of a subjective sense of deep relaxation and an unstressing of the body's musculature. Later, your practice can become more problematic as you proceed to the more psychological aspects of meditation. Thoughts, fantasies, images, personal difficulties, and novel internal distractions may press upon your consciousness and disrupt your attention away from a meditative focus. This can be a point of difficulty for many people and can be discouraging. At this point in particular a trained practitioner can be of invaluable assistance, especially if he is familiar with your personal psychological orientation and general expectations for meditation. Every individual is unique, and whether he enters into meditative practice specifically to unstress or for internal exploration of consciousness, minute but critical adaptations inevitably need to be made to suit his special needs.

Another point to bear in mind is that there is an attitudinal component to meditation which may have a great deal to do with its success or lack thereof for a particular individual. Those who meditate have chosen to do so. They are self-selected, and by virtue of this they start out with a positive predisposition toward meditative practice which may not exist among skeptics for whom it is suggested or for whom it remains mystical escapism. Obviously, such a predisposition is going to enhance one's chances of success and make the individual more likely to practice diligently and experience the cumulative benefits that elude both the dilettante and the skeptic. A person entering into meditation has already in some sense committed himself to an accompanying philosophical belief system. This factor of the individual's attitude as he approaches meditation practice cannot be underestimated in understanding the positive effects of such practice. It should be evident that these psychological changes interact with the physiological ones in a complex spectrum of phenomena ranging from simple training in deep muscular relaxation to religious conversion. Although the relative importance of these two variables in producing personality and behavioral change are as yet unknown, research on emotions and psychedelic drugs suggests that physiological and attitudinal components may combine synergistically and create greater effects than either factor alone.

Dramatic life-style changes are not inherent in effective meditation. Recently there has been a proliferation of human potential movements, quasi-religious mind-control systems, and self-help seminars, many of which rely heavily on a group gestalt and the adoption of certain attitudes and beliefs which contribute to a rather elitist superiority among members. Belonging to the movement becomes more important than any of the real benefits derived therefrom. This is most emphatically not an essential aspect of meditative practice. Although the meditative technique that is chosen may or may not be one associated with a particular religious discipline, it remains above all a highly individual and personal practice. You alone are responsible for making it work for you. Even if your chosen practice has a religious derivation, your commitment to it may range from simply using the technique for muscular relaxation all the way to religious conversion. The choice is yours. Effective meditation does not in any way require you to adhere to rigid group norms or abdicate your life to a spiritual or secular leader. It is something you do by yourself and for yourself in order to know yourself more fully.

Most of the forms of meditation which have been introduced most widely in Western culture are only of two particular kinds: Zen meditation, largely through the work of Alan Watts and D. T. Suzuki, and Transcendental Meditation, introduced to this country by Maharishi Mahesh Yogi. Both of these systems are characterized by a pattern of lowered arousal and a predominance of alpha waves in the individual's EEG pattern. These two meditative systems are in fact very appropriate for an overstressed culture, in the sense that they induce a state of relaxation. However, these are not the only patterns or approaches of meditative systems. There are systems such as Kriya yoga, Kundalini yoga, and Karma yoga which advocate a state of high arousal and extreme active involvement. The point here is that there are innumerable forms of meditation and those presented here represent only practices which appear to be particularly appropriate in our society.

One final observation should be kept in mind. Meditation is only one component of an individual's total behavior. Meditative practice is not a panacea which will resolve or satisfy an individual's life needs. Despite the fact that meditation can have a positive effect upon an individual's entire life, it is by no means a substitute for any other part of that individual's activity. Meditation practices, if utilized regularly and in moderation, enhance but do not replace all the other aspects of a person's life.

With these reservations and cautions kept clearly in mind, it can be said that meditative practices lead to the maintenance of health, going beyond a stage of average health to a state of increased health and activity. In the first part of this book a great deal of time was spent defining and clarifying psychophysiological pathology. There is a great deal that can be done to correct and prevent this stage of gross pathology from occurring. Among the most effective methods which can be employed are meditative practices. In this and the following chapters examples of these various methods are offered to help an individual reader make an appropriate individual choice.

SCIENTIFIC EVIDENCE FOR THE ROLE OF MEDITATION IN ALLEVIATING STRESS

Certainly there is no dearth of literature concerning the effects of meditation. There are over 400 articles and studies to date on the psychophysiological changes that occur during meditative practice. Early research was conducted primarily with Zen masters and Indian yogis who demonstrated marked degrees of autonomic control. More recently, research has been conducted with Western meditators, primarily those who practice Transcendental Meditation and an Indian practice called Shavasana or the "corpse pose." Later sections of this chapter describe the basic principles underlying Transcendental Meditation, Zazen or Zen meditation, and Shavasana, and convey enough information for you to begin experimenting with them yourself. At least you can decide which appeals to you most if you should undertake a serious meditative practice. For now, the focus is upon experiments undertaken to evaluate the potential of meditation in the clinical treatment of psychosomatic or stress-related disorders.

Numerous research projects have demonstrated that meditation is psychologically and physiologically more refreshing and energy restoring than deep sleep (Wallace, 1970; Stroebel, 1975). In fact, many meditators have reported that they required noticeably less sleep after they began meditating (Bloomfield, Cain, and Jaffe, 1975). This need for fewer hours of sleep each night is often one of the first benefits noted by novice meditators, and seems to suggest that a profoundly regenerative process occurs during meditation. Psychophysiological states achieved during successful meditation are quite markedly different from those of both normal waking consciousness and deep sleep. Its implications for stress reduction and improvement of one's health and energy level are great indeed.

As early as 1935, French cardiologist Therese Brosse (1946) recorded measures of heart-rate control in Indian yogis indicating an advanced voluntary capability to manipulate autonomic functions. This phenomenon has only recently been given credence in Western psychophysiology and medicine. Another early study with Indian yogis, most of whom practiced Hatha Yoga, had more specific significance for meditation as an aid in stress reduction (Bagchi and Wenger, 1959). In ninety-eight meditation sessions, these researchers noted the following characteristic pattern of physiological alteration during meditation: 1) an extreme slowing of respiration to 4 to 6 breaths per minute; 2) more than a 70 percent increase in electrical resistance (GSR), indicating a state of deep relaxation; 3) a predominance of alpha brain-wave activity; and 4) a slowing of heart rate to 24 beats per minute from the normal rate of 72 beats per minute. Each of these alterations in physiological activity indicated that the meditators entered into a profound state of relaxation during their practice. Drawing on this work, Anand, Chhina, and Singh (1961) monitored the EEG records of four yogis during samadhi, which is the state of total fulfillment or enlightenment. According to their research, the yogis produced an abundance of alpha waves during meditation periods and were not at all distracted by such external stimuli as strong light, loud banging noises, being burned with hot glass tubing, or vibrations from a tuning fork. This research appeared to indicate that alpha regulation was somewhat related to the ability to establish autonomic control.

More recently, two Japanese psychiatrists, Kasamatsu and Hirai (1966), undertook an extensive study of four adepts who practiced variations of the Buddhist meditation called Rinzai or Soto Zen. Today their work stands as one of the most definitive concerning the EEG correlates of meditation-induced states. Their results indicated: 1) alpha waves predominated in the EEG records of the Zen masters; 2) drowsiness was ruled out as being responsible for the state of deep relaxation achieved, since the EEG records were monitored for sleep onset; 3) alpha persisted with eyes open (predominant alpha is very difficult to maintain for most people with their eyes open); 4) there were no similarities to hypnotic trance in the EEG records of the meditators; 5) the more years of Zen training these men had had, the more changes were reflected in the EEG records; and 6) evaluation of the students' competence in meditation by the master correlated closely with the amount of alpha and theta found in the records. These Zen adepts were clearly in a state of profound relaxation, during which they remained relatively undistracted by external influences. Details and implications of these studies for transpersonal psychotherapy and in the exploration of human consciousness are discussed in *Consciousness: East and West* (Pelletier and Garfield, 1976). These experiments with Eastern meditators have given impetus to an investigation of the effects of meditation on Western practitioners. Although the results of these investigations have not been as pronounced as they were among the Eastern adepts, the data has been strikingly similar, and indicative of pronounced psychophysiological changes during meditation.

Since our main interest here is meditation as an aid in stress alleviation, there is one important question which should be considered. Most forms of meditation which are being practiced in the West involve one or two fifteen-to-thirty-minute sessions per day. The significance of meditation as a means of alleviating stress in daily life would be slight if its effects were temporary and limited to periods of meditation per se. In any clinical evaluation of a procedure like meditation, it is important to note that whatever positive improvement takes place in the clinic should be assessed in terms of its carry-over effect into the person's daily activities. If this carry-over does not take place, then despite the marked degree of improvement in the clinical situation, the therapy is probably minimally effective. Conversely, if the effects of the meditation carry over and transform the individual in a more permanent way, it is more likely to be of value in the clinical management of stress and stress-related disorders. Research evidence indicates that such a carry-over effect is a reality. Meditators have been found to be more psychologically stable (Schwartz and Goleman, 1974); autonomically stable (Ormé-Johnson, 1973); less anxious (Ferguson and Gowan, 1973; Linden, 1973; Nidich, Seeman, and Dreskin, 1973); and to experience an internal locus of control (Schwartz and Goleman, 1974), which indicates an individual's sense of being effective in the world rather than a passive victim of environmental circumstances. Improvement in each of these areas is an essential goal of psychotherapy and psychosomatic medicine.

One of the reasons why meditation produces this carry-over effect is that it helps an individual learn to maintain low arousal state of neurophysiological functioning. This may be used in response to stressful situations to minimize stress reactivity. One common denominator of most of the meditative practices is that they mitigate stress responses to threatening stimuli. One researcher who developed an approach of systematic desensitization for the treatment of phobias proposed the concept of "reciprocal inhibition" (Wolpe, 1958). In reciprocal inhibition relaxation is seen as the direct physiological opposite of tension and anxiety. According to Wolpe, the induction of the relaxed state in the presence of threatening stimuli inhibits stress reactivity.

This technique of inducing a relaxed state in the presence of stressful situations underlies all of the meditative approaches to stress and stress-related disorders.

Such a goal also characterized Edmund Jacobson's techniques of progressive relaxation developed in 1928, as well as many more recent therapeutic systems. If an individual can learn to respond to stressful stimuli, to which a fight-or-flight response would be inappropriate, by inducing a state of relaxed, non-aroused physiological functioning, he or she will be able to avoid the consequences of a prolonged stress reaction. Though there are many contributing factors, the ability of a trained meditator to initiate this state when required is the most important single factor in the success of meditation as a stress-reduction technique. There is also evidence that, with sufficient training, the ability to substitute a low arousal state for the normal response to a stressful situation can become habitual (Stoyva and Budzynski, 1973). In other words, when a trained individual is subjected to a threat that he has no means of avoiding or overcoming, he can shift almost automatically into a pattern of decreased sympathetic arousal. It is important to note that meditation produces additional cortical inhibitory effects beyond those induced by relaxation. The ability of a trained meditator to induce a state which is the exact physiological and psychological opposite of the fight-or-flight response is clearly a very beneficial kind of adaptation. Attendant upon this pattern of lowered neurophysiological arousal can be an increased emotional and psychological stability and a heightened capacity to cope with the pressure of everyday life.

Many of the research studies concerning meditation have employed a measure of skin resistance to an electrical current, or Galvanic Skin Response (GSR). Skin conductance is one of the variables measured by a polygraph machine or lie detector. When a person is nervous or anxious, he tends to perspire, although this may be so subtle a change that it is not noticeable to the naked eye. Moisture on his skin increases the electrical conductance of a current between any two points on the skin, measured in ohms by electrodes attached to a galvanometer. When moisture due to sweating increases conductance, the resistance to the flow of current decreases, so as a person becomes more anxious the resistance reading is lower. Conversely, a dry skin induced by relaxation increases the resistance to the current, and the reading is higher. An understanding of this inverse relationship is essential in considering several major research projects on meditation as an adaptive response to stress.

In a study entitled "Meditation as an Intervention in Stress Reactivity," (Goleman, 1976), Daniel J. Goleman relied heavily upon skin-conductance measures. Thirty of the sixty people in the experiment were meditators with more than two years of experience of Transcendental Meditation, and thirty were non-meditators who were interested in yoga and meditation but practiced neither. Subjects were assigned randomly to one of three conditions at the outset of the experiment: 1) meditations; 2) relaxation with eyes open; 3) relaxation with eyes closed. Those who were asked to meditate included both meditators and non-meditators. Experienced meditators practiced Transcendental Meditation, and the unexperienced controls were instructed in a simple meditation technique modeled on Transcendental Meditation. After twenty minutes of this procedure, all the subjects were asked to open their eyes and look at a video screen, on which a film would begin in five minutes. This film, entitled *It Didn't Have to Happen*, has been used as a stressor in a number of studies on autonomic reactions to stress (Lazarus et al., 1962). It was originally designed to impress safety practices on wood-mill workers, and its subject matter is such that it produces pronounced stress reactions among viewers. Through the use of actors in a dramatic setting, the film depicts three shop accidents which were caused by poor safety standards. In one incident the fingers of a worker are lacerated, in another a worker's finger is cut off, and in the third an innocent bystander is killed by a plank driven through his midsection as a result of his carelessness in coming near a circular saw. Needless to say, these three episodes bring about autonomic stress reactivity and emotional effects among those watching. During the meditation period and throughout the film, each individual was monitored for skin conductance and pulse levels, which were recorded at thirty-second intervals.

As anticipated, both heart rate and skin conductance rose and fell in direct response to the accident impacts. Interestingly, however, there was one unanticipated result of this study. Experienced meditators indicated a greater increase in skin conductance during the period just prior to each of the industrial accidents, but they also indicated a greater overall decrease after the accident episodes were shown. At first this might seem to suggest that the meditators had greater autonomic stress arousal than the non-meditators and that meditation therefore would seem to have little potential as a means of mitigating the adverse reactions of stress. But this is not necessarily the case. One interpretation of the pattern of their responses implies that they had increased reactivity to stimulus in the environment before and during the stress, but that this was followed by a rebound effect of greater relaxation and a quicker return to physiological homeostasis after the stress had passed. Significantly, this agrees with one of the primary goals of all meditative systems, which is to increase the practitioner's perception and sensitivity to both internal and external events (Pelletier, 1974). This enables the individual to be more reactive to his environment, while at the same time allowing him to recover more swiftly once the stressful situation has passed. According to Goleman:

> Had this initial anticipatory rise in meditators not been offset by a greater recovery, meditators' stress response would seem to be a debilitating pattern. The anticipatory spontaneous response frequency rise in meditators, however, was counter-balanced by greater subsequent decrease during post-impact recovery, a

pattern also true for heart rate . . . The effects of meditation as stress intervention are more completely understood in terms of this total pattern. The net
effect for meditators was a significantly greater recovery from anticipatory arousal, a pattern consistent
with their more positive affect and lower situational
and trait anxiety levels [Goleman, 1975].

This research would seem to indicate that meditators had a
higher level of arousal when it was appropriate, and perhaps
a greater potential range of response when such response
was warranted. Although Goleman's study has many interesting implications for the use of meditation in alleviating
stress conditions, there is as yet no experimental data on the
performance of meditators under active, real-life stress
situations. However, there is considerable evidence to indicate that there are positive long-term changes which take
place due to the practice of meditation itself. Studies which
have used longitudinal designs and pre- and post-test designs have found significant decreases in anxiety measures
in functions which are considered to be constant over the
life of the individual (Ferguson and Gowan, 1973; Linden,
1973; Pelletier, 1974). Implications of meditation as a
means of alleviating stress reactions have been evaluated
in terms of habituation rate, but so far there has been little
direct assessment of the interaction of the effects of meditation in a stress situation using complex emotional factors.

Many stress researchers have underscored the point that
anxiety and the accompanying physiological arousal is a
positive, adaptive phenomenon in a threatening situation.
(Lazarus et al., 1965; Folkins, 1970). Many studies of stress
reactivity have used the measure of increased skin conductance in response to stress as an index to the efficacy of
different intervention strategies. A rise in skin conductance
as an individual enters into a stressful situation is termed
"anticipatory arousal" and is interpreted as an indication
that the individual is becoming stressed in a situation in

which he finds himself. That response is perfectly functional and persists throughout an appropriate stress reaction, but must be followed by a rebound and homeostasis. Closely related to these changes induced by meditation is the phenomenon of *habituation*. If an individual is subjected to a repeated stressful stimulus such as a loud noise, his physiological response will become less pronounced with each repetition of the noise. Anxiety plays a part in a person's ability to habituate to stress triggers that occur repeatedly in the environment and are unavoidable. Habituation to repeated stressful stimuli is a vital coping mechanism. Continuing strong reactions to a repeated stress, such as a jackhammer outside an office window or an overcrowded subway, can induce neurasthenia or nervous exhaustion. Furthermore, when a person is able to habituate or diminish the intensity of his reaction to a repeated stressor, he frees himself to deal with other situations that may be more worthy of his energy and attention.

During a threat, the orienting response of the individual is manifested in the EEG as high-frequency beta activity and indicates an optimum coping strategy which prepares and focuses the individual for accurate perception of the stimulus and whatever situational changes there are. However, the maintenance of this orienting response for defense arousal to the threat beyond the time required for coping responses represents a dysfunctional response. This failure to habituate is a factor underlying stress-related disorders. Habituation of stress-induced physiological, psychological, and behavioral arousal is a direct index of the extent of recovery. In an extensive study of habituation experiments, Mackworth (1970) suggests that when the set to respond event diminishes or habituates, then the organism is free to consider another novel and potentially dangerous situation. Slower autonomic habituation has been associated with anxiety symptoms and poor prognosis among psychiatric patients (Lader and Wing, 1964; Stern, Surphlis, and

Koff, 1965; Martin, 1971). Patients diagnosed as having "anxiety reaction" or with prominent anxiety symptoms not only showed greater physiological arousal to stress but habituated more slowly to repeated stresses and had a slower recovery from stress in general. Again, this seems to underscore the fact that the response to stress alone is inadequate to account for stress disorders. In fact, the inability to respond appropriately to a stressful situation may be more rather than less stress-inducing. The stress-reactivity pattern in meditators, who recover or habituate rapidly after a stressful situation, is in direct contrast to that of the chronically anxious patient. There is another interesting sidelight to these observations. On a purely neurophysiological basis, it is very difficult to differentiate between excitement and anxiety, particularly in their anticipatory forms. It has been hypothesized that meditators enter into a state of hyper-activity in the manner of excitement rather than of anxiety, whereas the anxiety component will tend to be greater among non-meditators. It should be obvious that anxiety leads to more extreme stress reactivity, and that a psychological predisposition to become excited rather than anxious in anticipation of an event will enable the individual to unstress more easily than his anxious counterpart.

A study conducted by David Ormé-Johnson concerning the relationship between autonomic stability and Transcendental Meditation is another illustration of the fact that meditators habituate more quickly than non-meditators (Ormé-Johnson, 1973). Working with a group of TM practitioners and a group of non-meditating controls, Ormé-Johnson subjected his subjects to a noxious loud tone at regular 53-second intervals. Stress reaction to each tone was measured by means of galvanic skin response. Habituation, indicated by greater electrical resistance, was significantly faster for the meditators than for the controls. With each repetition of the tone, the meditators' stress reactions became less pronounced, while the controls took a longer time to habituate and exhibited increased GRS readings for a much longer time than did the meditators.

Other physiological effects of Transcendental Meditation were studied by Robert Keith Wallace in 1970 for his dissertation at the University of California at Los Angeles. Wallace's subjects were 15 college students who had practiced Transcendental Meditation for six months to three years. Each of the 15 students was asked to sit quietly with eyes open for five minutes, then with eyes closed for fifteen minutes, and then to meditate for thirty minutes. At the end of the meditation period, they again sat with eyes closed for ten minutes, then with eyes open for five more. Physiological indices that were monitored during that time were oxygen consumption, heart rate, skin resistance, and EEG. There were significant changes between the control periods and the meditation period in all measurements. During Transcendental Meditation, oxygen consumption was reduced by 16 percent, from 251 cubic centimeters per minute prior to meditation to 211 cubic centimeters during meditation. Similarly, carbon-dioxide elimination was reduced from 219 cc per minute to 187 cc. Interpreting these results, it was hypothesized that these reductions, and the essentially unchanged ratio of oxygen consumption to carbon-dioxide elimination, indicated a slowing of metabolic rate and a state of deep rest. Wallace also compared the 16 percent reduction in oxygen consumption during meditation with an average of only 8 to 10 percent reduction during a night's sleep. Based on this comparison, it appeared that in twenty minutes Transcendental Meditation produced almost twice the metabolic slowing of deep sleep. Evidently, a very profound state of relaxation could be achieved in a very short time through the conscientious practice of meditation. Wallace noted other physiological changes as well, all of which pointed to the same conclusion. Cardiac output was reduced by almost 30 percent, skin resistance increased markedly, sometimes as much as 400 percent, and the EEG recorded a shift toward predominance of alpha and theta waves.

These measurements indicated that, in addition to the physical state of deep relaxation, the mind was also in a relaxed but alert state.

MEDITATION AND PSYCHOSOMATIC MEDICINE

The preliminary research outlined above indicates that the conscientious practice of meditation increases autonomic stability, aids in the habituation to repeated stresses, and produces a state of relaxation deeper in some respects than that achieved during sleep. In addition, the characteristic physiological pattern of a person during meditation is virtually opposite to that of a neurophysiological stress pattern. These effects of the meditation can carry over and extend into the post-meditation stage of daily activity. These studies imply that regular meditation can be an effective means of stress alleviation.

There has been much anecdotal and some experimental evidence of improved health among individuals who practice meditation regularly. One researcher, Gary E. Schwartz of Harvard University, found a substantial drop in the frequency of such psychosomatic disorders as headaches, colds, and insomnia among experienced meditators as compared with non-meditators, and a lower incidence of somatic complaints (Schwartz, 1973). These changes were also accompanied by some important habit changes, including reduced usage of alcohol, cigarettes, coffee, and other drugs, and dietary changes (typically, eating less meat and candy). In addition, the group of meditators reported more positive mood states and more regular daily routines. Such changes in life style and habits seem often to be adopted by committed meditators, and may play a significant part in their improved reactivity to stress. Once again, researchers are confronted with the difficulty of isolating various factors to determine their effect. There is almost certainly some interaction among such factors as change in diet, drug use, sleeping patterns, life-style orientation, and the meditation itself in producing the end result of reduced stress and greater coping capability. These results and differences were also noted in Goleman's study with meditators and suggest the possibility that the difference in the stress reactivity of the meditation group is due to changes in life style rather than to practice of meditation. In experiments of this type it is extremely difficult to determine in any definitive way how much of a role individual variables in the complex interaction of meditation, dietary change, drug-use change, sleeping patterns, and life-style orientation have to play in terms of the individual's stress reduction.

By contrast to the purely experimental approach which seeks to isolate causative variables, a clinical approach seeks to obtain a beneficial outcome for the individual patient. Frequently the therapist suggests that numerous variables be modified simultaneously, with the end point being to establish a more generally positive life style for the individual patient. Therefore, in clinical work the issue of which of these changes specifically accounts for the stress reduction is simply not as important as it is in experimental research. In a clinical setting the fact that no specific cause of change can be isolated is often of secondary consideration if a positive oucome is observed for the patient. Suffice it to say in this regard that meditators seem to adopt better overall health habits of their own accord once they begin meditation. It is well documented that the meditative state itself produces distinct and positive physiological changes, and it is highly probable that these improved health habits contribute in some measure to sustaining the beneficial effects of meditation.

Perhaps the most important bias to remember in any research concerned with meditation is that the selection of those individuals who continue regular meditation over a prolonged period of time may in itself be the significant variable that correlates with reduced stress. It may be that the stress-reduction benefits are not due to meditation per se, but rather to self-selection in becoming a meditator or continuing as a meditator for a prolonged period of time. Even if longitudinal studies were conducted to see if in fact these patterns developed over time as an individual practiced meditation, they would not be sufficient to resolve this issue completely.

At this early stage in the clinical application of meditation there are only a few specific instances of meditation being used in psychosomatic medicine with marked success. Meditation has been used successfully in the treatment of asthma (Honsberger and Wilson, 1973), hypertension (Benson and Wallace, 1972), phobias (Boudreau, 1972), and numerous other psychosomatic disorders. In a recent study, Herbert Benson and Robert Keith Wallace designed an experiment to test whether Transcendental Meditation would lower blood pressure in hypertensive patients (Benson and Wallace, 1972). They worked with a group of 22 hypertensives over periods ranging from 4 to 63 weeks. Resting blood pressure prior to learning and practicing Transcendental Meditation averaged 150 ±17 mm mercury systolic, and 94 mm ±9 mm of mercury diastolic. After the subjects started Transcendental Meditation, resting blood pressures measured at times other than during the meditative period dropped down to 141 mm ±11 mm systolic and 88 mm ±7 mm diastolic. Although only a small number of people were involved in this experiment, it seems to indicate that meditation may have significant value in the treatment of hypertensive patients. Honsberger and Wilson (1973) have pursued this line of research in hypothesizing that Transcendental Meditation may have a beneficial effect on bronchial asthma. Individuals involved in their study were 22 asthmatic patients. Half of the patients began the practice of Transcendental Meditation for three months, while the other half read related material daily but did not meditate. Daily symptom and meditation information was kept in diaries, and pulmonary-function data were obtained at 0, 3, and 6 months. Ninety-four percent of the patients who meditated had improved airway resistance.

Additionally, the severity of symptoms was reduced in the meditation group. Although the number of individuals was rather small, this was a very well-designed and controlled study.

Other projects focus upon the biochemistry of stress and its alleviation. Experiments have been designed to measure concentrations of blood lactate, since high levels are indicative of stress and fatigue. It has also been demonstrated that infusions of blood-lactate ions produce symptoms of anxiety (Pitts and McClure, 1967). Experiments have shown that the average blood-lactate level in practitioners of Transcendental Meditation decreased markedly during meditation. In addition, the lactate level remained low for some time after the meditation was concluded (Wallace, et al., 1971). If high blood lactate generates anxiety, then it is very possible that the subjective feelings of alert tranquility which occur during and after meditation may result from the decreased lactate levels exhibited by meditators.

Meditative practice induces a generalized state of stress reduction, but most psychosomatic disorders are localized in a specific system. When meditative practices are applied in a clinical setting, alone or in conjunction with other therapeutic modalities such as clinical biofeedback, it is necessary for the individual to learn specific control as well as an overall self-regulatory pattern. In a classic study of symptom mechanisms of psychiatric patients under stress, Malmo and Shagass (1949) indicated that patients with somatic complaints manifested increased physiological responses to a stressor in the system assoicated with the complaint. This finding is in keeping with the neurophysiological stress patterns discussed in Chapter 2 on the neurophysiology of stress. In Chapter 8, dealing with clinical biofeedback and stress reduction, individual predisposition toward manifesting stress in a specific body system is discussed more fully. At this point, it is sufficient to note that it is possible to determine whether a psychological disorder is affecting an individual in his circulatory system, his digestive system, the reactivity of his brain waves, in muscle complexes, or in another specific system. This provides a means not only of identifying but of alleviating these systems before more severe symptoms are present, and certainly before a more severe psychosomatic disorder becomes manifest. In later research, Malmo (1966) has attributed this increased physiological responsiveness to a failure in the homeostatic regulatory mechanism in that system which is most reactive to the stress. A particular system in an individual's body will become affected by psychological stress to the point where it can no longer rebound of its own accord into a state of relaxation and habituation. When this occurs it becomes necessary to retrain or reeducate the individual and his entire psychophysiological system. Meditative techniques and clinical biofeedback work in different ways to restore a balance which has been disrupted in the course of the individual's life. Regulation of specific systems can be most efficiently accomplished with biofeedback, but a generalized meditative practice is an invaluable precursor or adjunct to treatments of psychosomatic disorder.

TYPES OF MEDITATION AND
THEIR EFFECT ON STRESS-RELATED DISEASE

Recent psychophysiological research has demonstrated the occurrence of unique physiological states achieved by meditators and the process leading to and the attainment of heightened awareness. It has been empirically verified that the meditative process relieves nervous-system stress more efficiently than either dreaming or sleeping. There are numerous examples of such marked physiological alterations which are accompanied by equally remarkable subjective reports such as 1) reduction of the metabolic rate, (Anand, Chhina and Singh, 1961; Kasamatsu and Hirai, 1966); 2) reduction of the breathing rate to four to six breaths per minute, from twelve to fourteen per minute (Allison, 1970); 3) an increase in the amount of alpha waves of eight to twelve cycles in the brain (Akishige, 1970; Kamiya, 1968; Pelletier, 1974); 4) the appearance of theta of five to eight cycles in the brain (Green, 1974; Pelletier, 1974); 5) a 20 percent reduction in blood pressure of hypertensive patients (Datey et al., 1969), and other related reports. Most of the above research has been conducted with meditators trained in Transcendental Meditation. This technique is unique, since it involves no autosuggestion, no adaption of a particular religious philosophy, and no physical manipulation. Control of attention is established by instructing the meditator to "turn the attention inward toward the subtler levels of a thought until the mind transcends the experience of the subtlest state of the thought and arrives at the source of the thought" (Maharishi Mahesh Yogi, 1969). There are two basic assumptions which establish the basis of TM. One is that subtler levels of thought are progressively more enjoyable to the mind. Secondly, the attention has a strong tendency to drift toward more enjoyable experience.

The technique of TM involves the repetition of a mantra for 15 to 20 minutes each day while the meditator sits in a comfortable position with eyes closed. First, the initiate seeks out the most comfortable position for himself, one which allows the spine to be in an upright position, either in a lotuslike sitting position on the floor, or in a straight-backed chair with feet firmly planted on the ground. With eyes closed, one begins by taking a few deep and well-modulated breaths to quiet down and then proceeds to the sub-vocal repetition of a mantra or specific sound. Instructors of TM insist that a mantra is a highly individual phenomenon and by understanding your particular needs and rhythms they will design the perfect mantra for you. Once you have received your mantra from your teacher, it is your secret.

Many people who have tried this form of meditation feel that each individual can devise his or her own mantra and work with it successfully. The main thing is that it be a short word or sound, usually of one syllable, that it contain no harsh sounds, and that it be devoid of any particular significance which may cause the meditator to make associations based on it. Herbert Benson of Harvard University, when instructing patients in his "relaxation response," which is modeled on TM, often suggests that they try out the word "one."

One purpose of a mantra is to absorb your attention so as to still the mind. However, Maharishi counsels TM practitioners not to be concerned when they find thoughts and images cropping up spontaneously over the rhythm of the mantra. He says the meditator should let the mind flow easily over these thoughts and images, but that it should not allow any of them to distract from the meditation. If the interlopers can be gently passed over, and the meditator can maintain the mantra as his primary focus, success will ensue. Breakthroughs to new levels of experience will come in various stages, until the practitioner finally achieves the ultimate goal of transcendental awareness.

In a recent article in *Psychology Today*, Leon Otis offered an overview of some recent TM studies being conducted at Stanford Research Institute. He speculated on some of the specific factors involved in the role of TM as a therapeutic agent:

> 1) Certain individuals may be more disposed to TM than others; i.e., those who get the most out of it are somehow predisposed in terms of personality characteristics; 2) it is people with these predisposed personality characteristics who tend to get highly involved in scientific studies on TM; 3) the person most predisposed to TM is one who is reasonably well integrated and yet bothered by neurotic anxieties, guilts, and phobias; 4) many individuals who begin TM tend to stop meditating (in the SRI sample, 50% had stopped after several months; 5) older meditators tend to keep meditating, whereas younger meditators tend to drop out; 6) the benefits that meditators experience may be actually due to high expectations [Otis, 1974].

These speculations and hypotheses indicate that a number of personality and psychological and self-selection variables play a vital role in the efficacy of TM. These factors obviously should be explored before any definitive statement can be made about the effects of meditation as such. Based upon research, it does seem that when an individual receives proper instruction and is motivated to maintain diligent meditative practice, psychological benefits can accrue through the practice of Transcendental Meditation. Therefore, it would seem to be a safe conclusion that for individuals who feel predisposed toward the methodology or the practice of TM, the regular practice of this form of meditation would be an effective means of reducing stress and anxiety. There have been numerous other studies with implications for stress reduction which employ TM as the primary meditative technique. There is no need to review this extensive literature of TM, since it is adequately considered in two recent books. One is entitled *TM: Discovering Inner Energy and Overcoming Stress*, by Harold H. Bloomfield, Peter Cain, and Dennis T. Jaffe (Delacorte Press, 1975). A second book, entitled *Scientific Research on Transcendental Meditation: Collected Papers*, has been edited by L. Domash, J. Farrow, and D. Ormé-Johnson (Maharishi International University, 1976) and contains articles concerning both the basic research on and clinical applications of Transcendental Meditation. These two books offer a comprehensive overview of the effect of TM on stress and stress-related disorders.

Another technique which has been demonstrated to affect general stress reduction is an ancient yogic one known as Shavasana or the "corpse pose" (described later in this chapter). This particular exercise has been employed by British cardiologist Chandra H. Patel in experiments reported in *Lancet*, the journal of the British Medical Association, under the title "Yoga and Biofeedback in the Management of Hypertension" (1973). Yogic relaxation and biofeedback were used with twenty patients. As a result of this intervention, five patients were able to stop anti-hypertensive medication therapy altogether, and seven others reduced their dosage by 33 to 60 percent. Blood-pressure control, with medication, improved in four patients, while four patients did not respond to therapy. Of those four patients who did not respond to blood-pressure control, at least one derived indirect benefit through the relief of migraine and depression. Previous research by K. K. Datey had demonstrated that the yogic exercise Shavasana, alone, significantly reduced blood pressure in hypertensive patients (Datey, 1969). Patel points out that anti-hypertensive drugs do in fact reduce the complications of hypertension and radically improve the prognosis. However, many of these drugs are far from ideal and have disadvantages or side effects, causing Patel to conclude that "any new method for reducing blood pressure is therefore welcome."

During Patel's experiments, the patients lay on a couch in a Shavasana position. At the same time, they were monitored by an audible signal from a galvanic-skin-response unit to determine to what extent they had succeeded in relaxing. When the patient was able to reduce the tone of the signal, it signified relaxation, while an increase in tone indicated increased arousal. (This biofeedback technique is described in more detail in Chapter 8). Patients were also instructed to concentrate on their breathing. After making their respiration smooth and regular, they were instructed to focus on various parts of the body to make them go limp and relaxed while repeating subvocally phrases such as "my arms are feeling very heavy and relaxed." During physical relaxation, most of the patients were able to forget the outside world and often were not even aware of their own bodies except in a detached manner. However, they found it difficult to forget their breathing movements, and began to use them as an object of meditation. They were also encouraged to choose other objects on which to focus their meditation. At the end of each session, the patient was told his blood pressure level before and after the session.

Analyzing the results of this study, Patel wrote:

> It is postulated that daily relaxation and meditation reduces the sympathetic discharge in response to the environmental stimuli, making the neurohumoral factors concerned with the production of hypertension ineffective. Mental concentration reduces the external interference, making the subject less aware of the external environment. This increases his perception of his internal environment. Additionally, helped by biofeedback, the subject becomes more aware of the smallest change in the autonomic function (in this case, blood pressure), which allows him to make the necessary changes in the control of that function [Patel, 1973].

Her experiments have been successful enough to stir much interest. That such a treatment, conducted in half-hour sessions three times a week for three months, should produce such substantial improvement in blood-pressure readings is certainly a convincing arugment for the use of techniques such as Shavasana and deep relaxation as therapy for psychosomatic disorders.

An important factor in this research is that a yogic technique was used in conjunction with biofeedback monitoring devices to obtain clinical improvement. The biofeedback in this case was not used to monitor blood pressure itself, but rather to assist in the attainment of deep relaxation states through the use of GSR feedback. It was probably the instruction in the yogic technique which was most directly responsible for the results, although certainly the biofeedback contributed to heightened autonomic sensitivity. The question as to whether the meditative technique or the biofeedback technique was the major factor in contributing to the outcome is a basic research issue. For now, we can say only that a clinical-intervention technique comprised of biofeedback in a clinical setting and the practice of relaxation in the Shavasana pose was effective in blood-pressure reduction.

Following the publication of this research report in *Lancet*, there was a rebuttal in the same journal by Thomas Pickering of Rockefeller University. Pickering raised issues involving some technical points, the role of the placebo effect in the patients' expectations, patient-therapist interaction, and other intangible variables which may have played a part in the experimental outcome. In response to Pickering's criticisms, Patel noted several points which are well worth repeating here. Among her observations were:

> My patients were not merely thinking of blood pressure during training sessions; efforts were made to change the behavior patterns of the patients to behavior that will, I hope, become part of their daily lives . . . Personally, I believe that to provide biofeedback instruments without providing a technique is like the tools without the skill . . . I would like to ask Dr. Pickering what in his opinion is a "proper control" when one is trying to change the behavior pattern of the patient: his personality, mental makeup, physician-patient relationship, and a host of other factors and interactions play their part [Patel, 1973].

Combining clinical biofeedback and meditative techniques seems to work very effectively. It is clear that the clinical use of any of these techniques involves extremely complex factors such as placebo effect, expectations, and patient-therapist interaction. The effectiveness of combining homework exercises such as meditation and yogic techniques with biofeedback therapy is discussed at greater length in Chapter 8.

Perhaps the most important aspect of Patel's findings is the statement that these techniques need to be integrated into the person's life and that some degree of life-style change is an inevitable result of attempting to achieve stress reduction. True stress alleviation, rather than symptom removal via anti-hypertensive medications, seems to require a change in the behavior of the individual. Stress-reduction techniques need to be incorporated into the patients' life styles after clinical treatment has ended.

More recently, Chandra Patel and Professor K. K. Datey extended this research in a study entitled "Yoga and Biofeedback in the Management of Hypertension: Two Control Studies," which was presented at the 1975 meeting of the Biofeedback Research Society. In this study they used behavior modification, relaxation, and meditation based on Shavasana and reinforced by biofeedback. Their results were striking. Twenty hypertensive patients were matched with twenty hypertensive controls on the basis of age and sex. At the end of the trial, the twenty patients who had been treated by Patel's method showed markedly reduced blood-pressure readings for both systolic and diastolic. Furthermore, there was a reduction in their requirement for anti-hypertensive drugs averaging 41 percent. These patients were followed up for the year following treatment, and showed satisfactory maintenance of both blood-pressure levels and drug reduction, indicating that they were able to integrate what they had learned in the clinic into their everyday life styles without difficulty. In another part of the study, sixteen patients were treated for six weeks, following a six-week control period during which they were observed for the sake of comparison. Again, blood pressures were significantly reduced, and their use of medications was reduced by 27.5 percent. Follow-up studies on these patients are in progress at the time of this writing.

The particular yogic technique used in these studies is the posture of Shavasana, known as the corpse pose. It can be practiced by anyone who wishes to reduce stress. Descriptions of meditative techniques are always deceptively simple. Diligent practice is of primary significance, and cannot be described in elaborate detail. Merely reading the description does not give an idea of the effect of the technique. Shavasana derives from the yogic tradition of India and is very straightforward.

To enter into the Shavasana pose, lie supine on a fairly

supportive surface (hard mattress or the floor) with your feet comfortably apart and relaxed. Your arms should lie easily at a natural distance from your body and along it, with the palms up and your eyes closed. You may open your eyes if you feel more at ease that way, but eyes closed is the recommended procedure. Then become aware of your breathing without controlling it and note the ingoing and outgoing flow. One useful method for monitoring the breath is to feel the flow of breath at the tip of your nostrils. Make this the object of your meditation. So far as your head is concerned, allow it to rest comfortably wherever it feels best. If you find you have a tendency to become drowsy during this particular practice, you can remedy this by bringing your feet closer together so that the effort required to hold the posture maintains alertness. Assuming this posture and concentration on breathing for fifteen minutes three times per day constitutes the entire meditative practice. Shavasana is very easy and extremely relaxing, and is particularly good for people who cannot sit for long without difficulty. However, some meditative effort is required to focus your attention and not let sleepiness, the intrusion of unsettling thoughts, or just the fact that you are lying down interfere with your concentration.

Another technique useful in stress reduction is Zazen or "sitting meditation." Despite the religious and philosophical complexity of Zen Buddhism itself, this particular exercise is simple and straightforward. Either the beginning Zen meditation posture or the more classical meditative posture can be used in order to enter into a state of deep relaxation and psychophysiological unstressing. According to the research literature, TM and Zazen meditation in their early stages appear to produce a comparable state of neurophysiological relaxation. Usually, one imagines a Zen student sitting for hours in a lotus position on a cushion on the floor. However, the classical Zen posture may be impossible or unnecessarily painful for many people. Nothing is gained in meditative practice by forcing one's body until it aches or cramps. Also, there is no stigma attached to the use of a chair in Zazen, since the primary requirement of correct back posture can be maintained just as easily in a chair. Meditation should be paced to each individual's ability. Following are instructions for a sitting posture in a chair, published in a small book entitled *Zen Meditation,* by Shasta Abbey in Mount Shasta, California:

> Sit forward on the front third of the seat, allowing the pelvis to rotate forward and the abdomen to relax forward. As in all meditation positions, the back should be straight but relaxed with a concavity in the small of the back. It may be necessary to employ a small cushion to assist in obtaining the best results for positioning the torso. In this case it should be fairly flat and hard, and one should sit on the fore-edge of it.
>
> The feet should be flat on the floor. Now the knees and upper legs have a natural tendency to fall apart when the feet and lower legs are together, but this requires a certain amount of concentration and physical effort. The more natural approach seems to be to let them relax, then move the feet apart until the lower legs are perpendicular to the floor and there is more or less a right angle at the knees. At this point the distance between the feet will be approximately 6 inches, though this may vary from person to person.

This posture seems to be easy for most people to feel comfortable in, although it may be helpful to have someone knowledgeable check to make sure you are doing it correctly. Above all, it should be comfortable, since the main purpose of meditation is to focus the practitioner's attention and not let it be drawn away from the object of meditation. An unnatural or painful position can be very distracting. However, your position should not be slouched or lazy. You are meant to stay alert and aware, and your position is one element in the practice which helps ward off drowsiness or sleep.

For those who wish to try the classical posture and procedure, here are detailed and easily followed directions from the Chief Abbess of the Shasta Abbey, Roshi Juju-Kennett:

Sit with a straight back, which means a back pulled in at the waist. It's very important that you get that right . . . It is pushing the lower back out, with a completely relaxed abdomen—that is what most people miss. Instead, they keep the abdomen tight and force the back out, and then get terribly stiff. Be completely relaxed. Carry your weight with the lower back muscles. You do tend to develop a nice front bulge, but that can't be helped.

You only sit the very tip of the bottom of the spine on the cushion so that you have a slight slope in the back as it moved down the zafu [cushion] . . . The head . . . should be in line, the ears in line with the shoulders, the nose in line with the navel, etc. Then you sway, starting with big sways and ending with smaller and smaller ones—you can do circular swaying as well if you like—and then you can find the exact position to rest, in which all your weight seems to drop straight down your spine and onto the zafu.

Then the hands—don't push them together, just hold them in your lap with the thumbs lightly touching each other. If you are left handed, lay the right hand over the left; if you are right handed, it is left hand over right. The reason is very simple one: one side of the body is always more active than the other, usually the side you use most, and that is the one you need to quiet the most, so you put the less active side superior to the active side so as to equate the body naturally. That is all.

Please do NOT close your eyes completely; have them lowered so that they are at a comfortable place on the floor, comfortable for you as an individual.

Breathe through the nose and not the mouth. . . . Don't do something that is unnatural for you. There are many, many forms of meditation which talk about counting the breaths, watching the inhalation, exhalation, etc. Yes, that is fine, but as a form of yoga and not Zen meditation. Take two or three deep breaths when you start, just to clear all the passages, and then breathe at what is natural for you.

Now don't deliberately try to think and don't deliberately try not to think; in other words, thoughts are going to come into your head; you can either play with them or you can just sit there and look at them as they pass straight through your head and out the other side. And that is what you need to do—just continue to sit; don't bother with the thoughts, don't be hijacked by them and don't try to push them away. Both are wrong.

When the meditation period is over, you sway the body starting with small sways or circles, getting larger and larger, so that you are able to get up quietly and walk around for a little while, and that ends the meditation period.

A number of problems frequently arise during the meditative practice. One is a tendency for an individual to breathe too deeply and induce a lightheaded high. Such a state is considered a distraction in the practice of Zazen, since the intention of meditation is not to induce states or sensations artificially. This feeling of lightheadedness is frequently due to hyperventilation. If this occurs, it is best to let the body breathe naturally, since when the posture is correct, with the lower spine forward, the breathing will naturally deepen as the diaphragm is given increased room in which to move. Meditative traditions also differ with regard to having eyes open or eyes closed during the meditative practice. Ordinarily, we use our eyes to dissect our visual environment into discrete pieces. This is an active form of visual perception which induces a state of beta activation in the neurophysiological system. During Zazen the eyes are held partially open, since Zen Buddhists believe that the closed eyes encourage withdrawal from life and drowsiness. Meditators are instructed to look with an attentive but unfocused gaze, as though the eyesight were a stream of water which flows out approximately three feet from the eyes and drapes over the objects in the field of vision. This non-analytic, un-focused way of looking at a limited space in front of you is both alert yet conducive to low-frequency activity in the brain. It may be slightly difficult to master at first. One of the basic philosophical tenets behind Zen is that the individual should live fully and completely in the present moment, involving himself deeply in everyday life and shunning withdrawal in any form. The eyes-open kind of meditation is, at least on one level, a reflection of this philosophy.

MEDITATION AS A REGENERATIVE PROCESS

Each of the three systems of meditation which have been discussed advocates sitting several times a day for a period of time ranging from fifteen minutes to half an hour. Many individuals say that they have an extremely busy schedule and simply do not have the opportunity to sit for such a long period of time each day. Very often, a realistic examination of a person's schedule indicates that in fact there is sufficient time if the individual is conscientious and serious in his efforts. To some extent, the minor life reorientation necessitated by meditative practice may be responsible for its success. It involves a commitment and a reordering of life priorities and behavioral patterns. At first the effects of your meditation period will probably be minimal or even imaginary. However, over time the benefits are quite real. As you become more adept, you will achieve the desired state of psychophysiological relaxation much more rapidly than you did at first. If you have periods in which your life is very hectic and you are legitimately having trouble making time and finding peace and quiet for twenty minutes twice a day, remember that it is better to meditate even for a few minutes every day than it is to skip whole days and then meditate longer at another time to compensate. If you meditate for no other reason than to alleviate stress, that is a worthwhile goal. Meditation breaks into the degenerative syndrome of prolonged stress reactivity very effectively. When you are able to reduce stress, the results will show up clearly in your energy level, your coping capability, and your personal over-all health.

The deceptively simple meditative practices outlined above can have a profound effect upon an individual's state of psychosomatic health. Certainly, the meditation itself produced beneficial neurophysiological activity, but meditation is a more holistic phenomenon. Contemplative introspection fosters an attitude of self-examination and detachment to see the interactions between self, others, and environment with greater clarity. From this state, life changes frequently ensue, such as dietary alterations, and these effects as a whole constitute the phenomenology of meditation. Considering the extensive research on meditation beginning as early as the 1930s, on the physiological correlates of the meditative state and on the results that have emerged from the clinical application of meditative techniques, it is predictable that the concept of meditation as therapy will continue to receive considerable research attention.

However, we must not forget that there is another very compelling reason why people in both Eastern and Western societies engage in meditation. Throughout the 2,500 years during which meditative techniques have been practiced, the primary goal has been the attainment of a state termed "cosmic consciousness" or "transcendental awareness." Mystics, religious leaders, and adept meditators from various meditative disciplines have attempted to describe this state, and yet it continues to defy rational definition. It remains a phenomenon that must be experienced directly to be truly understood. Buddhists call this state enlightenment or one-pointedness or satori. To the Indians, it is both total emptiness of the void and total fulfillment of samadhi. For practitioners of Transcendental Meditation, it is transcendental awareness or "bliss consciousness."

After long practice of a meditative discipline, through which the practitioner has achieved total stilling of the mind and total loss of self as a separate entity, during the meditation, he or she becomes open to a whole new order of reality. At this point, he is pervaded with the overwhelming and joyous knowledge that all of existence is a unity and that he is at one with it and one and the same as all else about him. There is no subject or object, no I or Thou, no Yin or Yang. With this powerful feeling comes a dissolution of all fear, including fear of death, and an inundation of warmth, joy, harmony, and absolute knowledge that there is an order to the universe. Mystical utterances may confound the man who approaches them armed only with his logic and rationality. But to one who has experienced this unity, it becomes the highest truth. He will retain the certain knowledge that it is the highest state of consciousness, even after passing through the direct experience of it and returning to the tasks of everyday life.

Autogenic Training and Visualization

7

Therapeutic use of deep-relaxation techniques predates the recent upsurge of interest in classical meditation by almost fifty years. In fact, it is surprising that some of the more systematic and well-proven methods have not generated more interest in this country. However, as history has demonstrated many times, a wave of belated popular interest is often required to bring to the fore concepts and attitudes which have existed for centuries but which have been neglected in the contemporary setting due to cultural myopia. Eastern philosophies and religions acquired an element of glamor during the sixties, primarily as a result of the use of consciousness-expanding drugs and the emerging anti-materialistic ethos. Hence, the interest in classical Eastern meditation, with its emphasis on the development of the inner person in contrast to the socially activist side of human nature. Yet, unbeknownst to most of those who were so quick to be attracted by the exoticism, glamor, and implicit rebelliousness against an existing order which were part of the meditation vogue, methods of developing the same kind of internal awareness and autonomic control that meditation affords were already available in the Western tradition.

These forms of Western meditation grew out of the need for both psychological and physical therapy in an over-stressed environment rather than being generated from a religious or philosophical belief system. Some of these Western techniques such as autogenic training are now being accorded a new respect. Furthermore, this revival of interest has prompted innovative clinical and experimental work applying these techniques to the treatment of specific dysfunctions. One of the most exciting applications, to be discussed in this chapter, has been by several cancer specialists such as Carl Simonton, who have used modified forms of meditation and visualization techniques as adjuncts to radiation or chemotherapy for the treatment of cancer, with some promising results.

Before we discuss the applications of these deep-relaxation or visualization procedures to the alleviation of disease, certain points must be made. First of all, at this early stage of research clinical applications of these methods must be considered adjuncts to traditional medicine rather than alternatives. Especially in the case of applying meditative or psychotherapy approaches with cancer patients, any clinical practitioner is ethically, legally, and morally obligated to be certain that the patient is receiving the most efficient traditional care prior to or simultaneously with any other form of therapy. This consideration cannot be overemphasized, since disease can range along the psychosomatic continuum from almost purely psychological to virtually totally physical. As any disorder tends toward the purely organic end of the continuum it may be increasingly counterproductive to employ relaxation or meditative approaches, since many of these disorders can and should be alleviated by the most expedient surgical or chemotherapeutic means. There is no readily available solution to this complex issue except to consider both the psychological and physical variables in any disorder and then to plan the most appropriate treatment for that individual patient.

It should also be made clear that the approaches described

in this portion of the book—meditation, autogenic training, and biofeedback—are not antagonistic to traditional medical or psychological therapies. There is no inherent conflict between traditional and meditative therapies unless it is created by practitioners maintaining rigid areas of specialization or denigrating the psychosomatic factors in all disease. No matter how organic a disease appears to be, there is inevitably an accompaniment of psychological and emotional stress which can aggravate the condition. Although it is highly premature to maintain that meditative or relaxation techniques can cure such disorders, it is certainly clear that such approaches can alleviate or eliminate the attendant anxiety and stress.

AUTOGENIC TRAINING

One of the most comprehensive and successful Western deep-relaxation techniques is autogenic training which was developed by the German psychiatrist Johannes H. Schultz in 1932. Ironically, autogenic training has been largely ignored in this country, as evidenced by the fact in a recent review of literature on the subject, only 10 out of 604 papers originated in the United States. There appears to be no reason for this neglect. Persons who, for whatever reason, are not inclined to engage in any of the Eastern meditative techniques discussed in Chapter 6 might do well to consider autogenic training. It is a remarkably thorough and systematically designed practice with an end result comparable to that of diligent meditation.

Schultz developed his system from his clinical experiences with hypnosis. Around the turn of the century, brain physiologist Oskar Vogt had observed that certain patients were able to place themselves in a hypnotic state for self-determined periods of time and termed this phenomenon "autohypnosis." Vogt noted several interesting patterns which occurred consistently among those who were able to achieve autohypnotic states, such as a substantial lessening of fatigue and tension as well as a reduction in the incidence and severity of psychosomatic disorders such as headache. Drawing upon these observations, Schultz combined the concept of autohypnosis with certain specific exercises designed to integrate mental and physical functions and above all to induce states of deep physiological and mental relaxation. Through his own work with hypnosis Schultz had noted that subjects who entered the hypnotic trance state experienced two overwhelming physical sensations. One was a pleasurable feeling of generalized warmth throughout the body, and the other a feeling of heaviness in the limbs and torso. Actually, the subjective sensation of warmth is the psychological perception of vasodilation in the peripheral arteries, and the sensation of heaviness is the perception of muscular relaxation. Both of these sensations are the psychophysiological correlates of the relaxation response. Schultz decided that if he could design exercises to teach people to induce these sensations in themselves, he might also be able to teach them to achieve the state of "passive concentration" which was characteristic of the hypnotic state.

One of the earliest definitive texts on Autogenic Training is Schultz's own (1953). In it he describes his system as a "method of rational physiologic exercises designed to produce a general psychobiologic reorganization [Umschaltung] in the subject which enables him to manifest all the phenomena otherwise obtainable through hypnosis." Schultz's purpose was to expand upon some of the positive effects Vogt had noticed in autohypnotic subjects, to improve functioning, and to help eliminate maladaptive behavior and its manifestations in neurotic and psychosomatic symptoms. Central to the success of autogenic training is the attainment of the "paradox of self-induced passivity," which is a concept very similar to that of "passive volition," which plays such a vital role in biofeedback and meditative training. Through this process, individuals learn to abandon themselves to an ongoing organismic process rather than exercising conscious will. Once again, too strong an effort of purposive volition immediately interrupts movement toward deep relaxation. What Schultz's method achieves, if practiced correctly and regularly, is a state of mind and body which has many of the same characteristics as the low arousal state achieved through meditation.

One primary difference between classical meditation and autogenic training is that the latter begins with exercises designed to induce distinct physical sensations, and leading to deep relaxation of a purely physical nature. After this initial stage and once the individual has developed the ability to enter the deeply relaxed state easily and rapidly, he is ready to graduate to the more subtle psychological aspects of autogenic training, through which he may be able to achieve unusual states of consciousness and a marked degree of autonomic control. Later stages of this meditative-like state have enabled people to perform remarkable feats such as self-anesthetization against a third-degree burn produced by a lighted cigarette placed on the back of the hand for one and a half minutes (Gorton, 1959). In one sense, the appeal of autogenic training is that it begins on a level easily understandable and easily learned and then progresses slowly to the more advanced and esoteric stages of accomplishment. It is designed literally to lead the practitioner step by step through physical relaxation procedures to a state wherein he becomes highly attuned to unconscious symbolism and fantasies and can interrogate his unconscious to resolve problems and profound internal dilemmas. Also, the system prescribes additional exercises which induce the type of autonomic control valuable in efforts at self-healing.

It is true that autogenic training depends to a great extent on the techniques of autosuggestion, and for this reason many people approach it with reticence. However, practitioners insist that there is a critical factor in distinguishing autogenic training from classical hypnosis. Patients in autogenic therapy are trained over a long period of time to enter into what constitutes a meditative state, and the initial use of autohypnosis is only a means of instructing and familiarizing them with their ability to enter into that state of their own volition (Schultz and Luthe, 1959; Gorton, 1959; Luthe, 1962). It is indeed from the lexicon of hypnosis that autosuggestion comes, but in this case it is used only for self-regulation away from a hyper-aroused and psychologically agitated state toward a state of increased physical and emotional normalization.

According to Schultz and Luthe, there are several essential requirements if an individual is to be successful at autogenic training and is to achieve the psychobiologic reorganization characteristic of hypnosis. These factors are: 1) high motivation and cooperation of the subject; 2) a reasonable degree of subject self-direction and self-control; 3) maintenance of a particular body posture conducive to success; 4) reduction of external stimuli to a minimum, and mental focusing on endopsychic processes to the exclusion of the external environment; 5) presence of a monotonous input into the various sensory receptors; 6) concentrated deployment of attention on the somatic processes in order to effect an inward focusing of consciousness. This is seen as a primal mode of experience in which an effacement of external stimuli is accomplished by attention deployment on bodily sensations. The result is a vegetative-passive level of functioning merging into a deeply focused meditative alteration of consciousness; 7) given these conditions, the occurrence of an overpowering, reflexivelike psychic reorganization; 8) the occurrence of disassociative and autonomous mental processes, leading to an alteration of ego functioning and dissolution of ego boundaries. The inner experiential and conceptual life assumes a plasticity of imagery, and a dreamlike state of consciousness results (Gorton, 1959). Schultz believes that any "normal" individual can experience this progression of change or *Umschaltung*. If he adheres to regular practice of the training, he will ultimately achieve self-regulation of a number of mental and physical functions.

In essence, the final stages of autogenic training may be compared to the breakthroughs of consciousness obtained through meditative techniques of various kinds. All of the procedures for deep relaxation have very similar effects both physically and psychologically. It is mainly the methods of attaining them that differ, and autogenic training's emphasis early in the learning process on strictly physical sensations may be easier for many people than plunging directly into attempts at contemplative meditations. Autogenic exercises were designed for Westerners unused to the kind of quietude that is so much a part of Eastern disciplines, and for this reason it may be a more accessible technique for those people living in Western environments.

BASIC POSTURES AND
EXERCISES OF AUTOGENIC TRAINING

Theoretically, autogenic training should be practiced with a minimum of external stimuli, and without the restrictions of tight or bothersome clothing, jewelry, glasses, and the like. However, once the basic warmth and heaviness techniques have been mastered, they can be practiced successfully even during quiet moments at the office or wherever and whenever one might feel the need. At first it is advisable to reduce distractions of all kinds until some measure of ease is acquired. Later and more advanced stages require a strictly controlled environment, since a more delicate and ephemeral state of consciousness is involved.

There are three basic postures which are recommended for autogenic training. Perhaps the easiest and the best one to start with is a lying-down position on a couch or bed, or the floor, if you prefer harder surfaces. The legs should be slightly apart and relaxed, with the feet inclined outward at a V-shaped angle. Sometimes it is a good idea to use support under the knees, such as a blanket or pillow, to provide maximum relaxation of the leg muscles. The heels should not be touching each other, and the trunk of the body and shoulders should be aligned symmetrically. Be especially careful to make sure the head is in a comfortable position which is not stiff or cramped in the neck or shoulders. One of the best ways to find your own particular preference for a thoroughly relaxed head is to experiment using pillows of different sizes in different positions under the head and neck. The key point to remember is that muscular tension should be totally absent in the position you finally choose for yourself. Your arms should lie relaxed and slightly bent at the trunk, with the fingers spread out and relaxed, not touching the main part of the body. This position is very similar to the Shavasana or "corpse pose" discussed in Chapter 6. It can be modified in any number of ways to facilitate total comfort, which is a luxury in itself, even before you begin the exercise.

In addition to the reclining position, there are two sitting postures recommended for autogenic training. They have the advantage of being applicable in a number of situations where it is not possible to lie down. There are many people who intuitively recognize the value of ten or fifteen minutes of "closing down" during the course of their work day, and the first stages of autogenic training are perfect for such times. In an office, a person could ask a secretary or switchboard operator to hold calls and seek out some quiet place where he can be relatively sure of being undisturbed. The lift and renewal of energy from just a short period of concentrated deep relaxation far exceeds the benefits gained from the ubiquitous coffee break. If you can master the first stages of the training while sitting, you will be able to use it almost anywhere. Some people have been able to engage in autogenic training in an upright, walking posture. Once again, the main point is to integrate your exercises into your life style as much as possible.

The sitting postures help to guard against sleep onset,

which can be a problem for many people if they are lying down. Sitting postures are favored by therapists in clinical biofeedback and during visualization techniques for these two reasons.

For the reclining chair posture, select an armchair with a high back so that the trunk of the body and the head are resting passively and comfortably against it while leaning back into the chair. The length of the seat should be equal to the length of the thighs so that the small of the back rests easily against it. Hands and fingers may be in a relaxed position on the arms of the chair or hang loosely on the inner side of the chair close to the body. The design of the chair is important, since the trunk should relax back into it so comfortably that you feel almost as if you are merging with the chair, and your head should be supported with no effort on your part to maintain its position.

If you are using a normal straight-backed chair, you will need to assume a more upright posture. This is also the posture used most commonly during clinical biofeedback. Straight-backed chair postures are simple, require no props, and can easily be transferred from the clinic to situations in the person's everyday life. Sit on the edge of the chair so that only the buttocks are on the seat and the thighs are touching the cushion only slightly. You may use a chair with cushion or without, depending on availability and your preference.

Specific instructions for entering into a balanced sitting posture are not provided in the standard training procedure. However, during the course of working with patients I have used the following instructions to enable an individual to attain a meditative posture. These instructions are not part of the autogenic procedure but are compatible with that method. When you first sit in the straight-backed chair your upper legs are at a 90-degree angle to the upright torso. While in this position, slide the left foot forward until you feel your weight shift to your heel. Then slide the foot back in toward your body until you begin to feel your weight pressing on the ball of your foot. Moving your foot in this manner, find the position in which your foot is flat on the floor with your weight evenly distributed on both the heel and the ball of your foot. In this position, your leg should be extended in front of you at approximately a 120-degree angle. Following this, do the same thing with your right foot. There should be no tension in the legs, and the knees should be approximately one foot apart. Hold your knees in your hands and wiggle them so that your legs move without resistance. The legs should now be in a stable position. The next step is to sit straight up in the chair without straining to hold your back secure. An upright posture can be maintained with a minimum of muscle tension if the position is correct. Now lean very far forward until you feel your lower back muscles pulling. Then allow yourself to lean back in the chair until you feel your abdominal muscles pulling. Next, as you did with your feet, rock back and forth until you find the position where neither set of muscles is strained and the spinal column feels as if it is poised perfectly on the pelvis. An image to keep in mind is that of a doll which is weighted in the center and returns to a balanced position whenever it is pushed in any direction. Now the legs and torso are in a state of balance. Turn your attention to your head and drop your head forward onto your chest until the back of your neck muscles pull. Then lean your head back until the muscles in front of your neck pull. Rock your head back and forth until you find the position in which it feels as if it is a ball balanced on the end of your spinal column, which is in turn balanced on your pelvis. Now drop your hands straight down by your sides. Raise the left hand and let it flop on your thigh as if it were a dead weight. Do the same with your right hand, and let them both relax where they fall. This is a very useful basic meditative posture which you may use to practice any one of the techniques discussed here, with the exception of Shavasana. This set of instructions for attaining a balance posture is my modification of the basic autogenic posture.

From this basic posture, the standard autogenic exercise proceeds in the following manner. The individual is instructed to imagine that there is a string from the top of his head to the ceiling and that this string is pulling him into an upright posture with both arms still hanging to the sides. Then the person is instructed to imagine that the string is cut and his head flops forward "like a rag doll." Generally, there is a vertical collapse of the trunk, shoulders, and neck into a relaxed posture. It is very important that the person does not collapse into such an extremely concave position that breathing is difficult. Any posture in this sequence should be maintained at a middle ground of minimum effort and minimum discomfort. After this relaxed posture is assumed, the hanging arms are allowed to swing upward and to be dropped on the thighs so that the hands and fingers hang loosely between the knees without touching.

A description of the concept of passive concentration will help you in clarifying your psychological orientation as you begin your exercises. According to Wolfgang Luthe, who was Schultz's student and is now the acknowledged authority on Autogenic Training:

> The decisive difference between [the] usual type of "active concentration" and "passive concentration" used during autogenic exercises lies in the person's attitude toward the functional result to be achieved. "Passive" concentration implies a casual attitude and functional passivity toward the intended outcome of his concentrated activity, whereas "active" concentration is characterized by the person's concern, interest, attention, and goal-directed active efforts during the performance of the task and in respect to the final functional result [Luthe, 1969].

In other words, let the sensations of being deeply relaxed come to you and take over, rather than striving for them too actively, since that will only interfere with the process. Imagine that you are like an empty vessel which is there to be filled through no conscious exercise of your own will. This state of open passivity is an expression of receptivity toward the inner dimensions of human consciousness, and an essential aspect of all meditative systems.

In this calm, passive stance you begin the first in a series of physical exercises. First, you focus your passive attention on whichever one of your arms is most active. For right-handed people, it is the right arm, and for left-handed people the left. While attending to this arm, you silently repeat to yourself the formula "My right [left] arm is heavy" approximately three to six times for 30 to 60 seconds. As soon as the 30-to-60-second period is over, you move yourself out of this state fairly vigorously by stirring about and opening your eyes. Flex your arms, and move your fingers, toes, feet, legs, shoulders, neck, and head. While you do this, you will notice that the arm to which you have been attending will retain residual feelings of heaviness and relaxation. Repeat this exercise four times in a row, allowing about a minute between each period for sensing its effects. What you do next depends largely on what you experience during this first exercise. Most people report that in addition to feelings of heaviness in the arm in question, they feel heaviness in the other arm or in certain parts of the right or left leg. This spreading of a sensation of heaviness to other parts of the body is termed a "generalization phenomenon," and it is an important aspect of the autogenic exercises. Next, focus your attention on your less active arm and repeat the same formula. Once you have obtained distinct feelings of increased weight in both arms, you may change the instruction to "Both arms are heavy," and then "cancel" after each series of repetitions with the phrase "Arms firm, breathe deeply, open eyes." As with any of the meditative techniques, it is as important to enter into a state of activation after the period of deep relaxation as it is simply to enter into a passive state. Deep relaxation is a precursor for more efficient activity and not necessarily an end in itself.

As during meditation, your mind may tend to stray as you

attempt to focus on the exercise, but there is no need to be disturbed by this. Merely direct your attention back to the task at hand in a gentle manner without getting upset at your vagrant imagination or trying too hard to hold your focus. It is a good idea to lengthen the periods of time you focus on both arms to anywhere from 60 to 90 seconds and to go through this procedure again at least four times. Once you feel that you have gained a measure of success with your arms, the generalized sensation of heaviness in other parts of the body will become more apparent. At that point, the individual begins focusing on sensations of heaviness in the legs. As with the hands, the person focuses first on the most active leg and then the other one before finally focusing on both of them together. Some people are able to induce feelings of heaviness immediately. For others, it may take as long as one or two weeks of practicing two or three times daily for fifteen minutes or so. As has already been noted, there is a distinct neurophysiological correlate to this subjective feeling of heaviness in the limbs. When the sensation of heaviness becomes more pronounced, the muscles in the limbs involved automatically become deeply relaxed. Each individual differs in regard to his ability to succeed at these exercises, and the help of a trained therapist is always useful in monitoring progress and determining at what point to move on to the next step in the training. However, the sensations of heaviness will be very real to you when you are doing the exercises correctly; you will not feel that they are just imaginary. You will know with certainty that you are mastering the technique. It all sounds deceptively simple, but can bring out a pronounced positive effect upon your entire psychosomatic state.

For the second stage in the physical part of autogenic training, the exercises focus on the induction of feelings of warmth. Typically, people will notice agreeable feelings of warmth spreading throughout their bodies even during the heaviness exercises. It is hypothesized that during the heaviness exercises numerous psychophysiological parameters move toward a state of balance. Warmth exercises compound this positive phenomenon and promote a "psychophysiologic state which enhances the recuperative efficiency of self-normalizing functions" (Luthe, 1969). After the individual has developed the ability to establish a sensation of heaviness almost instantly in all extremities, most instructors of autogenics will bring the idea of passive concentration into greater play. If the heaviness exercises have been successful, some degree of passive concentration is already mastered, and the person is ready to develop a fuller understanding of the nature of the state and move to later stages of the training. Warmth exercises are then done in exactly the same progression as the ones for heaviness, starting first with the more active arm, then both arms, then the legs both individually and together. Between each series of self-directed instructions, the person performs the same "cancellation" technique used for heaviness. On the average, from four to eight weeks are required for learning to establish warmth in all the extremities, but it may come more quickly to some people. It is usually surprising to people who take up Autogenic Training how amenable their bodies are to autosuggestion. For this reason, the recognizable physical effects of training encourage the person to maintain practice, whereas in classical meditation they might become discouraged by a lack of readily discernible progress.

Cardiac regulation is the third standard exercise in autogenic training. This exercise is an amplification of the heaviness and warmth exercises, applied to the area and action of the heart. For this exercise, the formula is to repeat mentally "Heartbeat calm and regular." During the early phases of this procedure, it is often easier for people to establish contact with the heart rate in a reclining position, with the right hand placed over the region of the heart. The formula is repeated longer at this stage, with 90 to 180 seconds being recommended. Again, this exercise is repeated four times in a row, with a vigorous effort to counterbalance its effects by using the invigorating phrase "Eyes open, breathe deeply" between exercises.

Respiration is the next focus. While practicing the first three exercises, most people notice a striking decrease in respiratory frequency and an increase in depth of respiration. In order to enhance this naturally occurring phenomenon, the individual focuses on his respiration and repeats to himself, "It breathes me." This is again repeated four times, for 100 to 150 seconds each time, with a cancellation period in between. After one to six weeks, the respiratory pattern responds quickly to the instruction.

Fifth is an exercise to induce a sensation of warmth in the abdominal region. This tends to induce a definite calming effect on central-nervous-system activity and to enhance muscular relaxation, and it may cause feelings of drowsiness. The exercise is not intended to warm the surface of the skin, but rather to establish a warmth in the depth of the upper abdominal cavity and focus on the solar plexus. The formula to use to achieve this is "My solar plexus is warm." It is helpful at this stage for either the therapist or the trainee himself to place a hand over the area of the solar plexus and imagine a sensation of heat radiating from that area. As with the previous exercises, the formula is repeated four times, with appropriate pauses in between.

Finally, the last stage in the strictly physical instructions of autogenic training involves the instruction of the phrase "My forehead is cool." Usually a lying-down posture is advised to start out on this exercise, since sensations of dizziness or fainting may be experienced. If it is not possible to lie down, passive concentration on the forehead should be developed slowly by beginning with periods of 10 to 20 seconds and building up a four-time repetition totaling two to four minutes.

Usually after anywhere from two months to a year, there comes a point in the practice of these six initial stages of autogenic training when the entire series can be done very quickly, between two to four minutes for induction of the complete sequence. Most trainers recommend practicing three times a day, after lunch and dinner and before going to sleep, in order that progress be made. However, there are frequent disturbing occurrences which seem to happen most often during the heaviness and warmth exercises. There are a number of motor tremors of physical sensations for emotional states which are called "autogenic discharges" and are considered to be the individual's attempt to self-regulate toward a state of increased health during the period of his relaxation. According to Luthe, autogenic discharges are "training symptoms which have no apparent relation to the formula and are considered as resulting from brain-directed processes which permit a brain-selected and physiologically adapted (non-damaging) release of disturbing quantities of neuronal impulses from various areas of the brain" (Luthe, 1969). Massive motor discharges may be quite pronounced in patients having a history of alcoholism, severe accidents, or incipient epileptic behavior. In other cases, violent crying spells may be associated with motor discharges in patients with a history of traumatized birth, abortion, traumatic dental surgery, or suppressed emotions over a significant incident such as the death of a relative. When these unexpected and distressing autogenic discharges occur, a trained therapist needs to assist the individual to work through them and remain in a state of passive concentration. According to Luthe, maintaining the autogenic posture and attitude will allow the person to dispel the troublesome thoughts or associations, and he advises "not to oppose such brain-directed self-normalizing processes which are self-terminating." Discharges are considered to be normal responses to the process of self-regulation.

Comparable experiences often confront people in other meditative disciplines and clinical biofeedback as well. There is a common occurrence refered to as the "get worse, get better syndrome," in which patients begin to experience an increase in pain after an initial period of improvement. Quite commonly, this secondary pain involves the entering into consciousness of a previously suppressed or denied psychological or physiological trauma. At this point, patients often feel worse, and the reacceleration of symptoms may even be more severe than the initial complaint. Interconnections between specific psychological difficulties and specific somatic disorders become quite graphic in this movement toward a state of psychosomatic health. Helping the individual to remain in a state of passive concentration and to confront these underlying problems is an effective means of truly alleviating the disorder rather than simply dealing with overt symptoms.

At the end of this first stage of training, the individual, by going through the phrases "My arms and legs are heavy . . . heartbeat calm and regular . . . it breathes me . . . my solar plexus is warm . . . my forehead is cool," should be able to accomplish all of these self-directed "commands" in only a few minutes. Once he has become proficient in achieving this process, he is ready for the next stage in the training, which is called "autogenic meditation." By this time, the person should be able to maintain a high degree of stability in the autogenic state for prolonged periods of time, ranging from thirty minutes to an hour. It has been demonstrated that if he is able to maintain this state, he is also capable of regulating a wide range of other physiological functions through autosuggestion. Schultz reports that some of his patients were able to self-induce an anesthetized state which enabled them to block the pain of dental drilling, while others were able to warm their feet by raising skin temperature as much as three degrees Fahrenheit. Hypertensive patients have achieved drops in systolic blood pressure of from 10 to 25 percent, as well as 5 to 15 percent in diastolic pressure. There is also a marked increase in alpha brain wave activity, which is associated with deep mental relaxation (Kamiya, 1968). As noted earlier, the neurophysiological mechanism by which autonomic control is achieved is not well understood. Luthe offers an explanation which is consistent with current neurological theories concerning the interaction of mind and body. According to Luthe's observations:

> Autogenic Training involves self-induced (autogenic) modifications of corticodiencephalic interrelations, which enables natural forces to regain their otherwise restricted capacity for self-regulatory normalization ... the function of the entire neurohumoral axis (cortex, thalamus, reticular system, hypothalamus) is directly unilaterally restricted to either bodily or mental functions [Luthe, 1969].

Based on this information, it is clear that autogenic training and meditation share a common orientation, a state of passive concentration which allows the mind and body to self-regulate toward a more harmonious state. When conflicting information between cortical and subcortical processes is removed, then the relaxation response induces a state of optimum psychosomatic functioning.

VISUALIZATION

A number of different stages in autogenic meditation may sound esoteric when described in words but immediately become less so when they are directly experienced. Most of these advanced stages involve visualization, or the summoning and holding of certain images in the mind for examination and exploration of their effects on consciousness. At this point many people may find the guidance of a therapist particularly useful, since the focus changes from physical to mental. However, the directives themselves are relatively simple, and if you feel you have mastered the physical relaxation of the first stage, you may not find it at all difficult to graduate to the visualization exercises. Once you have acquired some basic skills, these visualizations should be no trouble. Beginning the meditative stage is straightforward and involves the "voluntary rotation of the eyeballs upward and inward looking at the center of the forehead" (Schultz and Luthe, 1959). This procedure is often recommended in other forms of meditation, and has been demonstrated to induce an increase in the production of alpha rhythms in the brain (Kamiya, 1969), or to deepen a hypnotic, trance-like state of consciousness. Given the fact that this eye position aids in inducing a certain neurophysiological response, it is most interesting to note the paintings and statues of both Western and Eastern mystics with their eyes in such a position. A great deal of current neurophysiological research has confirmed the effectiveness of such meditative practices, which evolved out of practitioners' intuitive knowledge concerning psychosomatic regulation.

Meditation practices in autogenics are intended to produce an "intensification of psychic experience by increasing an individual's ability to visually experience endopsychic phenomena" (Gorton, 1959). Once the basic meditation posture and eye position has been achieved, the individual can proceed to the second stage of the visualization exercises, which involve color. You should try to hold in your mind's eye your choice of a static, uniform color which occupies your entire mental, visual field. Colors may be suggested by the therapist or they may occur to you spontaneously, based on your own preferences. Some colors, such as purple, red, yellow, and orange, apparently have a reinforcing effect upon the sensation of warmth, while others, such as blue and green, are likely to complement sensations of coolness on the forehead. If these associations hold true for you, then it is useful to keep them in mind while visualizing. From this basic exercise, you may go on to visualizing colors in formations, such as clouds, shadows, or various simple movements. Elaborating still further, you may then graduate to the visualization of polychromatic patterns and forms involving geometric figures, such as blue triangles. Also during this period, you can begin to experiment with movement, such as turning, falling, getting bigger or smaller, and other sensations of a quasi-physical nature. Practicing these visualizations is intended as a preliminary exercise in becoming familiar with the mind's capacity to produce vivid basic colors and imagery. Such processes occur spontaneously throughout waking and sleeping activity but do not receive adequate attention, since these subtle occurrences are overshadowed by the normal active mode of psychological functioning.

After you have explored your mind's capacity to create spontaneous imagery, the third meditative exercise step is to attempt to visualize and hold the image of a particular object, perhaps ornamental or symbolic, against a background mostly dark in color. Visualization objects should be static at this point in the training. Images such as faces, masks, statuettes, and the like are often chosen, but it is entirely a matter of personal preference. Choose an object to which your mind seems to gravitate most naturally. It is fairly common for people to have some degree of difficulty in visualizing static objects. They may have no trouble fixing on an object, and it may be a very vivid picture in their minds, but its appearance is often of short duration. In other cases, the object is elusive because the image is hazy or unclear. Fixing the mind on an immobile object can be an extremely difficult task, and progress in this stage of training is usually slow. It is useful to spend more time in practice sessions, perhaps as long as forty to sixty minutes. Cancellation formulas should be repeated after each effort at visualizing in all stages of advanced training, and they should also be used immediately if unpleasant or disturbing images persist in occurring. During the visualization exercises, the cancellation phrases recommended are: "The images [colors] gradually recede . . . they have become less clear . . . they have completely disappeared. The legs are light. The arms are light. Heart and breathing normal. Temperature of forehead normal. Arms firm, breathe deep, open eyes." Then, to reenter the visualization exercises, the trainee should go quickly through the litany of physical directives to achieve the deeply relaxed state and once again attempt to conjure up the image upon which he seeks to focus.

After some measure of success has been obtained at holding an object in the mind, the fourth stage of visualizing may be started. During this fourth exercise, the individual concentrates on the transformation of abstract objects and the progressive differentiation of subtle images. For instance, the visualization may involve abstract concepts such as justice, freedom, and happiness. For this stage, individual experience can range from simply seeing these words on a printed page to acoustic phenomena such as a voice repeating these words, or to vivid fantasies involving elaborate symbols and allegories pertaining to these concepts. It is pointless to weigh one form of experience against another, since elaborate fantasy is not a more effective means of exploring consciousness than a simplified phrase. Meditation upon these abstract concepts requires a training period of two to six weeks. As with any dream or fantasy material, it is very important to work with a skilled therapist at these advanced stages in order to integrate and comprehend these phenomena as fully as possible.

Following the several weeks of practice on the abstract ideas, the individual is encouraged to enter into the fifth meditation, involving a selective state of feeling. According to Wolfgang Luthe, "during this phase of meditative training, the trainee gradually learns to experience a psychophysiologic state which is in correspondence with his meditative intention. During prolonged training periods (30 to 60 minutes), passive concentration should focus on a specific state of overall feeling, for example, the feeling one experiences while looking over the wide and open ocean" (Luthe, 1969). Fifth-stage meditative experiences frequently involve such images as standing on top of a mountain, being on the moon, flying over clouds, or seeing a sunrise. Quite often, archetypal figures, religious themes, and situations of wishful concern play a prominent role. Additionally, vivid erotic and sexual themes may occur spontaneously. At this point, the individual may become an active participant in the material which comes to him and experience himself as an actor in the tableau which his mind presents. He becomes aware of his own dynamic role in the fantasy itself or sees himself in scenes more based on his real-life situation than on fantasy. For this stage, a person might call into mind an elaborate landscape or the interior of a house which is involved in some slow but recognizable change. You will probably be surprised to note that when some degree of movement occurs in the image you have chosen, it will be easier for you to maintain than a completely static image. The quality of the state the trainee achieves is very like that of dreaming and is at least equally vivid and real. He begins to experience the collective dimensions or the transpersonal dimensions of consciousness. When the mind calls up scenes in which the individual begins to see himself as an active participant, the exercises are called "film strips." Later, when there are prolonged periods of self-participation, the visualization is called "multi-chromatic cinerama." In this last, most elaborate phrase, where fantasy and reality alternate in the subject matter of what is "seen," both therapist and patient may derive significant insight into the patient's unconscious. Such insights can be of great use in resolving both psychological and physiological states of disorder and psychosomatic stress. Fifth-stage meditation exercises appear to mark a major transition of the individual's experience from a state of relative passivity into one of active participation. Involvement on the part of the individual in the healing process is an essential aspect of all meditative approaches and is clearly evidenced in this phase of autogenics.

Following the period of increased participation, the individual begins the sixth meditative exercise, which involves the visualization of other persons. In the sixth state of visualization there is a shift from the self-centered theme, and the individual learns to apply passive concentration to the visualization of other persons. At first the individual is instructed to visualize relatively neutral people, such as the postman, and then gradually to move toward other, more significant people with whom there might be conflict. It may require several weeks or months before such visualization can be maintained. Most individuals experience these images as rather hazy, indistinct and tending to fade quickly, especially when there are positive or loving emotions toward the person who is visualized. Images will gradually become clearer over the practice period and cease to fade away as rapidly. Eventually, they too will assume the realistic quality of dreams. In later stages of this exercise, the person is able to deduce valuable insight with respect to his affective relationships. Generally it is much easier for the trainee to visualize people toward whom there are hostile or negative feelings. Over time, however, he can stabilize any chosen individuals and derive insights concerning his relationships with them. Actually, this stage is intended to promote alterations in an individual's perception of these significant others. Through this meditative exercise, he can allow his relationships to become more realistic and to undertake these stages of training with the guidance of a knowledgeable psychotherapist. Autogenic training provides no adequate system for interpreting and analyzing repressed subjective material, and when such phenomena occur they can be extremely disconcerting and disturbing. Often a great deal of psychotherapy is required to help people work through such highly charged psychic material and come to see its significance without becoming severely disoriented. Well-integrated individuals can often resolve unconscious conflicts, achieve extensive emotional catharsis, and gain valuable personality insights. Experiences of such subtle levels of subjective reality may lead to the analysis of complexes, nuclear personal situations and problems, and the consideration of questions of fundamental existential value. Despite these positive outcomes, it is not unusual for people to regard their experiences at this stage as ego-alien and threatening. Therefore, it is of utmost importance that a trained therapist be present to guide the individual through his first encounter with deeper levels of consciousness. From the therapist's point of view, the benefits of autogenic training are obvious. Psychotherapeutic disciplines depend upon exploring the subjective thoughts and fantasies of individual patients, and the explicit directives autogenic training offers greatly facilitate this process.

Visualization, which plays such a key role in Autogenic Training, historically has been a central element in virtually all Eastern meditative techniques. Volumes of esoteric and psychological literature have been written over centuries regarding the processes and purposes of visualization methods. In the present work we cannot consider these myriad sources. However, I would like to pinpoint one central aspect of visualization which is common to all the literature: the detachment of the practitioner. Through visualization, an individual can achieve a focused awareness while remaining detached from thoughts, emotions, and the dispersion of energy characteristic of ordinary consciousness. By focusing upon symbolic representation of each aspect of physical and psychological functioning, the individual can derive profound insight.

Ordinarily, individuals are not aware of their spontaneous imageries. They occur haphazardly, with random associations, and are seldom deliberately induced or heeded. From a Western point of view, deliberate visualization can become a potent means of exploring psychosomatic interaction and inducing change in patterns of behavior. One hypothesis for the effectiveness of visualization practices is the principle that psychological energy follows patterns of thought. While Western science has concentrated upon the analysis of the energy underlying the elements of Mendeleev's Periodic Table, Eastern meditative practitioners have engaged in an equally subtle taxonomy of internal states of energy underlying psychological states. One of the most articulate discussions of this latter approach has been undertaken by Herbert V. Guenther in *The Mind in Buddhist Psychology* (1975), which is essentially a periodic table of consciousness. Central to this taxonomy of internal states are the descriptions of various spontaneous and induced mental images as a reflection of subtle psychological states.

Visualization is used at various stages of many types of meditation and for a myriad of purposes. In some instances, visualization is used to induce the initial meditative state or as a primary focus in and of itself. In other meditative systems, it is used during the meditation to deepen the state or to channel energy for a particular desired purpose. Induced visualization can be employed to stimulate the creative imagination, and when used while in a state of passive concentration, it is a very powerful tool to mobilize the resources of both the body and mind. Visualization has been aptly described as a bridge between the different levels of the self. Imagery is a means of discovering the dynamics of mind and of understanding the symbolic discourse between mental events and between mind and body. Where the mind tends to focus, the emotions and the physiology are likely to follow. Despite the fact that the link between visualization and neurophysiological alterations remains an enigma, there is increasing evidence that subtle mental phenomena can have a profound positive or negative impact upon an individual's entire psychophysiology. Exploring the potential of this impact is one of the most stimulating areas at the frontiers of holistic approaches to healing.

VISUALIZATION AND PSYCHOSOMATIC MEDICINE

One of the most striking uses of visualization has been its application to psychosomatic disorders for the purpose of self-healing. There is considerable anecdotal and research evidence underscoring the extent to which various forms of meditation alter psychophysiological functioning in the direction of increased health, sloughing off the effects of prolonged stress, bringing about a release from abnormal states of hyper-arousal, and restoring the body's natural ability to ward off disease through the immune system. Deep relaxation and meditative practices have also been shown to produce pronounced attitudinal changes among regular practitioners. They aid in restoring a sense of control to an individual's life, and can generally induce a more positive life outlook. More recently, Eastern techniques of meditation and visualization have been applied directly to disease, and it appears that this process of psychophysiological integration can have a dramatic effect upon the disease process.

Some of the most innovative work in this area so far has been done by O. Carl Simonton, a radiation oncologist in Fort Worth, Texas, and his wife, Stephanie Matthews-Simonton. In their clinical practice they have examined the psychosocial factors of cancer and sought a means of altering those in a positive direction. Inevitably, theoretical constructs are generated far in advance of the means to apply them. Research into psychosocial influences on the development of cancer has been going on for over sixty years, and the Simontons' work is the first to show that these factors can be influenced by stress reduction and visualization techniques. Due to the fact that cancer is not widely acknowledged to have a psychosomatic origin, their research is regarded with some degree of skepticism among their colleagues, but it is gaining acceptance. As more information points to the role of viruses in cancer, the failure of an over-stressed immune system to maintain surveillance over viruses and mutant cells is seen as a primary factor in cancer onset and treatment. Since psychologic stress has been shown to depress immune activity, it seems logical to postulate that stress reduction and the mobilization of positive psychological atitudes may be one means of restoring the body's ability to overcome invasive viruses and destroy mutant cells. This possibility is considerably more difficult for a professional clinician to entertain than it is for the layman, whose experience tells him that both psychological and physical factors influence his state of illness or health.

The diagnosis of cancer is virtually synonomous with death to the layman, even though advances in surgery, chemotherapy, and radiology have certainly demonstrated that the diagnosis does not necessarily imply terminal disease. A psychosomatic approach to treatment may be needed in order to eliminate that misconception. Unfortunately, at the present time standard practice divides individuals into those who receive one of the above treatments and those who are receiving maintenance care prior to death. This dichotomy neglects a vast middle ground in which psychotherapy and stress reduction can be an invaluable adjunct to standard treatment and may be a vital factor in swinging the balance between life and death. No responsible clinician would assert that such adjuncts actually cure cancer, but there is sufficient evidence concerning the benefits of stress-reduction procedures to merit their inclusion in a cancer-treatment program. Life is suspended in a delicate balance, and whatever benefits might be derived from stress-reduction techniques and psychosocial counseling should be considered in a holistic approach to the cancer patient.

During 1969, Carl Simonton began to develop his approach to cancer after hearing a prominent immunologist advance the still relatively unaccepted theory that cancer was due to a breakdown in the body's immune system. This man had applied an unorthodox method of treatment with terminal leukemic patients who had failed on all other forms of chemotherapy. For the treatment, he obtained a concentrated solution of the patient's abnormal white cells and applied the solution to a prepared area of the skin in hopes of evoking an immune response which would encourage the body's defenses to attack the foreign cells. There was a very high rate of remission among patients he treated in this manner, which is most unusual among people with the extent of disease these patients suffered. When other researchers followed his lead and tried to duplicate the results of this treatment, the positive outcome for patients was cut in half, but still it was impressive enough to warrant attention. Simonton began to suspect that this discrepancy in outcome was due to the fact that the initial experiments had been conducted with the patients' full knowledge and understanding of the potential of the treatment. Also, there was a considerable amount of excitement, enthusiasm, and belief among both the patients and the doctor.

Pursuing this observation, Simonton began to examine the histories of some of the 2 to 5 percent of patients with metastatic cancer who had had unexpectedly good response to treatment to see if he could find a common denominator which might explain their recoveries. Quite quickly, he discovered that the single factor that emerged among these patients was one of attitude. There was an extraordinary high correlation between positive response to treatment and positive attitudes, both to the disease and to life in a more general sense. Prospects of changing patients' attitudes, however, were not promising, especially with people already severely depressed and overwhelmed by the disease. At this point, Simonton began experimenting with both autogenics and biofeedback. He noted that relaxation in the true sense is not as easy as is normally assumed and that autonomic control depends upon achieving a relaxed state. If one could gain control over such functions as blood pressure, peripheral temperature, and other processes, he asked, then would it not also be possible to influence the immune mechanisms? During the same period he also took a course in mind control, which he approached quite skeptically. However, it was from this that he came to see that positive attitudes can in fact be taught. Out of these multiple sources, Simonton evolved a treatment which was based upon belief-system modification and stated, "I believe there are three extremely important factors that need to be recognized and brought to light. One is the belief system of the patient. The second is the belief system of the family and those people who surround the patient and are meaningful to him. The third is the belief system of the physician" (Simonton and Simonton, 1975). Paralleling John Lilly's concept that belief systems limit an individual's perception of reality and possibility, this approach to the psychosocial factors in cancer had to begin with an examination of fundamental assumptions regarding the disease.

By the middle of 1971, Simonton had evolved a unique method of treatment that he proposed to explore with his cancer patients when they were referred to him for radiology treatment. His first patient was a sixty-year-old man with widespread throat cancer, who had lost a great deal of weight, could barely swallow his own saliva, and could not eat. According to the diagnosis, this condition would have been incurable by radiation therapy. It was decided to use a combined treatment protocol involving both radiation and meditative techniques. Simonton explained to him that through relaxation and imagery, both of them were going to try to affect the disease. Also, he explained the mechanism by which radiation therapy worked and how the body could supplement the effect of radiation if its innate immune capacity could be mobilized. For the treatment, the patient was instructed to relax deeply three times a day while mentally picturing his disease and the treatment. Visualization was central to the process and involved picturing the destruction of cancerous material by the body's immunological system and disposal of it through the circulatory system. After three months of treatment, the patient recovered completely, and a year and a half later had no sign of throat cancer. As a further outcome, the patient, who had also suffered from both arthritis and impotence, overcame these through a modification of the same basic visualization technique. Of course, many therapeutic approaches can point to such dramatic outcomes, but that is not what is significant here. The success with this patient was an indication of a new direction, a method of focusing upon and rectifying the psychosocial factors of neoplastic disease.

Shortly after this initial case, Simonton was drafted, and his commanding officer at Travis Air Force Base in California was very receptive to this innovative approach. While at Travis, numerous cases involving various cancers were treated with this new approach, and significant outcomes were obtained. One case involved an Air Force navigator who had squamous carcinoma in the roof of his mouth and also a larger tumor in the back of his throat. Using radiation therapy alone, the estimated cure rate for these types of cancer was only around 5 to 10 percent. Again, using a combination of radiation, meditation, and visualization of both the disease and the healing process, plus the very enthusiastic cooperation of the patient, the cancers were virtually arrested after four weeks of treatment. By the end of ten weeks, both the mouth and throat were essentially normal in appearance. Three months after he had been relieved of duty as a result of his disease, the navigator reassumed a normal working status.

Another case involved a man with a large and painful wart on one finger. It had become progressively worse even after a number of medical treatments over the course of a year, and he returned from Vietnam to have the finger amputated due to the intense pain. He also had a lesser wart on the thumb, which Simonton initially was not going to treat. Again, the patient was receptive to Simonton's techniques. After one month of treatment, there was no evidence of any warty tissue on either the finger or the thumb, although the thumb had made slightly slower progress than the primary wart.

One other case involved a thirty-year-old woman who had cancer of the uterus. She had a bad infection at the time the diagnosis was made, and this is usually a serious sign, since patients whose lesions become infected tend to have a poorer prognosis. For this particular patient, no further treatment was advised, and Simonton acted as a consultant only. When Simonton later examined the patient with the gynecologist who had made the original diagnosis, the gynecologist remarked that the tumor seemed somewhat smaller than it had two weeks previously. After four weeks, both physicians were astounded to discover that her tumor had decreased by at least 50 percent of its volume. When he asked her if she had any idea why this was happening, she announced that she had heard that grape juice was good for cancer and that she had been drinking four glasses a day. Later, Simonton was discussing the possibility of beginning to use a treatment for her involving relaxation and imagery, and she seemed surprised that he was describing a meditative practice. She disclosed that she had been reading Edgar Cayce's work a year prior to this and had been meditating regularly since that time and it had changed her life. Simonton then asked if she had been meditating regarding her tumor, and she acknowledged that she had been. A further surprise was that the patient had been afraid to tell him about the meditation for fear of ridicule and had substituted the grape-juice story to avoid the subject. Here was a patient who had already been successful in treating her own illness through meditation and visualization without the reinforcement of any traditional therapy. Significant case histories such as these do not constitute proof of the efficacy of meditative approaches by any means. However, they are suggestive of directions which need to be further explored.

At the present time, there is a pressing need for controlled studies in order to determine the potential of meditative and visualization techniques as adjuncts to traditional cancer therapy. Such studies are now being conducted. Case histories such as these were necessary for their observations to be seriously considered. Admittedly, these outcomes were unexpected, and that is the very reason for focusing upon them. When patients deviate from expected norms in a positive direction, then it is imperative that healing professionals explore the factors which may have contributed to that outcome. Innumerable tables of actuarial statistics involve the morbidity and mortality of the average patient, but there is a virtual absence of information regarding the patients who outdistance these norms and who become well.

Suffice it to say at this point that, out of the first 152 patients Carl Simonton treated at Travis, 20 had an excellent response. These 152 patients were divided into attitude groups ranging from a very poor attitude indicated by double negative (− −) to a very positive attitude (+ +). Each patient was assessed by each staff member, who rated the patient's attitude by indicating a double positive, single positive, a positive and negative for a mixed attitude, a single negative, or a double negative. Then the staff members rated the clinical response of the patient from excellent to poor. In all cases, there was a direct correlation between good attitudes and good responses to treatment. Out of the 20 patients who had excellent responses to treatment, 11 had positive assessments, and 9 had doubly positive indicators. Even more significantly, 14 of these patients had less than a 50 percent chance of five-year cure and only 6 had better than a 50 percent chance of five-year cure. According to these findings, the correlation was with patient attitudes and was not dependent upon the severity of the disease (Simonton and Simonton, 1975). Obviously, issues of causality cannot be assessed here, and one can argue that positive attitudes were due to the fact that those patients were receiving effective treatment and were simply feeling better. Such debates continue but simply are not relevant here. These are mentioned not to demonstrate causality or as evidence of cure, but to stand as a clear, empirical body of evidence that psychological and physiological factors interact in the disease of cancer. Whether or not issues of causality are resolved through more intensive research, that degree of certainty is not necessary to justify the use of psychotherapeutic or meditative techniques in cancer therapy. Such measures are non-invasive and have no side effects. They are an important part of a holistic approach to cancer treatment.

Since these preliminary studies, the Simontons have refined and extended their treatment procedures. Once again it must be emphasized it is of utmost importance to bear in mind that the application of meditative and visualization techniques is as an adjunct to traditional treatment and is not proffered as an alternative. Furthermore, these stress-reduction approaches are only one aspect of a lengthy screening process and intensive psychotherapy sessions, with the visualization used primarily as homework exercises to keep the patient involved in the healing process.

As of this writing, the full therapeutic approach evolves in four steps. First, the patient entering the clinic engages in an orientation session and is encouraged to bring as many family members or friends as he or she might wish. All of the cancer patients and their families meet in a group session of twelve to fifteen people. Patients are introduced to concepts such as stress reduction, meditation, visualization, and the psychosomatic aspects of cancer involving both attitudes and immunological responses. For the second stage, the patients are instructed in a basic visualization exercise which will be more fully described below. Patients are instructed to listen to a tape of the visualization process three times a day and to read *The Will to Live* by Arnold Hutschnecker. Following this orientation, approximately 50 percent of the patients do not return for further treatment. For those patients who do return, the third stage of treatment is initiated. During this phase, the patients and families meet in group sessions every day for five days. The content of these sessions ranges from problems and prognostic indicators regarding the visualization to exploring the psychosocial and familial content of the patient. There is a great deal of rigorous psychotherapy during this week in order to help the patient discover and rectify the life patterns which have sustained his disease. Last, the fourth phase of treatment involves the patients' leaving the clinic and returning home to continue practicing their meditation and visualization. Also, they are encouraged to continue to seek and utilize insights regarding the carcinogenic aspects of their personality and life style. Each patient commits himself to one year of treatment and returns every three months for three days of intensive group sessions.

The visualization technique itself is so simple that it at first seems improbable that such dramatic results could come from such a deceptively simple procedure. First, patients are taught a simplified form of autogenic relaxation with a focus on breathing. Each person is instructed to repeat the word "relax" silently to himself and to let go of tension in various muscle complexes which are typically responsive to stress by focusing on them one at a time. When a state of physiological relaxation has been established, the patient visualizes a pleasant, natural scene such as a little brook in a meadow or whatever occurs to him. Patients are instructed to spend time and enjoy the scene so that they begin to experience the calming effect both of the fantasy and of holding it in the mind. After this stage, the patient is asked to visualize his illness in any way that it appears to him, and this ranges from seeing the cancer as a cauliflower to a piece of hamburger with strands extending out from it into other areas. Next, the patient visualizes his particular form of treatment. If it is radiation therapy, he imagines tiny bullets of energy hitting all the cells in the area of the tumor. Normal cells have the ability to repair the small amount of damage done, but the cancer cells do not regenerate as easily and they perish. Then the patient visualizes a great army of white blood cells as they perform their function of transporting the dead cancer cells through the blood, liver, kidneys, and then out of the system. Most importantly, the cancer is then visualized as shrinking or responding in some positive manner to the treatment. If the treatment is chemotherapy, then the chemical is seen as distributing itself through the blood and being picked up by cancer cells, which think it is food and are poisoned rather than nourished. Normal cells are able to resist the minor damage done to them by the toxic substance, and patients visualize these cells as thriving. Again, the cancer is visualized as shrinking and the white blood cells relieve the body of the dead cancerous material. Patients are also encouraged to visualize pain in much the same way. By directly confronting their pain, they are drawn further into the workings of the disorder and focus energy on its alleviation. Through this approach, patients become profoundly in touch with their entire psychophysiology and with the disease process itself and are thereby able to exert some influence over it.

Applying stress-alleviation techniques as an adjunct to cancer therapy is one of the most outstanding examples in current medicine of mobilizing the patient's volition in the healing process. Carl and Stephanie Simonton are among the few who have utilized the power of concentration that meditation affords and applied it specifically to cancer. In this way they offer the patient specific tools to work with in establishing contact with the disease process. Given the controversial nature of these approaches, the fact that cancer is still so little understood, and the inevitable presence of many variables affecting the progress of the disease, it is little wonder that these methods must be regarded as tentative directions.

Carl Simonton acknowledges that he is often confronted with the issue of scientific proof for his theories, given the large number of variables involved. In response to this, he cites the case of a psychiatrist who was having great success using an unorthodox approach to the treatment of schizophrenia. He was constantly queried by colleagues who insisted upon empirical verification. Finally he became interested in the question of precisely what constituted scientific proof and organized a symposium focused on the subject, asking several leading scientists to participate. In answer to one of his letters, he received a short note in which the writer stated, "The question is much too difficult for me," and went on to say that he doubted he could be of much help in the resolution of so complex an issue. According to Simonton, "This answer was more than the humility of a great man; it was more than the reflection of scientific honesty. It was at the root of a great man's whole philosophy of being. The letter was signed, 'Albert Einstein'" (Simonton and Simonton, 1975). It is hoped that in an era which has thrust open the very basis of scientific inquiry from quantum physics to the science of consciousness, researchers and clinicians can maintain consideration of the psychosomatic dimensions of cancer. Throughout the second chapter of this book, there is substantial evidence that subtle processes of imagery and emotion can have a profound impact upon the entire neurophysiological and immunological systems. Today scientists can only witness these events with curiosity and awe. Perhaps tomorrow researchers will unravel these enigmas and come to know the processes underlying their occurrence.

Certainly it would be a most formidable task to devise controlled experiments to determine the precise role of the mind in disease and health maintenance. When the subtle and invisible processes of the human mind are involved, we can expect many frustrations, since its functions are so resistant to quantitative and qualitative measurement. Yet it is clearly a primary factor, perhaps even the most crucial factor, in determining whether an individual is healthy or sick, whether he lives or dies.

The greatest potential of autogenic training and visualization, however, lies not in pathology correction but as a potent tool in a holistic approach to preventive medicine. Through the regular use of these self-regulatory exercises, it is possible to maintain health by recognizing and correcting subtle dysfunctions before they become more severe. Children in several European countries, including Germany and Holland, are taught such methods in elementary school as a means of achieving efficacy in stress reduction at an early age. Such straightforward procedures could be introduced into schools, hospitals, and recreation centers to help individuals practice and experience states of harmonious integration between mind and body.

Biofeedback

8

Clinical biofeedback and meditative practices share a common ground in that they both emphasize the attainment of a state of relaxed internal awareness as a prerequisite to achieving insight and growth. In both systems the person is asked to sit in a quiet environment in a state of passive attention. During this time, the individual attempts to identify and develop a harmony between mind and body. This practice is rare in the Western world, where a person usually does not sit, listen, or reflect upon himself, but continuously acts externally.

The growing interest in biofeedback has caused somewhat of a furor in the scientific community. Basic information is required to dispel some of the prevailing misconceptions among laymen and professionals. Unfortunately, laboratory and clinical research on biofeedback and on related areas such as meditation and deep-relaxation techniques are often tainted by simplistic and at times wild speculation both by scientists and by the journalists reporting on it. It is certainly understandable how research that challenges our basic conception of man's biological structure and psychological abilities can stimulate novel and overenthusiastic ideas. Unfortunately, such unfounded theorizing has tended to alienate an important segment of the scientific community. At one extreme are those who argue that biofeedback can help us literally control any aspect of our biology at will. On the other extreme is a dwindling number who dismiss biofeedback as a useless gimmick. Clearly, neither of these extremes is appropriate.

Prior to the last decade, the concept of the voluntary regulation of the autonomic nervous system was considered to be impossible by both researchers and clinicians. Today most researchers concede that autonomic control is a reality, but there is nonetheless a residue of resistance. Current research in biofeedback has been of a quality that is lending increased legitimacy to its techniques, expanding our understanding of the potential of human self-regulation, and also helping us to recognize both its applications and limitations in clinical application. This chapter will not attempt to review the extensive literature underlying the field of biofeedback. Both research and clinical literature relating to the basic issues of biofeedback are collected in a yearly anthology published by Aldine Publishing Company. These volumes are entitled *Biofeedback and Self-Control,* and are edited by an alternating board of editors. For those interested in pursuing the more fundamental issues in biofeedback they are the primary sources of information.

CLINICAL BIOFEEDBACK

Conceptually, biofeedback is based upon three basic principles: 1) any neurophysiological or other biological function which can be monitored and amplified by electronic instrumentation and fed back to a person through any one of his five senses can be regulated by that individual; 2) "every change in the physiological state is accompanied by an appropriate change in the mental emotional state, conscious or unconscious, and conversely, every change in the mental emotional state, conscious or unconscious, is accompanied by an appropriate change in the physiological state" (Green, Green, and Walters, 1970); and 3) a meditative state of deep relaxation is conducive to the establishment of voluntary control by allowing the individual to become aware of subliminal imagery, fantasies, and sensations.

Research and clinical practice with biofeedback and meditation have demonstrated that many autonomic- or involuntary-nervous-system functions can be brought under conscious control if an individual obtains information about that process. These functions include brain waves, heart rate, muscle tension, body temperature, and other more experimental applications such as stomach-acidity and white-blood-cell levels. Clinical biofeedback has an extensive potential, since the monitoring of these bodily functions is limited only by biomedical technology, and the regulation of that function is dependent upon the patient and therapist's ingenuity and creativity.

A single example of the learning process involved in biofeedback can provide a model which is applicable to virtually all instances of autonomic regulation. During the initial stages of electrocardiogram (ECG) or heart-rate feedback, patients are surprised to see how volatile their heart rates really are. At first the pattern seems random, since the heart rate appears to increase and shortly afterward decrease for no easily discernible reason. After a relatively short time the patient realizes that minor changes in his physical posture —even flexing an index finger, or changes in his breathing pattern—have a profound effect upon the heart. Breathing in a slow or regular manner or sitting in an upright posture helps to decelerate the heart rate, whereas slouching or breathing shallowly and quickly tends to accelerate it. This recognition is a first step in establishing the link between mind and body as their interaction affects the heart. After the initial stage, during which these rather obvious connections are made, the patient begins to realize that a more subtle level of regulation is possible. When thinking of a pleasant or relaxing vacation, he notes that his heart rate begins to decelerate. Conversely, when he thinks about a perplexing or stress-inducing situation like his income tax or an argument with a close friend, heart rate accelerates. Exploration of the interaction between psychological events and physiological changes are at first fascinating to the individual, and can preoccupy him for long periods of time. After this second stage has been investigated fully, the individual graduates to a still more sophisticated understanding of mind/body interaction. At this point, he begins to realize that feelings of heaviness and warmth in the area of the heart will allow the heart rate to decelerate, while feelings of lightness and constriction in the same area will actually produce acceleration. This is a very important step in the learning process, because the individual is able to remember and duplicate these sensations at any time throughout the day. Once this link between internal sensations and their effects upon the cardiovascular system is established, the individual has a means of regulating this critical autonomic function. This progression from unconscious physiological process to a conscious awareness of psychosomatic interaction, followed by a decreased reliance on the instrumentation, is a fundamental process in clinical biofeedback.

Clinical biofeedback can be integrated into other therapeutic techniques or used as a core technique through which other therapies and educational approaches are applied. Biofeedback is one of many approaches in the revolution of psychotherapy and medicine which places the responsibility of illness, health, and especially personal growth upon the individual. In this evolving model, the therapist acts as a guide or a teacher in order to maximize the conditions for the patient's growth and self-healing. Clinical biofeedback can be used in conjunction with a variety of methods such as traditional psychotherapy, psychosynthesis, hypnosis, behavior modification, meditation, and rational therapy (Peper, 1973; Pelletier, 1974). Like all other tools in education, psychotherapy, and self-exploration, biofeedback applications without a properly motivated person and without considering the multiplicity of physical and psychological factors of a disorder may be useless or potentially harmful. Emphasis in clinical biofeedback is upon a holistic approach to the individual and considers the patient's physical, psychological, spiritual, and environmental needs.

Although biofeedback and the successful practice of meditation achieve many of the same ends, the essential difference is that biofeedback amplifies biological signals. An advantage of biofeedback over non-feedback techniques is that the physiological information tells an individual precisely how he is functioning. Interpreting the feedback, a person knows exactly how tense he is in certain muscles, and through trial and error he can discover the means of relaxing those muscles. When he is successful, the feedback lets him know immediately. It is true that in a similar manner a meditation master or guru provides feedback to the novice meditator to gauge his progress and instruct him in more positive directions. However, the information received in biofeedback is neutral, since the technique involves no dogma. Meditation may also be engaged in without adherence to any of the accompanying belief systems, but that is the exception rather than the norm. In any teacher-student or therapist-patient exchange there is an element of feedback, and in clinical biofeedback this is supplemented by the information from the monitoring devices. Therapists can increase their own sensitivity to the patient's subtle levels of functioning, and thereby be better able to advise other therapies which might be helpful to that particular person. Biofeedback has been used in conjunction with the therapies mentioned above, as well as gestalt therapy, Reichian patterning, bioenergetics, the Alexander technique, and autogenic training. In all these therapies both therapist and patient need accurate, ongoing information in order to assess the patient's progress. Biofeedback is one highly effective means of obtaining objective information for such purposes.

Clinically, it is not important whether a person can perform autonomic-control gymnastics, since the question is whether he has such control in his daily life and whether that control is beneficial. Researchers have demonstrated that individuals can regulate certain biological functions without being consciously aware of how that control has occurred. One area of basic research has focused upon such neurophysiological gymnastics as warming one hand while cooling the other or eliciting specific brain-wave patterns from different areas of the brain. These research results raise important clinical issues. How often do such patterns become manifest without a person's awareness, as a first step toward the degenerative cycle of psychosomatic disorders? Such marked instances of biological regulation illustrates once again the profound influence of psychological factors upon the physiological system.

BIOFEEDBACK AND HEALTH MAINTENANCE

At the present time, a great deal of the clinical work in biofeedback is oriented toward the alleviation of pathology. However, the treatment of specific symptoms with specific modalities of feedback is only one limited application of biofeedback's potential. In a larger context, the greatest value of biofeedback may lie in its ability to introduce people to the concept of a relaxation response which would help them reduce daily stress prior to the development of a more severe psychosomatic disorder. Biofeedback has certain clear advantages over the meditative and deep-relaxation techniques which have been described in previous chapters. Stress reduction due to meditative practices is based on an overall response. This is certainly beneficial, but there is no conclusive evidence to indicate that an overall relaxation response has any effect upon the particular organ system in which that individual expresses his stress. There is a general tendency for all neurophysiological functions to move toward a state of deep relaxation during the meditative periods. However, the particular area of affliction, such as the high blood pressure of a hypertensive patient, may not necessarily drop during this overall relaxation period. Therefore, one major advantage of biofeedback is that the specific physiological function which needs to be corrected can be monitored, feeding information back to the patient to help him assess his progress in alleviating that dysfunction. This instantaneous feedback is a major asset in stress-reduction therapy.

There has been some concern expressed about the danger of patients becoming dependent on biofeedback instrumentation to achieve the desired specific correction or generalized state of relaxation. The instruments are hardly portable, and the problem of carrying over the skills learned in the clinic into the person's daily activity has received a great deal of scrutiny. Actually, there have been a number of cases in which patients have used portable, single-modality monitoring devices at home, but this is a needlessly complex solution for a difficulty which can be resolved through the combined use of biofeedback and meditative techniques. As always, the carry-over effect of what is learned in the clinic is critical in determining the ultimate outcome for the patient. Increasingly, biofeedback therapists are instructing patients in meditative techniques to reinforce the specific skills learned through the monitoring devices. Meditation and other relaxation techniques have been shown to reduce overall stress and thus ward off its many expressions in psychosomatic disorders. It is very efficient to combine these techniques with biofeedback technology in order to encourage the patient to depend not only on instrumental feedback, but also on the non-electronic, easily portable, and generalized machinery of his own biological system.

From previous chapters it is clear that individuals differ in their patterns of response to stress (Lacey, 1967) and that the same degree of overall physical stress will be manifested in a different organ system for each individual. Therefore, a comprehensive approach to clinical intervention using biofeedback techniques would have to include at least two components. One is to teach the individual a generalized meditative technique which can be applied for relaxation in specific situations. Secondly, monitoring of the specific system in which that person is manifesting his stress should be done to help the individual self-regulate that system as unequivocally as possible. One of the most important limitations to recognize in clinical biofeedback is that the simple self-regulation of a particular function such as heart rate or brain-wave activity is not necessarily adequate to produce a sufficient amount of neurophysiological change on the part of that individual on a generalized basis. One way of conceptualizing this total approach to treatment is to imagine a three-dimentional cone. At the base of the cone are all the neurophysiological functions of the individual, including his heart rate, blood pressure, brain-wave activity, muscle tension, skin conductance, and respiration pattern. All of these parameters are free to vary within quite a large radius at the base of the cone. At the top of the cone is a perfectly integrated and harmonious state in which a person is functioning in an unstressed condition. Any neurophysiological function which the individual self-regulates through biofeedback increases the probability of his obtaining this highest state of unstressed relaxation. Regulation of brain-wave activity toward lower frequency will tend to move an individual toward a state of deep relaxation. If he learns to self-regulate muscle tension in the direction of relaxation, then he will obtain an even greater state of integration. As various other functions are regulated toward a uniform and integrated state of relaxation, the likelihood of a harmonious mind/body state increases. By combining training in regulation of specific dysfunctional systems with overall relaxation methods such as autogenic training, meditation, and progressive relaxation, clinicians are creating a model of treatment that can truly be called holistic.

Biofeedback might be compared to a mirror which reflects the psychophysiology of the individual. In order to use the information from the mirror, the person needs to "1) be aware that the image reflected is his; 2) be aware that he might desire to change that image; 3) believe that he is capable of changing that image; and 4) experience the change, growth and control so that he knows he is changing" (Peper, 1974). How the individual changes depends upon how he uses the information presented in the mirror. Emphasis in clinical biofeedback, as in meditative practice, is on maximizing a person's self-awareness so that he can begin to see an alternative way of acting and being in his environment in order to maintain positive change in both physiologic and psychologic functioning.

Regulation of autonomic-nervous-system activity involves a subtle and little-understood psychological process of volition or will, about which we have much more to learn. Basically, there seems to be a two-step process involved in psychophysiological autoregulation. First, the patient learns to achieve deep relaxation through whatever biofeedback channel best enables him to achieve that state. Second, after the state is achieved, he becomes aware of the presence of his internal imagery, fantasies, and sensations, and the manner in which they affect physiological functioning. Passive attention to simple biological and psychological processes such as breathing, heart rate, muscle contractions, and thought patterns is basic to all meditative systems. Autonomic control in biofeedback involves this same principle, since learning depends upon focusing passive attention upon a simple function and creating a harmonious interaction of mind and body. The necessity of achieving this synchrony is clearly recognized in meditative systems, but it is often overlooked in purely technological, conditioning approaches to biofeedback. When the subtle interaction between mind and body is ignored in the course of biofeedback instruction, autonomic control is likely to be unsuccessful. Physiological monitoring devices alone cannot help the patient consciously to understand and integrate his sense of volition or the fantasy material which accompanies the states he achieves by means of deep relaxation or biofeedback, and this is where traditional therapies serve as an invaluable adjunct to biofeedback. The way in which the sense of volition is induced is virtually impossible to explain verbally. It is analogous to explaining how to stand up. We just do it, and are ill equipped to talk about it. The moment we attempt to analyze the task of standing up, our performance is hindered. So it is with the learning of autonomic control, since it is dependent upon internal processes involving attention and attitudes.

Basic clinical skill is invaluable to the therapist in biofeedback, since he needs to teach the skill, develop meaningful homework exercises for the patient, and help him integrate what he has learned into his life style through personal, family, and job counseling. Biofeedback itself is only one aspect of the therapy, and therapists often devote a great deal of energy to helping the patient restructure his life style so that illness-inducing patterns are not repeated. This orientation is very similar to that of the other self-regulatory therapies. Yoga, gestalt therapy, and autogenic training all try to give the person a new sense of himself and his body by teaching him not only the physical skills he can use to self-regulate but responsibility for his own learning process and ultimate success. Knowing that "I have control" is one part of the undefined healing quality often transmitted by "bedside manner" when a physician gives his patient the inner confidence that he can get well. This same mobilization of an individual's volition may also be one major aspect of the placebo effect. In biofeedback, the person can experience success in being self-regulatory, and one of the therapist's tasks is to develop feedback signals which are meaningful for the person so that he does not experience undue failure. Biofeedback, instead of being crisis-oriented and placing responsibility for illness on external circumstances, aims for self-control and individual responsibility. In the long run, this may involve changing one's concept of health in a very general way to include proper diet, social conditions, fresh air, exercise, and the correct mental, physical, and spiritual attitude. Biofeedback training often reduces the patient's feeling of helplessness once he sees that he can master enough autonomic control to correct a particular symptom. With his newfound sense of efficacy, he is encouraged to evaluate and rectify other aspects of his life.

Biofeedback therapy is radically different from classical conditioning in its emphasis on the use of subjective imagery and subtle internal states as a means of establishing voluntary control. This learning process is unique with each individual. According to psychophysiologist Elmer E. Green, "In actuality there is no such thing as training in brain wave control, there is training only in the elicitation of certain subjective states . . . what are detected and manipulated (in some as yet unknown way) are subjective feelings, focus of attention, and thought processes" (Green, Green, and Walters, 1970). Demonstrating the unequivocal interaction between psychological processes and physiological alterations provides a graphic means for the patient to experience himself as an integrated whole. Although these patterns may be initially pathological, the same interaction can be maximized toward health. In the newly emerging therapeutic systems there is an increasing involvement of the patient in his own treatment. Patients can gauge their success or failure via the feedback instrumentation, and, in the final analysis, only they can create the conditions in which success will be consistent. Biofeedback permits them to understand and utilize the link between their personal psychological and physiological processes. Since establishing this link is the key to exerting positive influence over mind/body interactions and breaking into the downward spiral toward psychosomatic illness, biofeedback systems have much to offer in preventive medicine and in the resolution of some major theoretical and clinical problems in health care. Symptoms operate in a cascading effect; when you recognize that you have a headache, you become even more tense, because of the recognition that this headache will not allow you to function as well as usual. This common degenerative cycle becomes the basis of all psychosomatic disorders in which the symptom, in and of itself leads to a further aggravation of the disorder. One of the most effective applications of clinical biofeedback is to instruct a person to recognize and alleviate the most minute initial symptoms before they lead to a more severe one which he will have to rectify by even more drastic measures. In other words, while the problem is still small, an individual is capable of altering the gradual progression toward more severe symptoms. When the individual recognizes excessive levels of tension, he can mobilize the mind/body complex to reverse undesirable change. By becoming increasingly sensitive to these early tension levels, an individual can begin to practice preventive medicine by being able to interrupt excessive stress before it can lead to more severe manifestations.

Homework exercises are an important part of successful biofeedback therapy, in order to insure that the patient will be able to generalize the skill learned in the clinic into his daily activity. Very often it is possible to attain dramatic instances of autonomic regulation in the clinical setting, and this can be misleading. It is very important to wait for a concrete behavior change as an index of whether the person has integrated his self-regulatory ability into his life style. Instances of this include an alcoholic who can pay his bills because he is spending less on alcohol, or a rehabilitation case who does not need to pry his fingers from the steering wheel but can voluntarily flex his hands open. Indicators such as these must be observed carefully in linking clinical practice with homework exercises. Most often these homework exercises consist of deep-relaxation techniques, such as observing respiration rate and patterns, various forms of classical meditation, progressive relaxation, autogenic training, and many other exercises designed to help the individual reexperience the state achieved during clinical sessions.

In many cases, giving the person a portable feedback unit to use at home and asking him to keep a daily log of his practice enhances his willingness to do the homework. This procedure can be both more gratifying and more economical in the long run, since the patient learns faster and the length of time he spends in therapy is considerably shorter. Inexpensive, portable thermometer units have been used successfully by migraine patients; portable muscle-feedback units (EMGs) are very effective for practice at home in dealing with neuromuscular disorders; and GSR (galvanic skin response) feedback is frequently recommended for home use by patients who must recognize levels of arousal and control skin resistance (Sargent, Green, and Walters, 1973; Johnson and Garton, 1973). Autonomic control does not come easily, and in order for biofeedback to be effective in the treatment of such problems as neuromuscular tics, spastic colon, tranquilizer dependency, tension headaches, stress control, and a host of other ailments, a great deal of conscientious work is necessary both in and out of the clinic. Usually the therapist needs to work with a patient once a week for approximately twelve to fifteen sessions, and this must be supplemented by daily work on the part of the patient at home. An interesting aside concerning the time required for successful autonomic control is that children between the ages of nine to fourteen learn more rapidly than do their parents. Perhaps this is due to the fact that they are more willing to experiment with methods of self-regulation and are less programmed into old behavior patterns. Younger children do not "know" that autonomic control is not possible, and this constraint upon their learning is not as stringent as it is with older adults. Also, children and young adults have not made an excessive level of neurophysiological arousal into a habitual life style, and it is easier to elicit and reestablish the relaxation response, which is an integral aspect of their functioning since birth.

The potential of clinical biofeedback as an educational device in preventive medicine is vast, and the most positive results are usually obtained with people who seek clinical help for minor symptoms before the onset of chronic disorders. These people can learn not only to alleviate their symptoms, but also to overcome habitual chronic stress responses in order to prevent more severe disorders from occurring. Biofeedback used with the ultimate end of teaching people relaxation has been extremely successful in helping them cope with both symptomatic manifestations of stress and with the more immediate problems of adjusting to the sources of stress in their lives. Muscle-feedback relaxation has been used to wean individuals from their tranquilizers and soporifics. Through a combination of EMG and breathing techniques to unstress, they learned to be more relaxed and resilient to the tensions of their offices and home lives so that they no longer needed the tranquilizers on which they had become dependent (Love, 1972; Love, Montgomery, and Moeller, 1974). Biofeedback training for deep relaxation cannot be underestimated, whether one uses EMG, GSR, or temperature as the means of indicating when a person has attained an unstressed, meditative state. To some extent, deep relaxation means setting the mind free and loosening the bonds of the ego. When this is accomplished, there are rewards that transcend the purely physical sensations. While deeply relaxed, a person listens more clearly to stimuli of every kind without preconceptions, and can stop the constant cerebral chatter of the brain in order to attain a state which gives him access to his unconscious. From this state of internal awareness an essentially healthy person can learn to recognize excessive stress and prevent its consequences. Hypo-aroused states, as indicated by theta waves or very low EMG levels, can be used as occasions for self-programming activity and sleep learning (Budzynski and Peffer, 1974). People can use this meditative state to interrogate their "unconscious" in order to obtain information concerning a pressing problem or concern before it leads to excessive anxiety or physical symptoms. In a further extension of this self-analytic aspect of meditative states, the pioneers of biofeedback, Elmer E. and Alyce Green (Green, 1974), are using theta-feedback training to develop imagery, creativity and integrative experiences. Individuals have learned to maintain a state of hypnagogic or dreamlike imagery by regulating their theta activity for prolonged periods of time. Theta activity appears to be a threshold between the conscious and the unconscious and permits a person to engage in an experience of subtle levels of psychological and physiological awareness. From that experience, these individuals learn a profound sense of trust in their own inner experience and ways to allow their unique creativity to unfold. As in all feedback training, the benefit the person gains from the newly achieved state is dependent on both the guidance of the therapist and the willingness of the individual to explore these subtle levels of experience. Such uses of biofeedback move the process away from pathology correction toward health maintenance and personal growth.

APPLICATIONS OF CLINICAL BIOFEEDBACK

Before proceeding to enumerate a few specific applications of clinical biofeedback, it is important to clarify the context in which biofeedback therapy occurs. In contrast to the medical model of diagnosing a specific disorder for which a specific procedure is then applied, biofeedback requires a more flexible systems approach. There are many instances in which a specific feedback mode, such as temperature training, is applied to a specific disorder, such as vascular migraine. However, more often the approach involves the learning of a generalized state of meditative relaxation, which then is focused upon a particular system, such as excessive muscle tension or peripheral vasoconstriction. Very often it is possible to use quite different instruments, such as the GSR and the EEG, to produce the same response, for instance a decrease in migraine incidence. Underlying this phenomenon is the fact that general stress is manifested in many physiological systems simultaneously. Since the nature of psychosomatic disorders involves this interconnectedness, they then can be alleviated by allowing an individual to self-regulate one particular function, which in turn affects the entire neurophysiological system. This self-regulatory capacity of the psychosomatic system is not produced by the instrumentation but is permitted to reemerge as an essentially normal response which has been disrupted or curtailed. Specific biofeedback instruments for specific disorders are a necessary but insufficient condition for clinical biofeedback procedures. Flexibility must be encouraged in order to adapt any given approach for a particular patient so that he or she can reestablish the relaxation response.

Despite the abundance of research articles, there are relatively few sources which have addressed themselves to the broader implications of biofeedback for psychosomatic medicine, the philosophical issues underlying biofeedback techniques, and the impact of these innovations upon health care. Therefore, this section will concentrate upon the relatively few studies which are indicative of important trends in clinical biofeedback and from which we can draw its broader implications.

Teaching relaxation through monitoring specific psychophysiological systems is the primary basis of clinical biofeedback's success in a wide range of applications. In referring to stress-related disorders, George B. Watmore and Daniel R. Kohli (1968) have used the term "dysponesis" (from *dys*, meaning "wrong" or "faulty," and *ponos*, meaning "effort" or "energy"). Misplaced efforts are capable of producing a variety of functional disturbances within the organism. Biofeedback instrumentation is designed to discover dysponetic functioning in specific systems and then help people adjust the faulty functioning before it develops into a chronic symptom or severe disorder. Using muscle electromyographic feedback, Kohli and Whatmore have treated patients with digestive-system disturbance, depression, eczema, and neurodermatitis. Muscle feedback has also been used successfully by Budzynski and Stoyva for systematic desensitization in the treatment of dysponetic, phobic responses. In such work, the person is asked to imagine a troubling scene. As the tension level increases, the EMG signals increase, indicating stress. When the stress level becomes excessive, he gradually relaxes and lets his fear or tension go until the low EMG criterion have been reached. Then he begins thinking of the scene again and repeats the process of freeing himself from its unwanted high-arousal effects. In this way, he learns to "desensitize" himself and slough off an undesirable stress reaction through the feedback. In this manner, biofeedback can be used as a valuable adjunct to behavior therapies. Doing away with dysponetic motions, such as unconsciously tensing one's shoulders under conditions of stress, contributes to overall improved performances. Improved performance after relaxing may be due to the fact that tension uses up some energy uselessly and that dysponetic motions create noise so that our attention and concentration is scattered, interfering with optimum functioning.

Unstressing through biofeedback therapy has also been successful in the amelioration of hypertension. Moeller and Love (1972) used EMG feedback from the frontalis muscle group of the forehead combined with autogenic homework exercises to teach nine hypertensive patients to enter into and maintain deeply relaxed states. These patients were given one half-hour of biofeedback once a week for seventeen weeks. They achieved an average of 15 percent decrease in both systolic and diastolic pressure after training. More recent evidence indicates that in such clinical trials training sessions were too far apart, homework exercises were not integrated into the life styles of the patients, and patients did not have the opportunity to deal with their personal problems in the context of psychotherapy. Such over-sights constitute a basic conceptual error in translating the applications of biofeedback from experimental to clinical contexts.

Electromyographic feedback has also been used to induce a specific relaxation response in the treatment of migraine, tension headaches, ulcerative proctitis, and spastic colon. All of these disorders are the result of classic fight-or-flight stress reactions which have become inappropriate due to being prolonged past their usefulness or elicited when they served no purpose. As is always the case, the breakdowns occurred in specific organ systems which were the most vulnerable. Muscle feedback is also a potent tool in re-habilitating patients with neuromuscular problems, espe-cially mild paralysis of spasticity. EMG feedback is used in cases of spasticity to let the patient "hear" his muscle spasm and thereby learn to decrease it through decreasing the feed-back tone.

A case history of one of my patients is useful in illustrat-ing the applications of EMG feedback. The patient was a nineteen-year-old man suffering from paralysis due to a cervical (neck) fracture. Function of the left side of his body was severely impaired in terms of muscular activity, and the entire left side of his body was approximately fifteen degrees lower in temperature than the right. This patient was first monitored for temperature feedback on his left side, and he learned to elevate and sustain the temperature until it was increased by thirteen degrees, leaving only a two-degree difference. Following temperature training, there was significant improvement in the muscular coordination of his left arm. Using EMG feedback from both extensors and flexors, he was then able to regain a significant amount of fine motor movement in the arm. In order to begin the neuromuscular reeducation, baseline readings were taken from the more functional right arm, and the patient was asked to duplicate those readings with the less functional left side. (Asking the patient to create analogous feedback between functional and dysfunctional parts of the body is a very effective tool in muscular rehabilitation.) In addition, the patient performed numerous exercises at home, such as repeatedly making a fist and then relaxing. In the course of therapy, he began to see the left arm, which he had previously regarded as a dead and useless appendage, as once again functional. Over time, he began to make a psychological reconnection with his arm. His progress was furthered by instructions to use his left arm as much as possible and avoid depending on his right arm. Also, he was asked to visualize and make mental reconnections with the arm, with the intent of seeing it heal and become more functional. In rehabilitation work such as this, small successes have a motivating effect. Even a minute change can be registered on the EMG instrument as an indication of clear progress, which is then an impetus for further effort.

Cases of neuromuscular rehabilitation are not simple matters involving a mechanistic application of electromyography. Even in instances of clearly organic dysfunction there are important elements of psychological disruption which must be resolved. Another case history involving EMG feedback points up the value of a holistic approach to another of my patients and the use of psychotherapy in conjunction with physical therapies. In this case, the patient was a woman of sixty who entered the clinic with spasmodic torticollis, commonly referred to as "wry neck." Her neck was chronically turned over the right shoulder, and she could not move it. She had been through surgical intervention, cortisone injections, hot packs, traction, chiropracty, and even biofeedback therapy, all with very little result. At the clinic she was taught to passively attend to relaxing the contracted left contralateral sternomastoid muscle and "allowing" her head to turn. She was also encouraged to act with passive rather than active volition. After five sessions, the patient was quite successful in doing this, and managed to turn her head to some degree. However, very shortly after her initial success and for no explicable reason, she was no longer able to move her head any farther than a forty-five-degree angle from her shoulder. At that point a spike in the EMG activity was noted, and the feedback was then set up so that whenever the spike occurred she would receive a feedback tone. She was asked to report any images, sensations, and thoughts which came to her when the tone came on. During one hour of this treatment, she became aware of a feeling of eyes looking at her and a deep sense of guilt and shame. Proceeding along these lines, she revealed that she had begun an affair five years previously with a much younger man who was married. This disturbed her greatly, due to her moral upbringing and belief structure. In discussing the affair, she stated, "If my neighbors ever found out, I could not look them straight in the face." At the moment that she made that statement, the muscle activity in her neck began to become more volatile, and she was able to move her head farther than she ever had before. That moment of insight did not instantly alleviate the torticollis, but it did enable her to make steady progress from that point on. Six months later she was able to turn her head in a three-quarters rotation. Her treatment is one further indication that the combination of feedback and psychotherapy is a most effective approach.

Biofeedback for neuromuscular reeducation is an area of considerable importance. It is a very efficient method of helping individuals regain control over their bodies following a period of dysponesis. Johnson and Garton (1973) have had encouraging results with ten hemiplegic patients, all but one of whom had been paralyzed for at least a year. Marinacci (1968), one of the most adventurous researchers in EMG muscle retraining, has had success treating partial paralysis due to stroke, and he has also used EMG feedback with some success in cases of Bell's palsy, causalgia, nerve injury, residual anterior poliomyelitis, and other muscular problems. Booker and his colleagues (1969) have successfully retrained the facial muscles in a patient with severance of the facial nerve following spinal accessory facial nerve anastomosis. One limitation of EMG feedback in neuromuscular rehabilitation is that therapy must be started quite soon after the injury, before bad habits have formed or there is muscular atrophy. Portable equipment for use at home is particularly desirable in neuromuscular rehabilitation, and the therapist becomes a guide with whom the patient develops new therapy procedures as functions are regained.

Disorders of the cardiovascular system have been treated effectively with biofeedback, since blood pressure and heart rate are amenable to biofeedback monitoring. Blood pressure poses some difficulty at present, however. Biofeedback has even been used with normo-tensive individuals who have learned to increase or decrease systolic pressures at will as a demonstration of the fact that voluntary regulation of cardiovascular activity is clearly possible (Brener and Kleinman, 1970; Schwartz, 1972). Biofeedback techniques whose primary aim is the attainment of deeply relaxed states elicit a generalized relaxation response which can aid in the treatment of cardiovascular disorders, particularly hypertension. In individual cases, it is usually advisable to determine early in the treatment to which modality or combination of modalities the patient is most sensitive. It is of utmost importance to determine which kind of feedback induces a deep relaxation state most effectively and thus affects blood pressure.

In one early study, Benson, Shapiro, Tursky, and Schwartz (1971) used biofeedback to obtain significant decreases in systolic blood pressures in patients with hypertension. However, no attempt was made to introduce the laboratory-designed exercises into the patients' daily lives or to evaluate the persistence of lowered pressure outside the laboratory. It is inadequate to train people to manipulate one parameter or simply to learn a particular feedback method in the laboratory. This approach may be self-limiting, because it does not consider a patterned response, nor does it consider the issue of integrating the learned behavior into the person's life style. Early in the development of bio-feedback technology, these carry-over effects were simply not judged to be important. Only within the last three years has it become evident that carry-over effect into the daily life of the patient has much to do with the ultimate success of the therapy. It has gradually become clear that those who consistently performed their homework exercises profited most from the clinical training. Those who did not practice or were not willing to adopt a new attitude toward themselves did not profit as much, and in many cases lost their regulatory ability after a period of time. Through a combination of physiological regulation and psychotherapy it is possible to approach the patient in a holistic manner and to use the therapy for particular symptoms as an occasion for personal insight and growth.

One researcher who has conducted extensive studies with biofeedback and cardiovascular functions is Gary E. Schwartz of Harvard University. Much of the significance of his work lies in the fact that he taught individuals to regulate several functions simultaneously. Schwartz focused his research design on what he calls "patterns of physiological responses in the generation of subjective experience" (Shapiro, Tursky, and Schwartz, 1970). This research is one of the most convincing and remarkable demonstrations of the specificity of human self-regulation. With his colleagues David Shapiro and Bernard Tursky, he began a series of experiments on systolic blood pressure and heart rate. Subjects in the experiment were given audio feedback indicating the regulation of one of four possible states: blood pressure and heart rate up; blood pressure up and heart rate down; blood pressure down and heart rate up; and blood pressure down, heart rate down. Quite quickly it was found that individuals could exert self-regulation in a single session over their blood pressure and that these changes were independent of heart rate. In fact, it appeared that systolic blood pressure and heart rate were related in a random manner. Elevation or decrease in one function did not necessarily produce equivalent changes in the other. One question which arose was whether a person could learn to control both processes simultaneously. In order to resolve this issue, subjects were given feedback only when a desired pattern occurred. When the subjects were required to produce an integrated pattern of either blood pressure and heart rate up or blood pressure and heart rate down, they showed simultaneous control of both functions in the same direction. This was in direct contrast to the previous findings which showed that specific control over either heart rate or blood pressure did not necessarily induce a simultaneous change in the other function. Still more important, the feedback for these integrated patterns produced more rapid learning and somewhat larger changes than the feedback for each function alone.

Perhaps the most significant finding, however was that when the subjects were taught to lower both heart rate and blood pressure together, they began, spontaneously and consistently, to report feelings of relaxation and calmness. Such subjective reports would be anticipated as consistent with a more generalized physiological relaxation. In other words, when the two parameters varied together, it was a significant enough change for the individuals to begin to recognize a psychological difference. Thus, a connection was made between mind and body as a critical step in helping carry over the learning from the clinic into daily life. A further implication of the initial finding that blood pressure and heart rate did not vary together is that it is possible for an individual to fragment the functions of his neurophysiological system and create a disruptive pattern. This fragmentation can occur entirely without the person's awareness. It may be true that these splits occur more frequently than current practitioners recognize and that discontinuities between psychological and physiological processes constitute the essence of psychosomatic disorders. Research concerning neurophysiological stress profiles supports this concept. If such fragmentations lead to dysfunction, a harmonious integration of mind and body functions should be an important goal of health maintenance.

Another area in which biofeedback can be used to integrate a psychological and a physiological process is in the use of the galvanic skin response, or GSR. Marjorie Toomin has identified three types of reactors, or three ways in which individuals can react to emotional or stressful material.

1) Over-reactors—people who respond excessively for a very long time.

2) Under-reactors—people who do not respond to ordinary emotional or exciting stimuli with a change in skin resistance.

3) Medial-reactors—people whose GSR pattern moves up and down in a pattern that clearly reflects changes in attention, excitation, and emotional involvement [Toomin and Toomin, 1973].

This feedback is used in two ways: 1) as a monitor to help assess the weight of spoken materials (i.e., Is the patient showing effect or body responses with the verbal responses?) and 2) as feedback for the patient to take home. Over-reactors are taught to lower their excitation levels and increase their skin resistance, while under-reactors are asked to decrease their skin resistance. One example of GSR under-reaction is the case of a manic young man who talked very fast and laughed as a punctuation to almost every statement. However, his GSR remained constant at a low resistance, indicating low arousal. When he was asked to stay quiet for a moment and pay attention to his feelings, he reported feeling relaxed but a little excited. He was then asked to see what he could do to alter the GSR feedback tone. He tried laughing, deep breathing, and thinking of his wife, but the tone remained constant. Then he was asked to talk more slowly about the problems that had brought him to therapy, meanwhile noting when the GSR tone did not respond to emotional material. Initially the GSR did not change as he laughed, but he stopped and attended to his feelings. He then found that he was masking his sadness and anger with this laugh. At that point the GSR began to respond appropriately to the emotional content of his thoughts, and he began to learn to recognize these feelings as they arose, even though they were not strong at first. In other cases, the increase or flattening (non-responsiveness) of the GSR signaled strong repression and withdrawal. As Toomin points out, feedback to both patient and therapist is advantageous, since the patient becomes increasingly aware of the connection between psychological and physiological processes and learns to integrate them. Also the patient becomes more willing to cooperate with the therapist in exploring repressed and frightening material. Skin-conductance biofeedback appears to be a useful device for helping patients recognize that they are experiencing different stages of psychophysiological arousal and become sensitive to the interaction of their emotions and physiological responses.

While many clinical applications of biofeedback are quite well developed, such as thermal feedback for vascular migraine, there are innovative areas at the frontiers of clinical biofeedback. Among these innovative approaches in clinical biofeedback is localized regulation of highly specific biological functions with increasingly precise sensors. In localized control, the emphasis is placed on developing the proper sensors for the specific functions to be regulated. One such application is the use of a small strain gauge around the penile shaft. This has been developed to give penile-erection feedback so that the person or the therapist can become aware of subtle penile changes in a process of overcoming impotence (Eversaul, 1975). Minute alterations in the engorgement of the blood vessels of the penis can be measured, and the individual can begin to recognize when he is sexually aroused. By recognizing the interaction between the biological function of erection and certain psychological states of arousal, individuals can work toward an integrated state of mind and body during sexual arousal and thus overcome impotence.

Another innovative biofeedback system has been developed by Paul Gorman and Joe Kamiya (1972), who have been teaching individuals to regulate their stomach acidity. This could develop into a treatment for ulcers. In other research laboratories, air-resistance feedback has been applied for teaching individuals to recognize changes in their bronchial-tube diameter, and this may have applications to asthma and other respiratory diseases (Vachon, 1973). More experimental methods of biofeedback are electro-occulographic or EOG feedback, which involves the feeding back of muscle tension around the eyes for the correction of visual disorders ranging from near- and far-sightedness to cases of glaucoma.

In a still more fascinating application, David French and his colleagues at Claremont College in Claremont, California, have successfully trained five students to induce hand warming, and subsequently to attain scrotal heating with thermal feedback (French et al., 1972). This research derived from evidence that external applications of heat to scrotum of a variety of animals and man would cause the sperm count to decrease. (The use of cotton batting in the loincloths of Indians and hot baths in geisha houses is recognition of this effect.) The researchers requested each student to engage in five consecutive daily training sessions, in which they learned to increase their scrotal temperature. For one week following the scrotal heating, the sperm count of all five students was reduced below fertility level. This data has obvious potential for non-pharmaceutical male birth control.

Another experimental use of clinical biofeedback is auditory feedback of the activity of the small intestines. Gastrointestinal feedback is used for the regulation of chronic diarrhea or chronic constipation when laxatives are no longer effective (Stroebel, 1975). Charles Stroebel of the

Institute of Living has used an amplified stethoscope and noted that patients can learn to discriminate between increased and decreased levels of peristaltic activity in the intestinal tract by listening carefully to these fluctuations. By noting an increase in this audible signal, a patient can learn to overcome chronic constipation or can decrease this activity in order to self-regulate diarrhea. Once an individual is made aware of the activity in his intestinal tract, he can then learn how to maximize or minimize it in order to allow that part of his body to function more freely and to recognize the stresses which caused those systems to become dysfunctional in the first place. Each of these instances of experimental biofeedback has clear implications for clinical practice and involves the patient in the process of self-regulation. Common to each application is a recognition of the interaction between stress and its effects upon a highly specific physiological system.

Regulation of epileptic-seizure activity is another innovative area of research. This research was initiated by M. Barry Sterman of the Veterans Hospital in Sepulveda, California. Sterman began his research with cats and noted a discrete 12–16 Hz rhythm over their sensorimotor cortex when the cats remained immobile. Since this frequency was characteristic of immobility and epilepsy can be considered as hyper-mobility, the deliberate induction of this 12–16-cycle activity might be a means of eliminating seizure activity. Following this observation, Sterman trained four psychomotor epileptics to produce this brain-wave activity, which he termed the sensorimotor rhythm, or SMR. Biofeedback training over six to eight months resulted in a significant decrease in seizure activity (Sterman, 1974 and 1975). Control of pain is another important medical problem to which biofeedback has been applied. Alpha feedback has been used to aid in the overcoming of intractable pain due to post-operative or phantom-limb syndromes (Pelletier and Peper, 1977). An abundance of alpha activity appears to help an individual remove himself from the pain and not react to it as intensely. Patients still feel the pain, but it is usually reported as a dull sensation rather than a sharp or throbbing one. Successful experimentation of this nature demonstrates the extensive applicability of biofeedback as a therapeutic tool.

Biofeedback uses still in the future could range from vaginal feedback systems to control fertility and yeast infections to the use of the thermographic photography for breast-cancer detection in order to help a person regulate the temperature and blood flow in the area of the tumor. In thermography units, surface tumors can be detected as hypothermic or blue areas in contrast to the reddish tones indicating normal tissue. Since this information is clear and can be monitored on an ongoing basis, it is potentially an excellent means of biofeedback. If a patient can increase the hypothermic activity in the region of the tumor, then perhaps the tumor can be starved of nutrients by shutting down its blood supply. On the other hand, perhaps increasing blood flow in the area may enhance the local immunological competence and curtail the tumor by that means. In either case, the possibility is suggested of non-surgical intervention with breast tumors. Many of the biological sensors mentioned here are experimental and are not available for clinical applications at the present time. However, just consider the fact that the EEG was developed in 1934 and did not achieve significant clinical application as a biofeedback instrument until 1974. Now, rather than a span of forty years, the rapid innovations in biomedical technology are making new biofeedback instrumentation widely available within a matter of a few years. Each innovative application should be carefully assessed and developed prior to its application in clinical settings. It is equally important to remember that such instrumentation ultimately involves the cooperation of the patient, and no degree of biomedical sophistication can afford to lose sight of the requirements of the individual patient.

HOLISTIC APPROACHES TO CLINICAL BIOFEEDBACK

It should be evident at this point that the more neurophysiological functions are regulated toward a state of mind/body integration, the more positive will be the individual's level of optimum functioning. This holistic goal is gaining increasing support from the clinical and research literature. Research results indicate that psychophysiological functions are not necessarily linked together, and that it is certainly possible for an individual to fractionate or fragment his neurophysiological system into a disruptive pattern. The fact that the individuals do not necessarily know that this is occurring is support for the hypothesis that these neurophysiological dysfunctions can occur out of awareness. In contrast to a fragmented neurophysiological response is the relaxation response, which can be induced in the use of clinical biofeedback and meditative techniques. One researcher at Harvard University, Herbert Benson, and his colleagues have described this overall relaxation pattern as reflecting a more centrally integrated "relaxation response" (Benson, Beary, and Carol, 1974). According to Benson, this relaxation response is an innate, neurophysiological pattern, which can be induced when an individual regulates a simple pattern of attention and cognition. According to their research, this pattern can be induced by having an individual attend passively to his breath and saying the word "one" after each breath. This modified version of a Zen meditative practice has been demonstrated to effect marked decreases in metabolism.

As another example, during episodes of sleep-onset insomnia a person may be physically exhausted but unable to fall asleep because his mind is racing with distracting images and thoughts. It is interesting to note that the popular means of resolving this problem is to visualize sheep and count them. This is a very effective deep-relaxation and self-regulatory procedure, which may derive its effectiveness from blocking the verbal activity of the left hemisphere while engaging the visual capacity of the right hemisphere. The single focal point of attention is an essential aspect of all meditative systems.

Holmes and Rahe (1967) have indicated that many illnesses were precipitated by prolonged or transient stresses and changes in the preceding two years, whether due to accidents, contagious infections, or chronic afflictions. It is hypothesized here that if a person can learn to unstress himself automatically from chronic pressure or trauma, he may be able to avoid chronic-stress-induced illness. As one example, deep-relaxation feedback training could be used before surgery, since it is frequently observed that tense individuals need more anesthesia than relaxed patients. Stimulated by such innovations and potential applications, many biofeedback researchers have formulated a hypothesis that since low-frequency EEG occurs in passive meditation, and subjects can learn with biofeedback to regulate such EEG patterns, biofeedback regulation of EEG frequencies will lead to deep relaxation. This can be referred to as the fallacy of "instant electronic yoga." The major fallacy in this logic, based upon the research concerning patterned responses in biofeedback and meditation, is that any single system of biofeedback training is more likely to emphasize specificity than to induce an overall pattern. As noted earlier, there were consistent reports of subjective relaxation when uninstructed individuals were simultaneously lowering blood pressure and heart rate. Decreases in either one alone, however, did not produce the same subjective phenomenon. Similarly, when other individuals regulated patterns of occipital alpha and heart rate, they reported that heart rate down and alpha on was quite relaxing. When this pattern was not present, individuals did not report a state of subjective relaxation. It would appear from the research evidence that deep neurophysiological relaxation is not simply low muscle activity, low heart rate, low occipital alpha, or slow breath, but rather an integrated combination of these functions. Laboratory experiments have demonstrated that the regulation of patterns of responses can produce neurophysiological and psychological effects that are different than those observed when any single function is self-regulated. During periods of fragmentation, an individual is more likely to develop a psychosomatic disorder, while an integrated psychophysiology appears conducive to health maintenance.

Through the use of a comprehensive diagnostic system in clinical biofeedback, it should become possible to classify various kinds of psychosomatic fragmentations due to stress. Stress comprises various patterns of psychological, attentional, and somatic components which are brought into play. Given this complex nature of stress, it is necessary to treat dysfunctional levels with a combination of generalized relaxation plus specific regulation in the particular system in which the stress is most clearly manifested. Since it may be possible to classify various kinds of stress, depending on the cognitive, psychosocial, and somatic components, this clinical intervention can have an objective basis (Pelletier, 1974). Once a fragmented, dysfunctional pattern has been identified, the most effective relaxation procedure may depend upon the specific type of stress the person is experiencing at that time. It is quite possible for a person to have a high level of psychological anxiety but a relatively low level of physiological or somatic stress. Such splits or fragmentation between mind and body are in polar opposition to the integrated level of functioning described by Elmer E. Green and noted earlier. Through the use of increasingly sophisticated instrumentation applied in a clinical setting, these splits can be detected and the means of self-regulation can be created for establishing integration. Consider a patient who feels somatically very tense and anxious but experiences no particular psychological cause for this anxiety. For this patient, relaxation strategies might include gardening, jogging, or other forms of somatic activities which help to channel the physical activity and induce a sense of relaxation.

Ideally, biofeedback therapy will maximize the intuitive means by which patients engage in stress reduction, Very often, when I begin work with particular patients, I observe them as they attempt to self-regulate a particular psychophysiological process. Some patients begin to breathe differently; a few change their posture or begin flexing various muscles; others engage in spontaneous visualization or attend to a rhythmic biological function such as heart rate or respiration. Each of these procedures suggests an intuitive direction for that person. The instruments can then be used to provide them with information on how to maximize that natural predisposition. For those patients who engage in an attempt to become psychologically quiet, the EEG is useful, while the electromyograph may be more appropriate for those individuals who move toward a more postural means of stress reduction. Each patient works toward that end in a unique fashion, and the specific method is that individual's means to achieve an integrated state. In its most simple terms, the principle underlying a holistic approach to clinical biofeedback is that the whole person can be qualitatively different from the sum of his parts, and yet be dependent upon the organization of those parts for his unique state of psychosomatic integration.

Before the advent of psychophysiological instrumentation, clinicians were entirely dependent upon their intuition and the patient's subjective reports for monitoring the interaction between mind and body. Now it is becoming possible to assess those states more objectively and to make more accurate inferences concerning the relationship between subjective imagery, fantasies, visualization, and their neurophysiological concomitants. Awareness of subtle imagery and sensations is not a prerequisite to autonomic control, although such recognition does speed up the process.

An innovative approach to the synthesis of biofeedback

and deep relaxation procedures was undertaken by Thomas Budzynksi and Johann Stoyva (Budzynski, Stoyva and Adler, 1970) of the University of Colorado Medical Center. Their approach combines three systems: 1) Jacobson's progressive relaxation; 2) autogenic training; and 3) biofeedback, especially the use of the electromyogram. Their major application of this combination has been to disorders such as bronchial asthma, sleep-onset insomnia, migraine headaches, angina pectoris, and peptic ulcers. In practice, Budzynski and Stoyva follow the first six stages of autogenic training as a prelude to therapy. Following this state of deep relaxation, they use techniques of behavior modification and systematic desensitization as their most common therapeutic technique. Deep relaxation is an essential feature of systematic desensitization, which involves the establishment at the onset of a hierarchy of scenes of an increasing anxiety-provoking quality, based on the patient's detailed account of his phobic experiences (Wolpe, 1958). The patient is encouraged to remain relaxed while imagining a graduated series of frightening events. What is critically different in the system of Budzynski and Stoyva is that the patient monitors his own anxiety level by means of EMG feedback, and emphasis is upon understanding and integrating the fantasy material rather than viewing it simply as a way of extinguishing unwanted behavior patterns. In such approaches, the inner world of the patient is endowed with meaning and respect. It is seen as a profound source of information regarding the therapeutic process. Subjective reports are taken as indicative of the patient's insight and creativity, rather than as another occasion for the clinician to demonstrate proficiency at categorization.

Subjective reports of visualization experiences and fantasies during biofeedback bear a striking resemblance to those of meditators who have learned to view their inner states with calm detachment in a mode of active passivity. Biofeedback and visualization techniques offer a means of inducing a meditation state plus a means of interpreting the contents which are elicited during those states. Through the language of images, fantasies, and sensations an individual's conscious/unconscious, voluntary/autonomic processes can be harmoniously integrated, in order to reduce conflicting or misinterpreted stimuli which induce stress. Biofeedback instrumentation offers a means of inducing deep relaxation and probing those states with unprecedented accuracy. Once in a meditative state, an individual is capable of observing and assessing his fantasies and thoughts with a measure of objectivity and detachment. Such a state is clearly a prerequisite of self-understanding and is the basis for constructive alterations in behavior. When such a discipline is undertaken on a regular basis, an individual can learn to recognize and act in accordance with his most fundamental psychological and physiological responses to personal, social, and environmental stimuli. Of course, these ideals are not achieved by any individual without great effort, but that does not lessen their value as goals worth seeking.

The emphasis in this chapter has been upon the philosophical and pragmatic issues concerning the clinical applications of biofeedback. One point which is very important to note is that these clinical applications are often accompanied by profound alterations in the individual's perceptions of himself and others. Although biofeedback is perceived as a scientific means to enhance "control," this simplistic formulation belies its complexity. In practice, an individual learns to allow internal phenomena to occur and ceases to operate in a mode of active manipulation. During the feedback learning or the recapitulating of the feedback learned state at home, the person does nothing except sit quietly. During a self-styled meditative practice, the person simply attends to himself and neither grasps nor suppresses any thoughts or emotions. After reaching a certain state of physiological relaxation, a person has entered into spontaneous meditation. Through the biofeedback learning and the homework exercises, such as the self-healing visualizations and the observation of the breath without striving or trying, the individual experiences the concept of passive volition, and he moves from a state of believing in this concept to knowing it as a reality. With this experience the person becomes aware of the rich potential of quietness, and often seeks additional guidance for internal development.

Self-healing by means of biofeedback inevitably involves the individual in a process of psychological development and may elicit profound experiences of altered states of consciousness. The effect of these on alleviation of many disorders should not be underestimated. Not only do they create a marked transformation of the personality, but they have pragmatic applications in holistic therapy. All too often such altered states are dismissed or ignored as simply interesting phenomena with few objective verifications or significant implications. Sensations such as floating, spinning, sinking, and enlargement of the limbs can also feel threatening. Patients may avoid feeling these sensations by tensing their muscles or blocking their alpha EEG at the end of the exhalation phase of their breath cycle. Possibly these sensations trigger a reexperience of past traumatic events in which consciousness was forcefully changed in the body, due to a fall from a bicycle, childhood beating, near-drowning experience, or gas anesthesia (Luthe, 1969). Fear of these sensations may be so strong that the moment the sensations come to awareness, the person avoids feeling them by tensing up. However, with a gentle attitude and encouragement from a therapist, the person may allow himself to pass through these sensations and literally to experience that there is nothing to fear but the fear itself. Often the patient realizes that the released pain and the strange body sensations do not automatically lead to reexperiencing the traumatic past events. During the deep relaxation which follows, the person may experience a unitive sensation in which he merges with the room, chair, light, or therapist. This process of release appears similar to the profound unitive experiences in meditation and occur when consciousness expands beyond its usual constraints and modes of functioning. Through clinical biofeedback combined with meditation or psychotherapy, these experiences can be of paramount importance in correcting, maintaining, and enhancing psychological and physical health.

The significant future directions of clinical biofeedback will not lead to the indiscriminate application of biomedical instrumentation but to increasingly sensitive holistic adaptations for each individual. Thus, the frontiers will be expanded not only by current technology but by the creativity of therapists in shaping a clinical practice in which the patient's dignity, self-regulation, and growth are enhanced and developed.

PART FIVE
CONCLUSION

Toward a Holistic Medicine

9

Holistic approaches lead not only to the prevention of stress disorders but to a whole array of new possibilities for the individual. When individuals cease living under conditions of extreme stress which impel them to the brink of physical and psychological disease, it is possible to reformulate their lives and to utilize the time and energy that they would normally spend combating illness to living as fully as possible. This fundamental reorientation of life style and personal philosophy is the greater issue, of which stress alleviation and the prevention of pathology is but one aspect.

Today there is a profound alteration taking place involving the nature of human consciousness. Disruption and upheaval are occurring on a planetary level as a precursor to a transformation of our most fundamental belief systems. When the *Tibetan Book of the Dead* is available in paperback in most bookstores and Carlos Casteneda's *Tales of Power* is widely read, a new age is at hand. Questions are being raised concerning the essential nature of reality, from quantum physics to the emerging science of consciousness. Individuals are seeking a fundamental understanding of themselves and their universe and are no longer satisfied by material saturation and traditional success. Indications of this transformation are clearly evidenced by a resurgence of humanistic concerns in the midst of the proliferation of industrial and biomedical technology. Advances in the material sciences and technology have failed to bring the panacea they promised. At hand now is the task of integrating technological sophistication with humanistic values and an improved quality of life.

Creating an effective holistic approach to health care is central to this process. Implications of a holistic approach to health range from the concerns of each individual who is seeking to live a meaningful life, through the concerns of health professionals and government planners, to the philosophical issues which underly our conception of reality. At each level of analysis there are more unresolved issues than answers, but also clear evidence of new directions. For the individual, there is the increasing recognition that health care is a matter of individual responsibility. As part of that responsibility, the individual must learn to recognize both the applications and limitations of medicine (Illich, 1976). Medicine is legally defined in terms of the diagnosis and treatment of disease. This is but one aspect of health. An individual must also assume the responsibility of educating himself concerning nutrition and exercise, as well as emotional and mental well-being. Many people seek such aid only in instances of crisis, when preventive measures are no longer appropriate. There is no way a person can be convinced or coerced into seeking this information, or engaging in a life-style reorientation. According to the ancient Chinese philosopher Lao-tse, "The journey of a thousand miles begins with one step," and that initial acceptance and commitment is a necessary prerequisite for individual growth and transformation.

Each of the meditative systems noted in Part Four is one means of beginning the personal quest. In their apparent simplicity lies a common search for deeper meanings in everyday experience. Living each moment as clearly and fully as possible allows the individual to know which step or direction is next in his life path. Being able to tolerate the ambiguity of not programming an entire life, nor following a preconceived pattern, but remaining open to innovation and insight, is the essential challenge.

In light of this profound transformation of human consciousness, it should be clear that meditation is more than a means of stress reduction. Fundamentally, it is a means of becoming more attuned to the self as well as the psychosocial and biological environment. Meditation opens our awareness to the fact that life is not an incessant zero-sum game where one person's gain is another person's loss. In an enlightened mode of existence perhaps the afflictions of civilization will no longer be a plague. Freedom from the fear of tuberculosis, polio, typhoid, and similar afflictions has had profound social impact. Alleviating or preventing the present afflictions of civilization which have their roots in our entire psychosocial matrix will entail an even greater degree of innovation. Our civilization's afflictions are symptoms of an entire cultural life style which has become increasingly pathological. The new sense of personal responsibility extends into the realization that one can exercise choice regarding whether to be subjected to the brutalization of the evening news, the monotonous routine of an occupation which has ceased to be anything other than monetarily rewarding, or the unduly restrictive censure of a partner or peer group. In 1890, William James roused himself from a prolonged depression with the realization that he had the infinitesimal but omnipotent freedom to choose between one thought and another. When this individual freedom is experienced as independent of any and all external circumstances, the specter of confinement, censure, neurotic anxiety, and death itself fades rapidly.

Innovations in health sciences are not inherently antagonistic to such humanistic values. Holistic or humanistic approaches to medicine have given rise to such innovations as more sensitive childbirth procedures, considerations of environmental factors in healing, and recent attempts to engage the patient's volition in the healing process. Innovations in childbirth are an excellent example. The French obstetrician Frederick Leboyer has reflected upon the excessive mechanization of the birth process, with its harsh noises, blazing lights, the terrifying dangle upside down followed by a jolting slap, and the instantaneous severing of the umbilical cord. Efficiency certainly promotes these procedures to the detriment of the sensitivity of the newborn infant. In *Birth Without Violence*, 1975, Leboyer formulates simple but revolutionary alternatives to traditional child-delivery methods. During birth, the child is delivered in a quiet room under dim light. Immediately the baby is placed on the mother's warm stomach, before the umbilical cord is severed. Gentle massage and immersing the baby in tepid water both serve to lessen the shock from the intrauterine period to the infant's first individual breaths. Sophisticated technology is thus not abandoned but placed in perspective, and the centrality of the new individual being ushered into the world is restored. The most eloquent testimonial to this humanistic rite of passage is the blissful smile on the infants delivered in this manner. Memories of the contorted anguish of moments-old infants have been replaced by a vision of a potentially ecstatic experience for mother and child. Such is one instance of our unbounded opportunities to improve the quality of life.

It would be possible to dismiss many such concepts as unscientific, prophetic, or impractical were it not for the fact that they are empirically testable. A fundamental aspect of the scientific method as applied to patient care is that the person is assessed to be in an initial state; then a treatment is performed upon or with that patient, and the same initial variables are once again assessed to determine if that intervention has had an effect on the desired system. This method in its most fundamental form can be applied to new approaches to health care as well as the exploration of higher states of consciousness. Many of these issues are addressed in an articulate manner in a recent article in the *Journal of the American Medical Association* entitled "What is a health care trial?" by Walter O. Spitzer, Alvan R. Feinstein, and David L. Sackett. These physicians distinguish two sorts of trials. A "Health Service Trial" is one in which the principal interventions which are assessed involve strictly medical aspects of health care, such as surgery, the pathological assessment, and other traditional medical factors. As an alternative, they propose the assessment term "Patient Care Trial," in which the patient's entire life history becomes the focus of the health-care system. In this approach the traditional variables are considered, but also included are factors such as psychology, sociology, and more personal data about the individual patient. They illustrate this difference by citing two well-designed and well-executed series of research studies concerning the effects of tonsillectomy and adenoidectomy on children. In both studies the principal treatment was identical, consisting of the removal of tonsils and adenoids. For the traditional therapeutic trial, the main variables which were assessed in one study were weight change, the frequency of attacks of sore throat, tonsillitis, colds, and several other factors (Mawson, Adlington, and Evans, 1967). Contrasted to this is the patient-care trial, in which the assessment included these variables plus psychological and sociological data, such as the use of medical service, days of confinement to bed, and absence from school. Essentially, this approach is concerned with how well the patient is performing, rather than how elegant was the surgical procedure. Emphasis is restored to the quality of a patient's life following an intervention. Examples of other data which might be included in a patient-care trial might consist of variables such as ability to return to work following heart attack, cost of hospitalization, and occupational disability. In concluding their article concerning health-care trials, the research team indicated that

> The omission of socio-personal data has made the results of many therapeutic trials difficult to interpret in clinical practice. For example, in studies of pharmaceutical agents for coronary artery disease, therapeutic accomplishment is often reported as a change in frequency of anginal attacks or in supplemental usage of nitroglycerin. A practicing physician may want to know, and is usually unable to find, any information about the occupational capacity, physical function, and general comfort of the treated patient. In the case of chemotherapy for advanced cancer, the customary emphasis is upon survival time and tumor magnitude. The patient's physical and emotional states are seldom described, and the assessments are rarely, if ever, concerned with the way the patient's family is affected in terms of energy, costs, and morale. Expensive or hazardous new forms of surgery, radiotherapy, are often tested in therapeutic trials that are sound in their scientific logic but sometimes depersonalized by restrictions in their scientific data.

It is evident from the work of Spitzer and other individuals in the area of prevention and health care that increased attention needs to be given to assessing the risks of therapeutic methods, the cost, and the benefits of therapy before any approach to either treatment or prevention of pathology can be assessed. Again, Spitzer and his colleagues note, "Many hypotheses about cellular, intracellular, and molecular phenomena can be scientificially tested in a sheltered laboratory environment and need not pertain to human reality. Hypotheses about the care of people, however, cannot receive a complete scientific investigation if the comparison of therapeutic efficacy does not include the total affects on the treatment of people." Despite the fact that modern medical technology has produced major advances in science and innovations in therapy, it has also created equally massive problems when medicine becomes increasingly dehumanized. By broadening the scope of scientific evidence to include psychological and sociological considerations, it may be possible to restore the therapeutic balance that serves the needs of both science and society. Approaches to preventive care need not be unscientific or untestable simply because they are also concerned with humanity.

In addition to the psychosomatic stress factors and the meditative stress-reduction techniques that have been discussed in this book, there are many other variables which should be considered in a program of preventive health care. Among these are exercise, diet, adequate sleep, and, most important, a philosophy of life in which an individual remains active and productive each day and does not feel limited in his creative capacities. The need for increased physical exercise is obvious all around us. According to recent research by psychologist Richard Driscoll, it is evident that physical activity enhances an individual's capacity to reduce stress (Driscoll, 1975). For his experimentation, Driscoll used forty minutes of stress treatment and a combination of physical exertion and positive imagery in order to determine its effect upon anxiety reduction. In this carefully controlled study, Driscoll tested high-anxiety students in six conditions, including one group that received standard systematic desensitization, another which received the exercise and imagery treatment, and a control group which received no treatment. After witnessing a sequence of stressful scenes, the group that succeeded in most effectively reducing their anxiety was a group that used the physical exertion of running in place plus positive imagery of themselves being calm and tranquil. According to Driscoll's findings, the combination of positive imagery and physical exertion reduced anxiety the most, with two positive-imagery groups reducing anxiety more than the equivalent group without positive imagery. According to Driscoll, the critical factor in his study was not increasing or decreasing stress during the anxiety scenes, but insuring that positive feelings followed immediately afterward. This experiment is a behavioral affirmation of the neurophysiological evidence that stress reduction does not mean reducing an individual's reactivity but simply giving him a means of recovering from a stressful incident.

A comprehensive discussion of both exercise and diet would require volumes. Basic advice concerning diet can be summarized simply as maximizing food rich in essential vitamins and minerals and reducing the amount of superfluous food high in sugars. An exercise program accompanying this dietary change need not be excessively rigorous; in fact, it is preferable that the individual spend two or three hours per week on an activity which he finds pleasurable. Such simple recommendations are often ignored. Research studies have demonstrated that many individuals live on a diet of less than two thousand calories per day. A diet which is rich in fats, sugar, sweets, snacks, drinks, cookies, and a whole host of modern convenience foods is certainly in excess of two thousand calories per day, but it does not provide the essential elements. With most modern eating habits, an intake of more than two thousand calories per day is necessary to satisfy the body's need for vitamins, minerals, and protein. Since the contemporary diet tends to have a predominance of foods with low contents of these vital substances, the risk of subtle malnutrition and psychosomatic disease increases. Clearly there is already a heightened awareness in society as a whole concerning exercise, nutrition, and their interaction. Jogging has become a commonplace event, and organic-food markets are increasingly evident. Such occurrences are not sufficient in and of themselves, but they are indicative of promising new efforts in preventive health care, in which each person needs to select appropriate means of health maintenance.

Addressing itself to these issues is a 1975 version of a report from the Department of Health, Education and Welfare entitled *Forward Plan for Health*. This report assesses the factors of individual behavior change and alteration of individual life styles as a way of preventing disease and improving the nation's health. Primary emphasis in this extensive report is on increased visibility of the notion of "health behavior," which has been receiving increasing attention among professionals. The authors of the publication emphasize that many major health problems are of a social, economic, and psychological nature, rather than purely organic. The report discusses smoking, drinking, overeating, and careless driving as well as other major health problems. Psychologist Steven Weiss, who is head of educational development of the National Heart and Lung Institute, raises another important question. Essentially, Weiss's concern is what strategies can be employed to raise general health consciousness without creating a nation of hypocondriacs, and to what extent non-medical means for health maintenance should be emphasized. Emphasis throughout this projective plan for the future of health care is upon psychosomatic factors in health and the restoration of individual initiative in health maintenance. Furthermore, Weiss raised an interesting challenge when he asks "to what extent do health care professionals create an atmosphere of dependency which negates personal responsibility?" (*Behavior Today*, October 6, 1975). Raising such issues is an essential prerequisite to formulating a system of preventive medicine. Inquiries such as these raise fundamental philosophical concerns as wells as pragmatic ones concerning the allocation of funding for future health-care systems.

Another recent report concerned with these issues appeared in *Science* on September 26, 1975, entitled "Preventive Medicine: Legislation Calls For Health Education." Leading off the article is the statement that "It appears that therapeutic medicine, as important as it is, may have reached a point of diminishing returns. The 12% to 15% increases that we are adding to our hundred billion dollar health care bill each year—even the portion that is not caused by inflation—apparently have only a marginal ability." This is the conclusion of the task force on consumer health education at the National Conference on Preventive Medicine in June of 1975. Dire projections such as this would do no more than compound the present difficult circumstances if there were not some promising alternatives in evidence. Preventive health care is not only a necessity but is a reality which can be achieved. The efficacy of preventive programs has been demonstrated in studies undertaken by Lester Breslow, Dean of the School of Public Health at the University of California, Los Angeles, and one of the leading proponents of preventive medicine (Culliton, 1975). For five and a half years, Breslow and his colleagues conducted a study of eleven thousand adults, and concluded that certain simple health habits are associated with a longer life. These health habits include three meals a day, with particular emphasis on breakfast; moderate exercise; seven or eight hours of sleep a night; no smoking; moderate weight; and moderate use of alcohol. According to Breslow's study, a 35-year old man who practices three or fewer of these health habits can expect to live to be sixty-seven, whereas a man who practices six or seven of them has a life expectancy of seventy-eight. With such deceptively simple practices, the return of eleven years of prolonged life expectancy certainly seems to be worth attempting. Surprisingly, many of the necessary life-style changes conducive to health maintenance are often this straightforward. The addition of stress reduction and meditative techniques could improve health maintenance even further.

Preventive health programs require planning and initially require governmental support, but the indications are that such programs can in fact save considerable suffering and money in the long run. An example of such a program is ongoing at the Los Angeles County Medical Center and is concerned with diabetic education. That program stresses that the individual should take responsibility for his own health and disseminates this information through pamphlets and life-style counseling by physicians and nurses. During the course of the program individuals learn how to take care of themselves by recognizing and learning to alleviate the dietary and psychosomatic stress factors which aggravate their condition. An evaluation of the program demonstrated that the number of diabetic comas among the educated patients dropped from 300 to 100 over a two-year period, emergency visits declined by half, and 2,300 clinic visits were avoided. The estimated savings from this program of education and stress reduction was 1.7 million dollars. Given the total expenditures on health-care systems in the United States, this figure is hardly significant, but it does point to the fact that health care and disease prevention through education of the individual are a reality and can in fact reduce costs and the burden of patient care on existing health-care systems.

To state the present predicament regarding health care most simply, people have been killing themselves by failing to alter self-destructive life-style habits. These habits invite premature disability and/or death. The psychosomatic factors recently discovered in cancer, heart disease, and other deadly disorders offer a definite possibility of extending our present models of holistic, preventive health care still further. One organization which is oriented toward the establishment of preventive health care is the Society of Prospective Medicine, located at the Methodist Hospital of Indiana in Indianapolis. They have initiated a four-stage program of patient care, with periodic assessments and improvements in their procedures. First, an individual is given an assessment of his ten-year chance of survival. This is derived from the administration of a "Health Hazard Appraisal" which compiles present risks to a person's health and estimates his future risks. Included in this assessment are such aspects of life style as weight, cigarette smoking, exercise, and an array of psychological factors. Health Hazard Appraisal systems are one of the most important tools now being developed for preventive medicine. Secondly, when this health hazard appraisal has been established, the practitioners initiate a series of preventive procedures, with the patient's cooperation, to reduce these risks. Third, they initiate a "health management program," in which other individuals are engaged to help the patient maintain health. This may require other members of the family, other health agencies, or a team of health practitioners. At the heart of this health-management effort is the patient's sense of responsibility for his state of health and the cooperation between the patient and health-care practitioners. Last, there is emphasis upon timing, since all of the risk factors cannot be changed simultaneously. As the practitioners of the society move an individual through a risk-education program, there is certain to be more than one problem area and certain to be more than one means of intervention. An individual entering this program is encouraged to move along one step at a time and is not asked to undergo any measures other than those which are reasonable and practical. Emphasis is upon pacing and critical timing as a means of alleviating that individual's predisposition toward disability or more severe psychosomatic disorders. Out of these four stages, a comprehensive profile of the patient is drawn, which makes it possible to detect dysfunctional systems in an individual before they lead to more severe pathology. Also, it helps to identify the most appropriate methods of intervention. Many of these interventions are straightforward modifications of excessive stress, reduction of excessive weight, or similar precursors of more severe disorders.

The Health Hazard Appraisal (Robbins, 1970) noted above was developed by the health-services research branch of the United States Public Health Services Hospital in Baltimore, Maryland, under the agency of the Department of Health, Education and Welfare. One of the doctors most active in the development and continued application of this technique is John W. Travis (1975). The Health Hazard Appraisal is set forth in a straightforward eight-page booklet which assesses an individual by means of a number of questions, ranging from a medical history, such as when the last chest X-ray or ECG was taken, and results of recent physical examinations, as well as a short life history. In addition to these variables, it also questions, for example, how many total miles a day a person drives and whether that person wears a seat belt. It assesses how many medications are being taken at the present time, the person's drinking habits, and a brief psychological profile intended to note such variables as disrupted sleep, potential depression, appetite alteration, and suicidal thoughts. Overall, the assessment attempts to address itself to medical, psychological, sociological, and behavioral characteristics that may predispose an individual toward a premature psychosomatic disorder or death.

Upon completion of this Health Hazard Appraisal, the booklet is computer-scored and is compared to the most recent Geller Table data to compare that individual to his own peer group to precisely determine potential risks to that person. Basically, the program is intended to determine whether the person is above or at an average in terms of risk as compared to his own peer. After this assessment is obtained, the individual is given a health-hazard age, which might be the same as or in excess of his chronological age. For example, an individual of age forty-five may in fact have a health-hazard age of fifty, in the sense that he is engaged in sufficient negative life-style activity at the present time to place him at the risk of a decreased longevity of five years. At this point the individual simply has the information that he is in fact living in a high-risk manner. Fortunately, the Health Hazard Appraisal proceeds one essential step further. Contained in the computer printout is a series of recommendations for reducing these health hazards and improving life expectancy. As one example, out of five of these excessive years of risk, four years might be recoverable for that person by altering his life style. Therefore, the computer breaks down the years which are recoverable and notes to the person the specific area in which he should alter his life style to decrease his health risk. Included in this risk-reduction procedure are such recommendations as start an exercise program, quit smoking, lose ten pounds, have a yearly physical checkup, or simply wear seat belts all the time while driving. Each of these factors is given a numerical value of how much could be regained by that person. Very often it is possible to regain or to decrease the risk by as much as 90 percent. This assessment is still in the preliminary stages, and research is ongoing.

Inherent in this appraisal system is the assumption that the etiology of a disorder is a long developmental process which can be altered toward increased health rather than disability. The developmental stages which underlie this appraisal system are strikingly parallel to the neurophysiological stress profile developed in earlier chapters. According to the Health Hazard Appraisal literature by John W. Travis and Susan E. Reichard, the natural history of a disease progresses in a series of seven stages. Stage one is no-risk category, which constitutes the early part of life, when an individual is least likely to have a severe disease. Stage two is termed an "at risk" category, when conditions such as age and environmental pollution exist, so that the individual may become increasingly vulnerable to a disease. At stage three a particular physical agent or psychosocial situation is present which is determined to cause excessive stress upon the person. During this third stage the patient might smoke or engage in another activity which is a precursor of disease and places that individual into a higher state of risk. The initial chapters of this book are a detailed examination of the neurophysiological and psychosocial factors which constitute this most critical stage. In stage four there are definite clinical signs that a disease is initiated, but the individual is as yet unaware of it. During stage five there are clear symptoms, such as pain, blood in the urine, or other unequivocal signs to the individual that lead him to his physician to seek help for his discomfort. At stage six there is disability, and at this point the individual has usually already sought medical care, since he is now in a stage of acute pain, disease, or disorder. If this stage is not adequately noted or treated, then the final stage, seven, results in death.

Practitioners do not usually concern themselves with the disease process until it reaches the signs characteristic of stage four. Clearly, there are two earlier stages to disease which can be considered in a preventive model. A Health Hazard Appraisal makes it possible to look at both stage two and three prior to the clear signs of disorder in order to initiate preventive techniques. During stage four, the traditional multiphasic testing in conjunction with a psychosocial appraisal can be of further use in introducing psychological, sociological, and situational variables into the traditional medical exam. Obviously, at stages five and six there is a pressing need for traditional medical care. Most important, detecting disease at early stages allows health practitioners to practice truly preventive medicine by giving ample warning both to the person and the practitioner before a disease becomes manifest.

According to the Health Hazard Appraisal brochure,

> ... a copy of the appraisal should be given to the patient with an adequate explanation of its meaning. If possible, the spouse should be present when a high risk individual is counseled, since investment on the spouse's part will help the patient make the needed changes. Compliance with the recommendations is difficult to achieve with many individuals, but the satisfaction of seeing some patients respond positively rewards the user of the HHA.

This is a sensitive acknowledgment of the fact that the individual should be considered in the context of his whole life style if these changes are to be initiated. As has been noted throughout previous discussions, these life style changes are not slight or superfluous alterations which can be easily undertaken. All too often, leisure time for relaxation or prevention receives negative reinforcement from the people around the individual. It appears as self-indulgence, narcissism, or very simply laziness on the part of the person. Many individuals in a credit-fixated society believe in the eternal tomorrow, when they will alter or rectify life styles that they know are destructive, paying their debts later. Unfortunately, the later comes all too soon, with increasing frequency, and it is incumbent upon individuals to rectify their life styles on an ongoing daily basis rather than wait for the elusive future. One of the clearest messages from all meditative systems ranging from Zen Buddhism to Michael Murphy's *Golf in the Kingdom* is to live in the now, to appreciate each moment in and of itself without reference to the past or anticipation of the future. This orientation of living in the immediate present as fully and completely as possible is one means of establishing an increased self-awareness which is at the heart of preventive care.

Certainly, the present research and clinical programs focusing upon holistic health care are more suggestive of a direction than an accomplished fact. Perhaps the most important aspects of this renewed concern over the etiology of disease and its prevention are the fundamental, philosophical revisions which are taking place in our healing paradigm. Central to this revision is the concept that all stages of health and disease are psychosomatic in etiology and duration, and in the healing process. Both psychological and medical factors should be considered in any system of holistic medicine. Among the organizations which are attempting to place this holistic orientation into practice is the Psychosomatic Medicine Center of Gladman Memorial Hospital in Berkeley, and the Institute for the Study of Humanistic Medicine in San Francisco (Remen, 1975).

Each system of healing is based upon certain philosophical assumptions. Before any significant progress can be made, these biases need to be examined and evaluated. One assumption is that if you are not sick then you are well. Although this statement does not necessarily hold true, it is one of the most commonly held definitions of health by laymen and professionals. In these terms, good medical care in and of itself should produce better health. Often this is not the case. In fact, unrealistic expectations by patients are found to be the single most common factor in malpractice suits (Green, J. A., 1976). If both patients and physicians clearly recognized that the doctor's function is simply to diagnose and treat disease, then the medical profession could again receive the respect and dignity which their work deserves. A second assumption is that agent "x" will produce health—this single factor being nutrition, self-knowledge, stress reduction, meditation, finding God, sex, health foods, or any single variable that an individual believes will lead to a state of health. Any single-factor approach to health and health maintenance is too narrow and constricted and is unlikely to be any more effective than the approaches focusing on single causes of disease. Another assumption in traditional approaches to healing is that health or disease is totally dependent upon outside factors, such as bacteria, radiation, crowding, poverty, and all of the other factors which have been clearly related to stress and stress-related disorders. Obviously, there can be no doubt that external issues such as these can in fact predispose individuals toward a state of ill health or can inhibit a person's normal progress of maintaining health and growth. However, one of the most important factors to note in the systems which have been discussed for stress alleviation is that the emphasis is upon internal volition in an individual as the ultimate point of resolution. It is quite evident that two individuals confronted with virtually the same external circumstances react quite differently. Individuals can become aware of and create an alternative to even the most pressing of external circumstances.

Another important concept to consider in traditional concepts of health is that of bacterial infection. That disease is caused by germs which infect an individual's system is a theory, but it is not a proven fact. Undoubtedly bacteria play a major role in the disease process, but it would be a gross mistake to assume that germs alone cause disease. Research indicates that when an individual is faced with a stressful situation there is a response which mobilizes him to action. When the person cannot adequately cope with the stress, the body breaks down at a weak point which is determined by an interaction of genetics, past experience, and other psychophysiological factors. In this model, illness is part of an adaptive response and is not produced by bacteria in a cause-and-effect manner. Rather, the bacterial infection may be activated at the weakest point of the system when the organism can no longer cope with the stress.

Complementary to these philosophical assumptions underlying traditional healing practices is another set of orientations which constitutes the basis of a holistic perspective. Drawing upon numerous sources, it is possible to formulate several criteria for a fundamental working definition for holistic medicine. First, all states of health and all disorders are considered to be psychosomatic. Given this fundamental orientation, patients are more than culture plates bearing a particular disease, and healing involves far more than removing the overt manifestations of a disease process. Furthermore, the clinician cannot limit his expertise to biomedical technology, since a psychosomatic orientation requires treating the whole person through an integrated approach. Through considering the psychosomatic process in man, it becomes possible to consider the extent to which an individual can exert volition in the course of health and disease.

Second, and related to this, is that each individual is unique and represents a complex interaction of body, mind, and spirit. According to Stuart Miller and his colleagues at the Institute for the Study of Humanistic Medicine, "Illness can best be understood as a disturbance within the dynamic balance of these relationships" (Remen, 1975; Miller et. al.,

1975). This observation supports the concept that states of health exist when these elements function in harmony and disorders are evident when stress disrupts this complex balance. Third is the fact that the patient and the health practitioners share the responsibility for the healing process. Through this mutual interaction, the clinician's responsibility is to maximize the psychological and biological conditions to insure the patient's health maintenance or to promote the healing process. The patient's responsibility is to become an active participant, exercising his volition in regard to his own health, life style, and further development.

Growing out of this third point is a fourth aspect of holistic medicine: health care is not exclusively the province or responsibility of orthodox medicine. Diagnosis and treatment of pathology is obviously a medical concern, but the creation of a life style conducive to health maintenance and personal fulfillment is beyond the limited scope of pathology correction. Orthodox medicine is only one part of this process. It is increasingly evident that though people can be assisted medically, their health or sense of well-being is not necessarily enhanced. The physician and the medical-care institution are concerned only with attempting to remove the overt manifestations of disease. What is frequently ignored is that the individual's psychosocial environment may be more central to his distress than the symptom itself. Perhaps the mechanism of classical "symptom substitution" may be due to the very factor that one symptom or one disease can in fact be alleviated but when the underlying problem remains untreated or unexamined, it is quite likely that the person will manifest a further symptom of the disease process. What are healthy solutions and what constitutes the nature of health are the most pressing issues confronting the healing professions today. Working within a holistic approach to healing are professionals who have skills related to health in an essential but often unacknowledged manner. Among these practices are instructors of various physical exercises ranging from gymnastics to Tai

Chi, nutritional counselors, meditation teachers, and all other instructors of skills intended to enhance the quality of an individual's life. Health care is an area requiring mutual interaction and enrichment among these professions.

A fifth characteristic of holistic medicine is seeing illness as a creative opportunity for the patient to learn more about himself and his fundamental values. Illness needs to be viewed within the context of the entire life span of the patient. Identical disorders need to be considered quite differently in view of the person's psychological state, age, socioeconomic status, familial context, and many other factors which can govern the course of both the disorder and the healing process. Confrontations with pain, disease, and the possibility of death can be profoundly useful. Sages of all civilizations have noted that pain is a great teacher, since it informs the person that he must change his life and grow. A holistic approach helps patients tolerate the psychological dimensions of pain and use it creatively for their growth. Generally, the thrust of contemporary medicine is toward the annihilation and denial of pain, disease, and death. Bellicose approaches to disease are not sufficiently broad to constitute the whole of the healing process. Patients can and do emerge from psychological and physical disorders with increased rather than impaired functioning. It is incumbent upon the healing professions to examine these instances in order to help others reach such an outcome. For the present time, all that being healthy means is that a person will become ill or die within the average number of years for his peer group. Due to this emphasis upon pathology and mortality, there is virtually no systematic information on longevity, spontaneous remission, people with marked psychosomatic regulation, or concerning the individual who dies beneficently after a century of life. Determining the parameters of health by examining pathology is rather like peering through the wrong end of a telescope. Researchers and clinicians need to consider healthy, well-functioning individuals from many realms of life in order to initiate a true profile of health and well-being. There is a pressing need to know much of health as is already known of pathology.

A sixth and final consideration of holistic medicine is that the practitioner must come to know himself as a human being. Anyone in a healing profession must become acquainted with his own emotional nature, his personality conflicts, his strengths and weaknesses, and generally to engage in a process of self-exploration. Treating only specialized disease, as many practitioners do, and performing the same routine on an ongoing basis is certainly not satisfying to the human spirit. Specialization seems to demand such total involvement that many clinicians work too hard to fulfull their role, and die at an increasingly young age (Miller, et al., 1975). It is hoped that the practice of preventive medicine which focuses on the entire person will also help practitioners themselves become more fulfilled in their lives.

Inevitably, even in a system of preventive care, the factors of aging and death must be considered. Recently, our society has been obliged to begin an agonizing reappraisal of its private attitudes and public policies toward aging and death. Individuals over the age of sixty-five are living longer and enjoying better health care than ever before. However, there has been a tendency for isolation and decreased function on their part and an agonizing boredom. Aging is an irreversible process, but it is not inevitable for the individual to suffer from the degenerative diseases which can make advanced age an onerous time of life. It is possible to live fully throughout life, and if that is accomplished, death need not be feared. An ancient anecdote of Zen literature is most illustrative here. A novitiate asked a Zen master, "What is death?" and the master responded, "I do not know." With surprise, the initiate responded, "But you are a Zen master." To this, the master responded, "Yes, but I am not a dead Zen master." It seems that our preoccupation with disease and death is largely contingent upon misunderstanding and lack of education, and a fear more of helplessness than of death itself. For individuals who live a full life, death need not become a dreaded specter, but rather another stage in the evolution of life itself.

To see beyond the constraints of disease and death itself is to "follow the path of the heart," according to the teachings of Don Juan. Each individual who embarks upon that path is an active participant in the profound transformation of human consciousness that is now underway. Holistic approaches to healing are one major aspect of this transformation. The sixteenth-century physician and alchemist Paracelsus invoked the power of dreams, light from a clear morning sky, and the patient's visualizations as adjuncts to his medical interventions. Paracelsus envisioned the vital role of such factors and the influence of symbolic visualization in a healing process which involved body, mind and spirit. Many innovations in the healing profession and in basic research into the nature of consciousness itself have rediscovered this ancient wisdom. Prior to Leboyer's humanistic approach to childbirth, infants were brought into the world harshly, presaging immersion in an environment which had to be subdued and conquered. In an age that is discovering the unitary quality of Spaceship Earth and the interdependence of all living systems, perhaps it is altogether timely that our newborns are brought gently into a world where they will learn respect and love for themselves, others, and the entire planet.

Bibliography

ABESHOUSE, B. S., and I. SCHERLIS. "Spontaneous disappearance or retrogression of bladder neoplasm: Review of the literature and report of three cases." *Urol. Cutan. Rev.,* 55 (1951): 1.

AKISHIGE, Y., ed. *Psychological Studies on Zen.* Tokyo: Zen Institute of Komazawa University, 1970.

ALEXANDER, F. *Psychosomatic Medicine.* New York: W. W. Norton, 1950.

ALLEN, E. P. "Malignant melanoma, spontaneous regression after pregnancy." *Brit. Med. J.,* 2 (1955): 1067.

ALLISON, J. "Respiration changes during transcendental meditation." *Lancet,* 1 (1970): 833–34.

ALVAREZ, W. C. "The spontaneous regression of cancer." *Geriatrics,* 22 (September 1967): 89–90.

AMKRAUT, A., and G. F. SOLOMON. "From the symbolic stimulus to the pathophysiologic response: Immune mechanisms." *Int. J. of Psychiatry in Medicine,* 5, No. 4 (1975): 541–63.

ANAND, B. K., et al. "Studies on Shri Ramananda Yogi during his stay in an air-tight box." *Indian J. Med. Res.,* 49 (1961): 82–89.

————, G. S. CHHINA, and B. SINGH. "Some aspects of electroencephalographic studies in yogis." *Electroencephalography and Clinical Neurophysiology*, 13 (1961): 452–56. Reprinted in Charles Tart, ed., *Altered States of Consciousness*. New York: John Wiley & Sons, 1969, pp. 503–506.

ANDERVONT, H. B. "Influence of environment on mammary cancer in mice." *J. Nat. Cancer Inst.*, 4 (1944): 579–81.

APPLEY, M.H.E., and R. TRUMBULL. *Psychological Stress*. New York: Appleton-Century-Crofts, 1967.

ASSAGIOLI, R. *Psychosynthesis*. New York: Viking Press, 1965.

AX, A. "Electric Therapy." Paper presented to the Biofeedback Research Society, Clayton, Missouri, October 25, 1971.

BACON, C. L., R. RENNECKER, and M. CUTLER. "A psychosomatic survey of cancer of the breast." *Psychosom. Med.*, 14 (1952): 453–60.

BADGLEY, C. E., and M. BATTS, JR. "Osteogenic sarcoma: An analysis of eighty cases." *Arch. Surg.*, 43 (1941): 541.

BAGCHI, B. K. and M. A. WENGER. "Electrophysiological correlates of some Yogi exercises." In L. van Bagaert and J. Radermecker, eds., *Electroencephalography, Clinical Neurophysiology and Epilepsy*, Vol. 3 of *The First International Congress of Neurological Sciences*. London: Pergamon, 1959.

BAHNSON, C. B., and M. B. BAHNSON. "The role of ego defenses: Denial and repression in the etiology of malignant neoplasm." *Ann. N.Y. Acad. Sci.*, 125, 3 (1966): 827.

————. "Ego defenses in cancer patients." *Ann. N.Y. Acad. Sci.*, 164 (1969): 546–59.

BAKER, H. W. "Spontaneous regression of malignant melanoma." *Amer. Surgeon*, 30 (1964): 825–31.

BAKKER, G. B., and R. M. LEVENSON. "Determinants of Angina Pectoris." *Psychosomatic Medicine*, 29 (1967): 621–33.

BARDAWIL, W. A., and B. L. TOY. "The natural history of

choriocarcinoma: Problems of immunity and spontaneous regression." *Ann. N.Y. Acad. Sci.*, 80 (1959): 197.

BARTLEY, O., and G. T. HULTQUIST. "Spontaneous regression of hypernephromas." *Acta Path. Microbiol. Scand.*, 27 (1950): 448.

BATESON, G. *Steps to an Ecology of Mind.* New York: Ballantine Books, 1972.

BECKER, R. O. "Augmentation of regenerative healing in man: A possible alternative to prosthetic implantation." *Clin. Orthop.*, 83 (March–April 1972): 255–62.

———. "The basic biological data transmission influenced by electrical forces." *Ann. N.Y. Acad. Sci.* 238 (1974): 236–41.

——— and J. A. Spadaro. "Electrical stimulation of partial limb regeneration in mammals." *Bull. N.Y. Acad. Med.*, 48 (May 1972): 627–41.

BEECHER, H. K. "The powerful placebo." *J.A.M.A.*, 159 (1955): 1602–1606.

BENSON, H., J. F. BEARY, and M. P. CAROL. "The relaxation response." *Psychiatry*, 37 (1974): 37–46.

BENSON, H., and H. D. EPSTEIN. "The placebo effect: A neglected asset in the care of patients." *J.A.M.A.*, 232 (1975): 12.

BENSON, H., B. A. ROSNER, and B. R. MARZETTA. "Decreased systolic blood pressure in hypertensive subjects who practice meditation." *Journal of Clinical Investigation*, 52 (1973): 80.

BENSON, H., D. SHAPIRO, B. TURSKY, and G. E. SCHWARTZ. "Decreased systolic blood pressure through operant conditioning techniques in patients with essential hypertension." *Science*, 173 (1971): 740.

BENSON, H., and R. K. WALLACE. "Decreased drug abuse with transcendental meditation: A study of 1862 subjects." In C.J.D. Zarafonetis, ed., *Drug Abuse: Proceedings of the International Conference*. Philadelphia: Lea and Febiger, 1972.

BESWICK, I. P., and G. QVIST. "Spontaneous regression of cancer." *Brit. Med. J.*, 2 (1963): 930.

BIERMAN, E. O. "Spontaneous regression of malignant disease." *J.A.M.A.*, 170 (1959): 1842.

BLACKWELL, B. "Minor tranquilizers, misuse or overuse?" *Psychosomatics*, 16 (January–February 1975): 28–31.

BLADES, B., and R. G. McCORKE, JR. "A case of spontaneous regression of an untreated bronchiogenic carcinoma." *J. Thorac. Cardiov. Surg.*, 27 (1954): 415.

BLOOM, H.J.G. "The natural history of untreated breast cancer." *Ann. N.Y. Acad. Sci.*, 114 (1964): 747.

BLOOMFIELD, H., M. CAIN, and R. JAFFE. *TM: Discovering Inner Energy and Overcoming Stress*. New York: Delacorte Press, 1975.

BLUMBERG, E. T., R. M. WEST, and F. W. ELLIS, "A possible relationship between psychological factors and human cancer." *Psychosom. Med.*, 16 (1954): 277–90.

BONIUK, M., and L. T. GIRARD. "Spontaneous regression of bilateral retinoblastoma." *Trans. Amer. Acad. Ophthal. Otolaryng.*, 73 (1969): 194–98.

BOOKER, H. E., R. T. RUBOW, and P. J. COLEMAN. "Simplified feedback in neuromuscular retraining: An automated approach using electromyographic signals." *Archives of Physical Medicine and Rehabilitation* (1969): 615–21.

BOUDREAU, L. "Transcendental meditation and yoga as reciprocal inhibitors." *Journal of Behavior Therapy and Experimental Psychiatry*, 3 (1972): 97–98.

BOYD, W. "The spontaneous regression of cancer." *J. Canad. Assn. Radiol.*, 8 (1957): 45, 63.

———. *The Spontaneous Regression of Cancer*. Springfield, Ill.: Charles C. Thomas, 1966.

BRENER, J., and R. A. KLEINMAN. "Learned control of decreases in systolic blood pressure." *Nature*, 226 (1970): 1063.

BRETTAUER, J. "Spontaneous cures of carcinoma." *Amer. J. Obstet.*, 57 (1908): 405–406.

BRINDLE, J. M. "Spontaneous regression of cancer." *Brit. Med. J.*, 2 (1963): 1132.

BROSSE, T. "A psychophysiological study." *Main Currents in Modern Thought*, 4 (1946): 77–84.

BROWN, B. "Awareness of EEG-subjective activity relationships detected within a closed feedback system." *Psychophysiology*, 7 (1970): 451–68.

————. *New Mind, New Body*. New York: Harper and Row, 1975.

BROZEK, J., A. KEYS, and H. BLACKBURN. "Personality differences between potential coronary and non-coronary subjects." *Annals of the New York Academy of Sciences*, 134 (1966): 1057–64.

BRUDNY, H., B. B. GRYNBAUM, and J. KOREIN. "New therapeutic modality for treatment of spasmatic torticollis." *Archives of Physical Medicine and Rehabilitation*, 54 (1973): 575.

BRUNSCHWIG, A. "Spontaneous regression of cancer." *Surgery*, 53 (1963): 423.

BUDZYNSKI, T. H., and K. PEFFER. "Twilight state learning: The presentation of learning material during a biofeedback-produced altered state." *Proceedings of the Biofeedback Research Society*. Denver: Biofeedback Research Society, 1974.

BUDZYNSKI, T. H., J. M. STOYVA, and C. ADLER. "Feedback-induced muscle relaxation: Application to tension headache." *Journal of Behavior Therapy and Experimental Psychiatry*, 1 (1970): 205–11.

BUTLER, B. "The use of hypnosis in the care of the cancer patient." *Cancer*, 7 (1954): 1–14.

CAFFREY, B. "Factors involving interpersonal and psychological characteristics: A review of empirical findings." *Milbank Memorial Fund Quarterly*, 45 (1967): 119–39, Part 2.

CANNON, W. B. *The Wisdom of the Body*. New York: W. W. Norton, 1932.

CAPLAN, R. D. "Organizational stress and individual strain: A social-psychological study of risk factors in coronary heart disease among administrators, engineers, and scientists." University of Michigan Ph.D. dissertation. *Dissertation Abstracts International*, May 1972, Vol. 32 (11-B), 6706–6707.

————. "Job demands and worker health: Main effects and occupational differences." Institute for Social Research, Box 1248, Ann Arbor, Mich. 48106, 1975.

————, and J. R. FRENCH, JR. "Physiological responses to work load: An exploratory study." Unpublished manuscript. Institute for Social Research, Box 1248, Ann Arbor, Mich. 48106.

CASTANEDA, C. *Tales of Power*. New York: Simon and Schuster, 1974.

CHAMBERLAIN, D. "Spontaneous disappearance of carcinoma." *Brit. Med. J.*, 1 (1938): 508–509.

"Changing Health Directions." *Behavior Today*, June 30, 1975.

CHARALAMBIDIS, P. H., and W. B. PATTERSON. "A clinical study of 250 patients with malignant melanoma." *Surg. Gynec. Obstet.*, 115 (1962): 333.

CHAUCHARD, P. *The Brain*. Translated by David Noakes. New York: Grove Press, 1962.

COHEN, L. "Immunity and resistance in clinical cancer." *South African M.J.*, 30 (1956): 161–67.

CORSON, S. A. "Psychological stress and target tissue." In E. M. Weyer and H. Hutchins, eds., *Psychophysiological Aspects of Cancer*. New York: New York Academy of Sciences, 1966, pp. 890–915.

CULLITON, B. J. "Preventive Medicine: Legislation calls for health education." *Science*, 189 (1975).

CUTLER, M. "The nature of the cancer process in relation to a possible psychosomatic influence." In J. A. Generelli and F. J. Kirkner, eds., *The Psychological Variables in Human Cancer*. Berkeley: University of California Press, 1954.

CZACZKES, J. W., and F. DREYFUSS. "Blood cholesterol and uric acid of healthy medical students under stress of an examination." *Archives of Internal Medicine,* 103 (1959): 708–11.

DAO, T. L. "Regression of pulmonary metastases of a breast cancer." *A.M.A. Arch. Surg.,* 84 (1962): 574.

DATEY, K. K., S. M. KESHMUKH, D. P. DALVI, and S. L. VINEKAR. "Shavassan, a yogic exercise in the management of hypertension." *Angiology,* 20 (1969): 325–33.

DECOURCY, J. L. "Spontaneous regression of cancer." *J. of Med.,* 14 (1933): 141.

DETRY, J. M. R. *Exercise Testing and Training in Coronary Heart Disease.* Baltimore: Williams and Wilkins, 1973.

DODGE, D. L., and W. T. MARTIN. *Social Stress and Illness.* Notre Dame, Ind.: University of Notre Dame Press, 1970.

DOHRENWEND, B. S., and B. P. DOHRENWEND, eds. *Stressful Life Events: Their Nature and Effects.* New York: Wiley-Interscience, 1974.

DOMASH, L., J. FARROW, and D. ORMÉ-JOHNSON. *Scientific Research on Transcendental Meditation.* Los Angeles: Maharishi International University, 1976.

Dorland's Illustrated Medical Dictionary. Philadelphia: W. B. Saunders Co., 1974.

DRISCOLL, R. "Exertion therapy." *Behavior Today,* 6, No. 6 (1975).

DUBOS, R. J. *Man Adapting.* New Haven: Yale Univ. Press, 1965.

———. "Medicine's Living History." *Medical World News* (May 5, 1975): 77–85.

DUHL, L. J. "The process of re-creation—the health of the 'I' and the 'us'." Unpublished paper. University of California, Berkeley: 1975.

DUNBAR, F. *Emotions and Bodily Changes.* New York: Columbia University Press, 1954.

———. *Psychosomatic Diagnosis.* New York: Harper and Row, 1954.

DUNPHY, J. E. "Some observations on the natural behavior of cancer in man." *New Eng. J. Med.*, 242 (1950): 167.

EASSON, E. C. "False notion: Cancer = incurable." *UNESCO Courier*, 23 (1970): 23–26.

ECCLES, J. C. *Facing Reality: Philosophical Adventures by a Brain Scientist.* New York: Springer-Verlag, 1970.

ELIASBERG, W. G. "Psychotherapy in cancer patients." *J.A.M.A.*, 147 (1951): 525–26.

ENGEL, G. L. "Studies in ulcerative colitis: The nature of the psychologic process." *Am. J. of Med.*, 19 (1955): 231.

EVANS, E. A. *A Psychological Study of Cancer.* New York: Langmans, 1928.

EVERSAUL, G. A. "Psycho-physiology training and the behavioral treatment of premature ejaculation: Preliminary findings." *Proceedings of the Biofeedback Research Society.* Denver: Biofeedback Research Society, 1975.

EVERSON, T. C. "Spontaneous regression of cancer." *Conn. Med.*, 22 (1958): 637–43.

————. "Spontaneous regression of cancer." *Ann. N.Y. Acad. Sci.*, 114 (1964): 721–35.

————. "Spontaneous regression of cancer." *Progr. Clin. Cancer*, 3 (1967): 79–95.

———— and W. H. COLE. "Spontaneous regression of cancer: Preliminary report." *Ann. Surg.*, 144 (1956): 366.

————. "Spontaneous regression of malignant disease." Guest Editorial, *J.A.M.A.*, 169 (1959): 1758.

————. *Spontaneous Regression of Cancer.* Philadelphia: W. B. Saunders Co., 1966.

Exercise Testing and Exercise Training in Coronary Heart Disease. New York: Academic Press, 1973.

FERGUSON, P. C., and J. GOWAN. "The influence of transcendental meditation on aggression, anxiety, depression, neuroticism, and self-actualization." Unpublished manuscript, 1973.

FIER, B. "Recession is causing dire illness." *Moneysworth*, June 23, 1975.

FINN, F., R. MULCAHY, and E. F. O'DOHERTY. "The psychological assessment of patients with coronary heart disease: A preliminary communication." *Irish Journal of Medical Science,* 6 (1966): 399–404.

FISHER, S., and S. E. CLEVELAND. "Relationship of body image to site of cancer." *Psychosom. Med.,* 18 (1956): 304–309.

FOLKINS, C. H. "Temporal factors and the cognitive mediators of stress reactions." *Journal of Personality and Social Psychology,* 14 (1970): 173–84.

FOOT, N. C., G. A. HUMPHREYS, and W. F. WHITMORE, "Renal tumors: Pathology and prognosis in 295 cases." *J. Urol.,* 66 (1951): 190.

FORKNER, C. E. "Spontaneous remission and reported cures of leukemia." *Chinese Med. J.,* 52 (1937): 1–8.

FRANKENHAESER, M. "Looking at stress." *Behavior Today,* 6, No. 23 (June 1975): 499.

FRENCH, J. D. "The reticular formation." *Scientific American,* May 1957, pp. 2–8.

―――――, C. S. LEEB, S. L. FAHRION, T. LAW, and E. W. JECHT. "Self-induced scrotal hyperthemia in man: A preliminary report." Paper presented at the Biofeedback Research Society Meeting, Boston, November 1972.

FRIEDMAN, M., and R. H. ROSENMAN. "Type A behavior pattern: Its association with coronary heart disease." *Annals of Clinical Research,* 3 (1971): 300–312.

―――――. *Type A Behavior and Your Heart.* New York: Alfred A. Knopf, 1974.

―――――― and V. CARROLL. "Changes in the serum cholesterol and blood clotting time in men subjected to cyclic variation of occupational stress." *Circulation,* 18 (1958): 852–61.

FRIEDMAN, S. B., and L. A. GLASGOW. "Psychologic factors and resistance to infectious disease." *Ped. Cl. N. Amer.,* 13 (1966): 315–35.

―――――― and R. ADLER. "Psychosocial factors modifying host resistance to experimental infections." *Ann. N.Y. Acad. Sci.,* 164 (1969): 381–92.

FULLERTON, J. M., and R. D. HILL. "Spontaneous regression of cancer." *Brit. Med. J.*, 2 (1963): 1589.

FUNKENSTEIN, D. H., S. B. KING, and M. DROLETTE. *Mastery of Stress.* Cambridge, Mass.: Harvard University Press, 1957.

GALIN, D. "Implications for psychiatry of left and right cerebral specialization." *Arch. Gen. Psych.*, 31 (1974): 572–83.

GALLAGHER, R. E., and R. C. GALLO. "Type C RNA tumor virus isolated from cultured human acute myelogenous leukemia cells." *Science*, 187 (1975): 350–53.

GANNON, L., and R. A. STERNBACH. "Alpha enhancement as a treatment for pain: A case study." In J. Stoyva et al., eds., *Biofeedback and Self-control.* Chicago: Aldine-Atherton, 1971.

GARB, S. "Neglected approaches to cancer." *Saturday Review*, June 1, 1968.

GARDNER, E. *Fundamentals of Neurology.* Philadelphia: W. B. Saunders Co., 1968.

GATTOZZI, A. A. "Program reports on biofeedback." *N.I.M.H. Program Reports*, 5 (December 1971): 291–388.

GAYLORD, H. R., and G.H.A. CLOWES. "On spontaneous cure of cancer." *Surg. Gynec. Obstet.*, 2 (1906): 633–58.

GELLHORN, E., and G. N. LOOFBOURROW. *Emotions and Emotional Disorders.* New York: Harper and Row, 1963.

GLEMSER, B. *Man Against Cancer.* New York: Funk & Wagnalls, 1969.

GODFREY, F. "Spontaneous cure for cancer." *Brit. Med. J.*, 4 (1910): 2027.

GOLDFARB, O., J. DRIESEN, and D. COLE. "Psychophysiologic aspects of malignancy." *Amer. J. Psychiat.*, 123 (June 1967): 1545–51.

GOLEMAN, D. "Meditation and consciousness: An Asian approach to mental health." *American Journal of Psychotherapy*, 1975.

———— and G. E. SCHWARTZ. "Meditation as an intervention in stress reactivity." *J. of Consulting and Clinical Psychology*, 44, no. 3 (1976): 456–466.

GORDON-TAYLOR, G. "The incomputable factor in cancer prognosis." *Brit. Med. J.*, 1 (1959): 455–62.

GORMAN, P., and J. KAMIYA. "Voluntary control of stomach pH." Research note presented at the Biofeedback Research Society Meeting, Boston, November 1972.

GORTON, B. "Autogenic Training." *Amer. J. Clin. Hypn.*, 2 (1959): 31–41.

GOULD, A. P. "Cancer." *Lancet*, 2 (1910): 1665.

GREDEN, J. F. "The caffeine crazies." *Human Behavior*, April 1975.

GREEN, A. M. "Brainwave training, imagery, creativity and integrative experiences." *Proceedings of the Biofeedback Research Society*. Denver: Biofeedback Research Society, 1974.

GREEN, E. E., A. M. GREEN, and E. D. WALTERS. "Voluntary control of internal states: Psychological and physiological." *Journal of Transpersonal Psychology*, 2 (1970): 1–26.

————. "Biofeedback for mind-body regulation: Healing and creativity." Paper presented at symposium on "The Varieties of Healing Experience," De Anza College, Cupertino, California, 1971.

GREEN, H. N. "An immunological concept of cancer: A preliminary report." *Brit. Med. J.*, 2 (1954): 1974.

GREEN, J. A. "Medicine and the responsibility for health." San Francisco: unpublished paper, 1976.

GREENE, W. A., JR. "The psychosocial setting of the development of leukemia and lymphoma." In E. M. Weyer and H. Hutchins, eds., *Psychophysiological Aspects of Cancer*. New York: New York Academy of Sciences, 1966, pp. 794–801.

————and MILLER, G. "Psychological factors and reticuloendothelial disease. IV. Observations on a group of children and adolescents with leukemia. An interpretation of

334   BIBLIOGRAPHY

disease development in terms of the mother-child unit."
Psychosom. Med., 20 (1958): 124–44.

GREENE, W. A., L. YOUNG, and S. N. SWISHER. "Psychological factors and reticuloendothelial disease. II. Observations on a group of women with lymphomas and leukemias." *Psychosom. Med.*, 18 (1956): 284–303.

GRUNDY, S. M., and A. C. GRIFFIN. "Effects of periodic mental stress on serum cholesterol levels." *Circulation*, 19 (1959): 496–98.

GUNDERSON, E. K., and R. H. RAHE, eds. *Life Stress and Illness.* Springfield, Ill.: Charles C. Thomas, 1974.

GUYTON, A. C. *Textbook of Medical Physiology.* 4th ed. Philadelphia: W. B. Saunders Co., 1971.

HAMPTON, J., C. STOUT, E. BRANDT, and S. WOLF. "Prevalence of myocardial infarction and reinfarction and related diseases in an Italian American community." *J. Lab. & Clin. Med.*, 61 (1964): 866.

HANDLEY, W. S. "The natural cure of cancer." *Brit. Med. J.*, 1 (1909): 582–88

HARDYCK, C. D., L. F. PETINOVICH, and D. W. ELLSWORTH. "Feedback of speech muscle activity during silent reading: Rapid extinction." *Science*, 154 (1966): 1467–68.

HARNETT, W. L. "The relation between delay in treatment of cancer and survival rate." *Brit. J. Cancer*, 7 (1953): 19.

HERSHKOWITZ, M. "Disappearance of metastases." *J.A.M.A.*, 170 (1959): 996.

HESS, W. R. *Functional Organization of the Diencephalon.* New York: Grune and Stratton, 1957.

HOFFMAN, F. C. *The Mortality from Cancer Throughout the World.* Newark, N.J.: Prudential Press, 1915.

HOLMES, T. H., and M. MASUDA. "Life change and illness susceptibility, separation and depression." *A.A.A.S.* (1973): 161–86.

HOLMES, T. H., and R. H. RAHE. "Schedule of Recent Experience (SRE)." Department of Psychiatry, University of Washington School of Medicine, 1967.

———— "The social readjustment rating scale." *J. Psycho-somatic Res.*, 11 (1967): 213–18.

HOLMES, T. S., and T. H. HOLMES. "Short-term intrusions into the life style routine." *J. Psychosomatic Res.*, 14 (1970): 121–32.

HOMBURGER, F. *The Biological Basis of Cancer Management.* New York: Harper and Row, Hoeber Medical Division, 1957.

HONSBERGER, R., and A. F. WILSON. "Transcendental meditation in treating asthma." *Respiratory Therapy: The Journal of Inhalation Technology,* 3 (1973): 79–81.

HOUSE, J. "Occupational stress and coronary heart disease: A review and theoretical orientation." In O'Toole, ed., *Work and the Quality of Life.* Cambridge, Mass.: M.I.T. Press, 1974.

HOXWORTH, P. I., and J. B. HAMBLETI. "Unexplained twelve year survival after metastatic carcinoma of the colon." *Amer. J. Surg.*, 105 (1963): 126.

HUGGINS, C. "Endocrine-induced regression of cancer." Address of Dec. 13, 1966. *Science,* 156 (1967): 1050–54.

HUTSCHNECKER, A. *The Will to Live.* New York: Thomas Y. Crowell, 1953.

ILLICH, I. *Medical Nemesis: The Expropriation of Health.* New York: Pantheon Books, 1976.

INSEL, P. M., and J. CHADWICK. "Work stress and cardiovascular disease: A social ecological view." *Western Journal of Medicine,* 1974.

JACOBSEN, O. *Heredity in Breast Cancer.* London: H. K. Lewis & Co., 1946.

JACOBSON, E. *Progressive Relaxation.* 2nd ed. Chicago: Chicago Press, 1938.

————. *Modern Treatment of Tense Patients.* Springfield, Ill.: Charles C. Thomas, 1970.

JENKINS, G. D. "Regression of pulmonary metastasis following nephrectomy for hypernephroma: Eight year follow-up." *J. Urol.*, 82 (1959): 37.

————. "Final report—regression of pulmonary metastases following nephrectomy for hypernephroma: 13 year follow-up." *J. Urol.*, 94 (1965): 99–100.

JOHNSON, H. E., and W. H. GARTON. "A practical method of muscle reeducation in hemiplegia: Electromyographic facilitation and conditioning." Unpublished manuscript. Casa Colina Hospital for Rehabilitative Medicine, Pomona, Calif., 1973.

KAMIYA, J. "Conscious control of brain waves." *Psychology Today*, 1 (1968): 57–60.

————. "Operant control of the EEG alpha rhythm and some of its reported effects on consciousness." In C. T. Tart, ed., *Altered States of Consciousness*. New York: Wiley & Sons, 1969.

KASAMATSU, A., and T. HIRAI, "Studies of EEG's of expert Zen meditators." *Folia Psychiatrica Neurologica Japonica*, 28 (1966): 315.

KATZ, D., and R. L. KAHN. *The Social Psychology of Organizations*. New York: Wiley & Sons, 1966.

KEITH, R. A., B. LOWN, and F. J. STARE. "Coronary heart disease and behavior patterns: An examination of method." *Psychosomatic Medicine*, 27 (1965): 424–33.

KESSEL, L. "Spontaneous disappearance of bilateral pulmonary metastases." *J.A.M.A.*, 169 (1959): 1737.

KEYS, A., ed. "Coronary heart disease in seven countries." *Circulation*, 1 (1970): 41.

KIEV, ARI. *Magic, Faith, and Healing*. New York: The Free Press, 1969.

KISSEN, D. M. "The significance of personality in lung cancer in men." In E. M. Weyer and H. Hutchins, eds., *Psychophysiological Aspects of Cancer*. New York: New York Academy of Sciences, 1966, pp. 933–45.

————. "Psychosocial factors, personality and lung cancer in men aged 55–64." *Brit. J. Med. Psychol.*, 40 (1967): 29.

———— R. I. F. BROWN, and M. KISSEN. "A further report

on personality and psychosocial factors in lung cancer."
Ann. N.Y. Acad. Sci., 164 (1969): 535–45.

———— and H. J. EYSENCK. "Personality in male lung
cancer patients." *J. Psychosom. Res.* 6 (1962): 123–27.

KIVETSKY, R. E., N. M. TURKEVICH, and K. P. BALITSKY. "On
the psychophysiological mechanism of the organism's
resistance to tumor growth." In E. M. Weyer and H.
Hutchins, eds., *Psychophysiological Aspects of Cancer*.
New York: New York Academy of Sciences, 1966, pp.
933–45.

KLOPFER, B. "Psychological variables in human cancer."
Journal of Projective Techniques, 21 (1957): 331–40.

KORNEVA, E. A., and L. M. KHAI, "Effects of destruction of
hypothalamic areas on immunogenesis." *Fizio. Zh. SRR.
Sechenov*, 49 (1963): 42.

KOWAL, S. J. "Emotions as a cause of cancer: Eighteenth
and nineteenth century contributions." *Psychoanalyt.
Rev.*, 42 (1955): 217–27.

KRAUT, A. I. "A study of role conflicts and their relationships
to job satisfaction, tension, and performance." University
of Michigan Ph.D dissertation. University Microfilms,
No. 67-8312 (1965).

LACEY, J. "Somatic response patterning and stress: Some revisions of activation theory." In M. Appley and R. Trumbull, eds., *Psychological Stress*. New York: Appleton-
Century-Crofts, 1967.

LADER, M., and L. WING. "Habituation of the psycho-
galvanic reflex in patients with anxiety states and in
normal subjects." *Journal of Neurology, Neurosurgery,
and Psychiatry*, 27 (1964): 210–18.

LAING, R. D. *The Politics of Experience*. New York: Ballantine Books, 1969.

LANSKY, S., E. GOGGIN, and K. HASSANEIN. "Male child with
cancer the more anxious? Yes and no . . ." Roche Pharma-
ceuticals: *Psychiatric News*, 1975.

LAZARUS, A. A. "Broad-spectrum behavior therapy." *News*

338   *BIBLIOGRAPHY*

letter of the Association for the Advancement of Behavior Therapy, 4 (1969): 5–6.

LAZARUS, R. S., E. M. OPTON, M. S. NOMIKOS, and N. O. RANKIN. "The principle of short-circuiting of threat: Further evidence." *Journal of Personality*, 33 (1965): 622–35.

LAZARUS, R. S., J. C. SPEISMAN, A. M. MORDKOFF, and L. A. DAVIDSON. "A laboratory study of psychological stress produced by a motion picture film." *Psychological Monographs*, 76 (1962): whole no. 553.

LEBOVITS, B. Z., et al. "Prospective and retrospective psychological studies of coronary heart disease." *Psychosom. Med.*, 29 (1967): 265–72.

LEGIER, J. F. "Spontaneous regression of primary bile duct carcinoma." *Cancer*, 17 (1964): 730.

LEIZON, K. "Spontaneous disappearance of bilateral pulmonary metastases: Report of case of adenocarcinoma of kidney after nephrectomy." *J.A.M.A.*, 169 (1959): 1737–1919.

LESHAN, L. "A psychosomatic hypothesis concerning the etiology of Hodgkin's disease." *Psychological Reports*, 3 (1957): 565–75.

————. "Psychological states as factors in the development of malignant disease: A critical review." *Nat. Cancer. Inst. J.*, 22 (1959): 1–18.

————. "A basic psychological orientation apparently associated with malignant disease." *The Psychiatric Qtly.*, 36 (1961): 314–30.

————. "A emotional life-history pattern associated with neoplastic disease." *Ann. N.Y. Acad. Sci.*, 125 (1966): (3) 780–93.

———— and M. GASSMAN. "Some observations on psychotherapy with patients with neoplastic disease." *Am. J. Psychotherapy*, 12 (1958): 723–34.

LESHAN, L. and R. E. WORTHINGTON. "Some psychologic correlates of neoplastic disease: Preliminary report." *J. Clin. & Exper. Psychol.*, 16 (1955): 281–88.

————. "Loss of cathexes as a common psychodynamic characteristic of cancer patients: An attempt at statistical validation of a clinical hypothesis." *Psychol. Rep.*, 2 (1956): 183–93.

————. "Personality as a factor in the pathogenesis of cancer: A review of the literature." *Brit. J. Med. Psychol.*, 29 (1956): 49–56.

————. "Some recurrent life history patterns observed in patients with malignant disease." *J. Nerv. Ment. Dis.*, 124 (1956): 460–65.

LEVI, L. *Stress: Sources, Management and Prevention; Medical and Psychological Aspects of the Stress of Everyday Life.* New York: Liveright, 1967.

————. "Sympatho-adrenomedullary and related reactions during experimentally induced emotional stress." In R. P. Michael, ed., *Endocrinology and Human Behavior.* London: Oxford University Press, 1968, pp. 200–219.

————. *Society, Stress and Disease.* London: Oxford University Press, 1971.

LEVIN, E. J. "Spontaneous regression (cure?) of a malignant tumor of bone." *Cancer*, 10 (1957): 377.

LIEF, A., ed. *The Commonsense Psychiatry of Dr. Adolf Meyer.* New York: McGraw-Hill, 1948.

LINDEMANN, H. *Relieve Tension the Autogenic Way.* New York: Peter H. Wyden, Inc., 1973.

LINDEN, W. "Practicing of meditation by school children and their levels of field independence-dependence, test anxiety, and reading achievement." *Journal of Consulting and Clinical Psychology*, 41 (1973): 139–43.

LLOYD, O. C. "Regression of malignant melanoma as a manifestation of a cellular immunity response." *Proc. Roy. Soc. Med.* 62 (1969): 543–45.

LOVE, W. A., JR. "Problems in therapeutic application of EMG feedback." *Proceedings of the Biofeedback Research Society.* Denver: Biofeedback Research Society, 1972.

————, D. D. MONTGOMERY, and T. A. MOELLER. "A post hoc analysis of correlates of blood pressure reduction."

Proceedings of the Biofeedback Research Society. Denver: Biofeedback Research Society, 1974.

LUCE, G. G. *Body Time.* New York: Bantam Books, 1973.

————. "Muscle and EEG feedback." In J. Segal, ed., *Mental Health Program Reports.* Rockville, Md.: National Institute of Mental Health, 20852 (1973): pp. 109–21.

LUTHE, W. "Method, research and application of autogenic training." *Am. J. Clin. Hypnosis,* 5, No. 1 (1962): 17–23.

————, ed. *Autogenic Training.* New York: Grune and Stratton, 1965.

————, ed. *Autogenic Therapy.* Vols. I & III. New York: Grune and Stratton, 1969.

LYNN, R. *Attention, Arousal and the Orienting Response.* Oxford: Pergamon Press, 1966.

MACKWORTH, J. F. *Vigilance and Habituation.* Baltimore: Penguin, 1970.

MACMILLAN, M. B. "A note on LeShan and Worthington's 'Personality as a factor in the pathogenesis of cancer.'" *Brit. J. Med. Psych.,* 30 (1957): 49.

MAHARISHI MAHESH YOGI. *On the Bhagavad-Gita: A New Translation and Commentary.* Baltimore, Md.: Penguin Books, 1969.

MALMO, R. B. "Studies of anxiety: Some clinical origins of the activation concept." In C. D. Speilberger, ed., *Anxiety and Behavior.* New York: Academic Press, 1966.

———— and SHAGASS, C. "Physiologic study of symptom mechanisms in psychiatric patients under stress." *Psychosomatic Medicine,* 11 (1949): 27–29.

MANNHEIMER, D. I., S. T. DAVIDSON, B. B. BALTER, G. D. MELLINGER, I. H. CISIN, and H. J. PARRY. "Popular attitudes and beliefs about tranquilizers." *Am. J. Psychiatry,* 130 (1973): 1246.

MARGOLIS, J., and D. WEST. "Spontaneous regression of malignant disease: Report of three cases." *J. Am. Geriatrics Society,* 15 (March 1967): 251–53.

MARINACCI, A. A. *Applied Electromyography.* Philadelphia: Lea and Febiger, 1968.

MARTIN, B. *Anxiety and Neurotic Disorders.* New York: Wiley, 1971.

MAWSON, S. R., ADLINGTON, P., and EVANS, M., "A controlled study evaluation of adeno-tonsillectomy in children." *J. of Laryngology and Otolaryngology,* 81: 777–790, 1967.

MCQUADE, W., and A. AIKMAN. *Stress.* New York: E. P. Dutton and Co., 1974.

MEERLOO, J. "Psychological implications of malignant growth: Survey of hypotheses." *Brit. J. Med. Psych.,* 27 (1954): 210–15.

MELLORS, R. C. "Prospects for the biological control of cancer." *Bull. N.Y. Acad. Med.,* 38 (1962): 75.

MERCK SHARP & DOHME COMPANY. *The Hypertension Handbook.* West Point, Pa.: Merck Sharp & Dohme, 1974.

MEYER, R. J., and R. J. HAGGERTY. "Streptococcal infections in families." *Pediatrics,* 29 (1962): 539–49.

MIKURIYA, T. H., K. R. PELLETIER, and A. E. GLADMAN. "Unstable sub-beta EEG with beta tracking failure in psychiatric dysfunction." *Proceedings of the Biofeedback Society of California.* San Diego: Biofeedback Society of California, December 1976.

MILLER, F. R., and H. W. JONES "The possibility of precipitating the leukemic state by emotional factors." *Blood,* 3 (1948): 2880–84.

MILLER, N. E., L. V. DICARA, H. SOLOMON, J. M. WEISS, and B. DWORKIN. "Learned modification of automatic functions: A review and some new data." In T. X. Barber et al., eds., *Biofeedback and Self Control.* Chicago: Aldine-Atherton, 1970.

MILLER, S., N. REMEN, A. BARBOUR, M. A. NAIRLES, S. MILLER and D. CARELL. *Dimensions of Humanistic Medicine.* San Francisco: Institute for the Study of Humanistic Medicine, 1975.

MINC, S. "Psychological factors in coronary heart disease." *Geriatrics,* 20 (1965): 747–55.

MOELLER, T. A., and W. A. LOVE, JR. "A method to reduce

arterial hypertension through muscular relaxation." Paper presented at the Biofeedback Research Society Meeting, Boston, 1972.

MOORMAN, L. T. "Tuberculosis on the Navajo Reservation." *American Review of Tuberculosis*, 61 (1950): 586.

MOOS, R. H., and G. F. SOLOMON. "Psychologic comparisons between women with rheumatoid arthritis and their non-arthritic sisters." *Psychosomatic Medicine*, 2 (1965): 150.

MORRIS, J. N., et al. "Incidence and prediction of ischaemic heart disease in London busmen." *Lancet*, 2 (1966): 553–59.

MOSS, G. E. *Illness, Immunity, and Social Interaction: The Dynamics of Biosocial Resonation.* New York: John Wiley and Sons, 1973.

MUSÉS, C. M., and A. M. YOUNG, eds. *Consciousness and Reality.* New York: Outerbridge and Lazard, 1972.

NARANJO, C., and R. E. ORNSTEIN. *On the Psychology of Meditation.* New York: Viking, 1971.

NELSON, D. H. "Spontaneous regression of cancer." *Brit. Med. J.*, 2 (1960): 670.

NELSON, D. H. "Spontaneous regression of cancer." *Clin. Radiol.*, 13 (1962): 138.

"The nervous factor in the production of cancer." Editorial, *Brit. Med. J.*, 20 (1925): 1139.

NIDICH, S., W. SEEMAN, and T. DRESKIN. "Influence of transcendental meditation: A replication." *J. Counseling Psychology*, 20 (1937): 565–66.

ORMÉ-JOHNSON, D. W. "Autonomic stability and transcendental meditation." *Psychosomatic Medicine*, 35 (1973): 341–49.

OTIS, L. S. "The facts on transcendental meditation: If well-integrated but anxious, try TM." *Psychology Today*, 7 (1974): 45–46.

PARKER, W. *Cancer: A study of ninety-seven cases of cancer of the female breast.* New York, 1885.

PATEL, C. H. "Yoga and biofeedback in the management of hypertension." *Lancet* (November 10, 1973).

———— and K. K. DATEY. "Yoga and biofeedback in the management of hypertension: Two control studies." *Proceedings of The Biofeedback Research Society.* Monterey, Calif., 1975.

PAUL, G. L. "Physiological effects of relaxation training and hypnotic suggestion." *Journal of Abnormal Psychology,* 74, No. 4 (1969): 425–37.

PAYKEL, E. S., J. K. MYERS, M. N. DIENALT, G. L. KLERMAN, J. J. LINDENTHAL, and M. P. PEPPER. "Life events and depression." *Archives of General Psychiatry,* 21 (1969): 753–60.

PEARSON, H. E. S., and J. JOSEPH. "Stress and occlusive coronary-artery disease." *Lancet,* 1 (1963): 415–18.

PELLETIER, K. R. "Altered attention deployment in meditation." In D. Kanellakos and J. Lucas, eds., *The Psychobiology of Transcendental Meditation.* Reading, Mass.: W. A. Benjamin Press, 1974.

————. "Influence of transcendental meditation upon autokinetic perception." *Journal of Perceptual and Motor Skills,* 39 (1974): 1031–34.

————. "Neurological, psychophysiological, and clinical differentiation of the alpha and theta altered states of consciousness." *Dissertation Abstracts International,* 1974, 35/1, 74–14, 806.

————. "Neurological, psychophysiological, and clinical parameters of alpha, theta, and the voluntary control of bleeding and pain." *Proceedings of the Biofeedback Research Society.* Denver: Biofeedback Research Society, 1974.

————. "Psychophysiological parameters of the voluntary control of blood flow and pain." In D. Kanellakos and J. Lukas, eds., *The Psychobiology of Transcendental Meditation.* Reading, Mass.: W. A. Benjamin, 1974.

————. "Diagnosis, procedure, and phenomenology of clinical biofeedback." *Proceedings of the Biofeedback Research Society*. Denver: Biofeedback Research Society, 1975.

————. "Diagnostic and treatment protocols for clinical biofeedback." *Journal of Biofeedback*, 2, No. 4 (Fall/Winter 1975)

————. "I shall feel no pain and bleed no blood." In P. G. Zimbardo and F. L. Ruch, eds., *Psychology and Life*. Glenview, Ill.: Scott, Foresman, 1975.

————. "Mind as healer, mind as slayer." *Lifelong Learning*. Berkeley: University of California, 45 (August 6, 1975) No. 11.

————. "Neurological substrates of consciousness." *Journal of Altered States of Consciousness*, 2 (1975) No. 1.

————. "Theory and applications of clinical biofeedback." *Journal of Contemporary Psychotherapy*, 7 (1975) No. 1.

————. "Applications of meditative exercises in enhancing clinical biofeedback outcome." *Proceedings of the Biofeedback Research Society*. Denver: Biofeedback Research Society, 1976.

————. "Holistic applications of clinical biofeedback and meditation." *Journal of Holistic Health*, 1 (1976).

————. "Increased perceptual acuity following transcendental meditation." In L. Domash, J. Farrow, and D. Ormé-Johnson, eds., *Scientific Research on Transcendental Meditation: Collected Papers*. Los Angeles: Maharishi International University Press, 1976.

————. "What to tell your patients when they ask about biofeedback." *Extension Division Catalog*, University of California School of Medicine, Los Angeles, 1976.

————. *Toward a Science of Consciousness*. New York: Random House. In preparation, 1977.

———— and C. GARFIELD. *Consciousness: East and West*. New York: Harper & Row, 1976.

PELLETIER, K. R., A. E. GLADMAN, and T. H. MIKURIYA.

"Clinical protocols: Professional group specializing in psychosomatic medicine." *Handbook of Physiological Feedback.* Berkeley: Autogenic Systems, Inc., 1976.

PELLETIER, K. R., and E. PEPER. "The chutzpah factor in psychophysiological parameters of altered states of consciousness." *Proceedings of the Biofeedback Research Society.* Denver: Biofeedback Research Society, 1974.

————. "The chutzpah factor altered states of consciousness." *Journal of Humanistic Psychology,* 17 (1977) No. 1.

————. "Developing a biofeedback model: Alpha EEG feedback as a means for pain control." *Biofeedback and Self Regulation.* In press, 1977.

PELNER, L. "Host-tumor antagonism. 111. Prolonged survival of certain patients with cancer. Fortuitous occurrence or immunity mechanism." *J. Amer. Geriat. Soc.,* 4 (1956): 1126.

PENDERGRASS, E. Presidential Address to the American Cancer Society Meeting, 1959.

PEPER, E. "Reduction of efferent motor commands during alpha feedback as a facilitator of EEG alpha and a precondition for changes in consciousness." *Kybernetik,* 9, No. 6 (1971): 226–31.

————. "Biofeedback as a core technique in clinical therapies." Paper presented at the Biofeedback Research Society Meeting, Boston, 1972.

————. "Biofeedback as a core technique in clinical therapies." Paper presented at the 81st Annual Convention of the American Psychological Association, Montreal, 1973.

————. "Applications of biofeedback to reduce stress and for preventive health." Paper presented at the 82nd Annual Convention of the American Psychological Association, New Orleans, 1974.

PERLS, F. S. *Gestalt Therapy Verbatim.* Lafayette: Real People Press, 1969.

PERRY, J. W. "Reconstitutive process in the psychopathology of the self." *Ann. N.Y. Acad. Sci.,* 96 (1962): 853–76.

PICKERING, T. "Yoga and Bio-Feedback in Hypertension." *Lancet,* December, 1973 (letter).

PITTS, F. N., JR., and J. N. MCCLURE, JR., "Lactate metabolism in anxiety neurosis." *New Eng. J. Med.,* 277 (1967): 1329–34.

RAHE, R. H. "Life crisis and health change." In *Psychotropic Drug Response: Advance in Prediction.* Springfield, Ill.: Charles C. Thomas, 1969.

————. "Life-change measurement as a predictor of illness." *Proceedings of the Royal Society of Medicine,* 61 (1973): 1124–26.

————, et al. "Social stress and illness onset." *J. Psychosom Res.,* 8 (1964): 35–44.

RAHE, R. H., and M. ROMO. "Recent life changes and the onset of myocardial infarction and coronary death in Helsinki." In E.K.E. Gunderson and R. H. Rahe, eds., *Life Stress and Illness.* Springfield, Ill.: Charles C. Thomas, 1974, pp. 105–20.

RAKSTIS, T. J. "Helping cancer victims come back." *Today's Health,* 46 (1968): 40–41.

RASHKIS, H. A. "Systemic stress as an inhibitor of experimental tumors in Swiss mice." *Science,* 116 (1952): 169–71.

RAY, B. S. "Discussion of Everson, T. C. and Cole, W. H.: Spontaneous regression of cancer." *Ann. Surg.,* 144 (1956): 366–83.

REMEN, N. *The Masculine Principle, the Feminine Principle, and Humanistic Medicine.* San Francisco: Institute for the Study of Humanistic Medicine, 1975.

RICHARDS, V. "On the nature of cancer: An analysis from concepts in current research." *Oncology,* 21 (1967): 161–88.

RILEY, V. "Mouse mammary tumors: Alteration of incidence as apparent function of stress." *Science,* 189 (1975): 465–67.

ROBBINS, L. C. *How to Practice Prospective Medicine.* Indianapolis: Methodist Hospital, 1970.

ROSENMAN, R. H., R. J. BRAND, C. D. JENKINS, M. FRIED-
MAN, R. STRAUSS, M. WORM. "Coronary heart disease in
the western collaborative group study: A follow-up experience of 4½ years." *Journal of Chronic Diseases*, 23
(1970): 173–90.

———. "Coronary heart disease in the western collaborative group study: final follow-up experience of 8½ years."
J.A.M.A., 8 (1975): 233.

ROXBURGH, D. "Spontaneous regression of cancer." *Brit.
Med. J.*, 1 (1935): 39.

RUSSEK, H. I. "Stress, tobacco, and coronary heart disease
in North American professional groups." *J.A.M.A.*, 192
(1965): 189–94.

SACKS, O. W. *Migraine.* Berkeley: University of California
Press, 1970.

SALES, S. M. "Differences among individuals in affective, behavioral, biochemical and physiological responses to variations in workload." University of Michigan Ph.D dissertation. University Microfilms No. 69-18098, 1969.

——— and HOUSE, J. "Job dissatisfaction as a possible risk
factor in coronary heart disease." *Journal of Chronic Diseases*, 23 (1971): 867–73.

SARGENT, J. D., E. E. GREEN, and E. D. WALTERS. "Preliminary report on the use of autogenic feedback techniques
in the treatment of migraine and tension headaches." *Psychosomatic Medicine*, 35, No. 3 (1973): 129–35.

SCHACTER, S. "The interaction of cognitive and physiological
determinants of emotional states." In L. Berkowitz, ed.,
Advances in Experimental Social Psychology. Vol. I. New
York: Academic Press, 1964.

SCHEFLEN, A. E. "Malignant tumors in the institutionalized psychotic population." *Arch. Neurol. Psychiat.*, 64
(1951): 145–55.

SCHILDKRAUT, J. J., and S. S. KETY. "Biogenic amines and
emotion." *Science*, 156 (1967): 21–30.

SCHMALE, A. H., JR., and G. L. ENGEL. "The giving up–given

up complex illustrated on film." *Arch. Gen. Psychiat.*, 17 (1967): 135–45.

SCHOFIELD, J. E. "Teratoma of testis: Spontaneous disappearance of lung metastases." *Brit. Med. J.*, 1 (1947): 411.

SCHULTZ, J. *Das autogene training.* Stuttgart: Geerg-Thieme Verlag, 1953.

SCHULTZ, J., and W. LUTHE. *Autogenic Training: A Psychophysiologic Approach in Psychotherapy.* New York: Grune and Stratton, 1959.

SCHWARTZ, G. E. "Biofeedback as therapy: Some theoretical and practical issues." Paper delivered to the third annual Brockton Symposium on Behavior Therapy, April 1972.

———. "Pros and cons of meditation: Anxiety, self-control, drug abuse, and creativity." Paper delivered at the 81st annual convention of the American Psychological Association, Montreal, 1973.

——— and D. J. GOLEMAN. "Meditation as an alternative to drug use: Accompanying personality changes." Unpublished paper, 1976.

SCOTT, J. B. "Spontaneous regression of cancer." *Brit. Med. J.*, 1 (1935): 230.

"Seeking Cancer Cures." *Newsweek*, 76 (August 31, 1970): 48.

SEGUIN, C. A. "Migration and psychosomatic disadaptation." *Journal of Psychosomatic Medicine*, 18 (1956): 404–409.

SELIGMAN, A. M. "A review of Everson, Tilden, Cole, Waner: Spontaneous regression of cancer: A study and abstracts of reports in the world medical literature and of personal communications concerning spontaneous regression of malignant disease." *J.A.M.A.*, 198 (1966): 680.

SELYE, H. *The Physiology and Pathology of Exposure to Stress.* Montreal: Acta, 1950.

———. *The Stress of Life.* New York: McGraw-Hill, 1956.

————. *Stress Without Distress*. Philadelphia and New York: J. P. Lippincott, 1974.

SHAPIRO, D., and G. E. SCHWARTZ. "Biofeedback and visceral learning: Clinical applications." *Seminars in Psychiatry*, 4 (1972): 171–84.

SHAPIRO, D., B. TURSKY., E. GERSON, and M. STERN. "Effects of feedback and reinforcement on the control of human systolic blood pressure." *Science*, 163 (1969): 588.

SHAPIRO, D., B. TURSKY, and G. E. SCHWARTZ. "Differentiation of heart rate and systolic blood pressure in man by operant conditioning." In T. X. Barber et al., eds., *Biofeedback and Self Control*. Chicago: Aldine-Atherton, 1970.

SHAPIRO, S. I. "Spontaneous regression of cancer." *Eye ear nose throat monthly*, 46 (October 1967): 1306–10.

SHASTA ABBEY. *Zen Meditation*. Mount Shasta, California: Shasta Abbey publications.

SHEVRIN, H. "Brain wave correlates of subliminal stimulation, unconscious attention, primary- and secondary-process thinking, and repressiveness." *Psychological Issues*, 8, No. 2, Mono 30 (1973): 56–87.

SHIMKIN, M. B. "Duration of life in untreated cancer." *Cancer*, 4 (1951): 1.

————, M. H. GRISWOLD, and S. J. CUTLER. "Survival in untreated and treated cancer." *Ann. Intern. Med.*, 45 (1956) 255–67.

SHRIFTE, M. "Toward identification of a positive variable in host resistance to cancer." *Psychosom. Med.*, 24 (1962): 390.

SIMEONS, A.T.W. *Man's Presumptuous Brain: An Evolutionary Interpretation of Psychosomatic Disease*. New York: Dutton and Co., 1961.

SIMMONS, L. W. "The relation between the decline of anxiety reducing and anxiety resolving factors in a deteriorating culture and its relevance to bodily disease." *Proc. Ass. Res. Neuro, Ment. Dis.*, 29 (1950): 127.

SIMONTON, O. C., and S. SIMONTON. "Belief systems and

management of the emotional aspects of malignancy."
Journal of Transpersonal Psychology, 7, No. 1 (1975):
29–48.

SLOANE, R. B. "Some behavioral and other correlates of
cholesterol metabolism." *Journal of Psychosomatic Research*, 5 (1961): 183–90.

SOLOMON, G. F. "Emotions, stress, the central nervous system, and immunity." *Ann. N.Y. Acad. Sci.*, 164, No. 2
(1969): 335–43.

————, A. A. AMKRAUT, and P. KASPER. "Immunity, emotions and stress (with special reference to the mechanisms of stress effects on the immune system)." *Psychotherapy and Psychosomatics*, 23 (1974): 209–217.

SPITZER, W. O., A. R. FEINSTEIN, and D. L. SACKETT. "What
is a health care trial?" *J.A.M.A.*, 233, No. 2 (July 14,
1975): 161–63.

"Spontaneous regression of cancer." Editorial, *Brit. Med. J.*,
2 (1962): 1245.

STEIN, J. "Meditation, habituation, and distractability." Unpublished undergraduate honors thesis, Harvard University, 1973.

STEIN, M., R. C. SCHIAVI, and M. CAMERINO. "Influence of
brain and behavior on the immune system." *Science*, 191
(February 6, 1976): 435–40.

STEPHENSON, H. I., and W. J. GRACE. "Life stress and cancer
of the cervix." *Psychosom. Med.*, 16 (1954): 287–94.

STERMAN, M. B. "Neurophysiological and clinical studies of
sensorimotor EEG biofeedback training: Some effects on
epilepsy." In L. Birk, ed., *Seminars in Psychiatry*. New
York: Grune and Stratton, 1974, Vol. 5 (4), pp. 507–25.

————. "Clinical implications of EEG biofeedback training: A critical appraisal." In G. E. Schwartz and J. Beatty,
eds., *Biofeedback: Theory and Research*. New York: Academic Press, 1975, Chapter 18.

————, L. R. MACDONALD, and R. K. STONE. "Biofeedback
training of the sensorimotor electroencephalogram

rhythm in man: Effects on epilepsy." *Epilepsia,* 15 (1974): 395–416.

STERN, J. A., W. SURPHLIS, and E. KOFF. "Electrodermal responsiveness as related to psychiatric diagnosis and prognosis." *Psychophysiology,* 2 (1965): 61–66.

STERNBACH, R. A. *Principles of Psychophysiology.* New York: Academic Press, 1966.

STEWART, F. W. "Experiences in spontaneous regression of neoplastic disease in man." *Texas Rep. Biol. Med.,* 10 (1952): 239.

STONE, H. B., R. M. CURTIS, and J. H. BREWER. "Can resistance to cancer be induced?" *Ann. Surg.,* 134 (1951): 519–28.

STONE, H. B., and L. SCHNAUFER. "Attempts to induce resistance to cancer." *Ann. Surg.,* 141 (1955): 329.

STOUT, C., J. MORROW, E. BRANDT, and S. WOLF. "Unusually low incidence of death from myocardial infarction: Study of an Italian American community in Pennsylvania." *J.A.M.A.,* 188 (1964): 845–49.

STOYVA, J., and T. BUDZYNSKI. "Cultivated low arousal—an antistress response?" In L. V. DiCara, ed., *Recent Advances in Limbic and Autonomic Nervous System Research.* New York: Plenum, 1973.

STROEBEL, C. Personal communication to author. Institute of Living, Hartford, Connecticut, 1975.

SUMNER, W. C., and A. G. FORAKER. "Spontaneous regression of human melanoma: Clinical and experimental studies." *Cancer,* 13 (1960): 79–81.

TARLAU, M., and I. SMALHEISER. "Personality patterns in patients with malignant tumors of the breast and cervix: Exploratory study." *Psychosom. Med.,* 13 (1951): 117–21.

THEORELL, T., and R. H. RAHE. "Behavior prior to myocardial infarction." In T. Theorell, ed., *Psychological Factors in Relation to the Onset of Myocardial Infarction and to Some Metabolic Variables: A Pilot Study.* Stockholm: Karolinska Institute, 1970.

THOMAS, C. B., and K. R. DUSZYNSKI. "Closeness to parents and the family constellation in a prospective study of five disease states: Suicide, mental illness, malignant tumor, hypertension and coronary heart disease." *The Johns Hopkins Medical Journal*, 134, No. 5 (May 1974): 251–70.

THOMAS, C. B., and E. A. MURPHY. "Further studies on cholesterol levels in the Johns Hopkins medical students: The effect of stress at examinations." *Journal of Chronic Diseases*, 8 (1958): 661–68.

TINBERGEN, N. "Etiology and stress diseases." *Science*, 185 (1974): 26.

TOOMIN, M. K., and H. TOOMIN. *GSR Biofeedback in Psychotherapy: Some Clinical Observations*. Los Angeles: Biofeedback Research Institute, 1973.

TRAVIS, JOHN W. "Wellness Inventory." Wellness Center, Mill Valley, California, 1975.

TSUJI, K., S. ASHIZAWA, H. SASA, et al. "Clinical and statistical observations on spontaneous regression of cancer." *Jap. J. Cancer Clin.*, 15 (1969): 729–33.

TUKE, DANIEL HACK. *Illustrations of the Influence of the Mind upon the Body in Health and Disease Designed to Elucidate the Action of the Imagination*. 2nd ed. London: J. and A. Churchill, 1884.

U.S. Government Printing Office. *The Framingham Study: An Epidemiological Investigation of Cardiovascular Disease*. Washington, D.C.: U.S. Government Printing Office, Section 10, September, 1968.

VACHON, L. Cited in "Biofeedback in Action." *Medical World News*, March 9, 1973.

VAN DER VALK, J. M., and J. J. GROEN. "Personality structure and conflict situation in patients with myocardial infarction." *Journal of Psychosomatic Research*, 11 (1967): 41–46.

WALLACE, R. K. "Physiological effects of transcendental meditation." *Science*, 167 (1970): 1751–54.

———— and H. BENSON. "The physiology of meditation." *Scientific American,* 226 (1972): 84–90.

———— and A. F. WILSON. "A wakeful hypometabolic state." *Amer. J. Physiology,* 221 (1971): 795–99.

———— and M. D. GARRETT. "Decreased blood lactate during transcendental meditation." *Federation Proceedings,* 30 (1971): 376.

WEIL, A. *The Natural Mind.* Boston: Houghton Mifflin, 1973.

WEISS, E., et al. "Emotional factors in coronary occlusion. *Archives of Internal Medicine,* 99 (1957): 628–641.

WEISS, T., and B. T. ENGEL. "Operant conditioning of heart rate in patients with premature ventricular contractions." *Psychosomatic Medicine,* 33, No. 4 (1971): 301–22.

WERTLAKE, P. T., et al. "Relationship of mental and emotional stress to serum cholesterol levels." *Proceedings of the Society for Experimental Biology and Medicine,* 97 (1958): 163–65.

WEST, P. M. "Origin and development of the psychological approach to the cancer problem." In J. A. Gengerelli and F. J. Kirkner, eds., *The Psychological Variables in Human Cancer.* Berkeley: University of California Press, 1954.

————, E. M. BLUMBERG, and F. W. ELLIS. "An observed correlation between psychological factors and growth rate of cancer in man." *Cancer Res.,* 12 (1952): 306–307.

WEYER, E. M., and H. HUTCHINS, eds. *Psychophysiological Aspects of Cancer.* New York: New York Academy of Sciences, 1966.

WHATMORE, G. B., and D. R. KOHLI. "Dysponesis: A neurophysiologic factor in functional disorders." *Behavioral Science,* 13, No. 1 (1968): 102–24.

WHEATLEY, D. "Evaluation of psychotropic drugs in general practice." *Proceedings of the Royal Society of Medicine,* 65 (1972): 317.

WHEELER, J. I., JR., and B. M. CALDWELL. "Psychological evaluation of women with cancer of the breast and of the cervix." *Psychosom. Med.,* 17 (1955): 256–68.

WICKRAMASKERA, I. "Effects of EMG feedback training on susceptibility to hypnosis: Preliminary observations." *Proceedings of the American Psychological Association* (1971): 783–84.

WILLIAMS, M. "Psychophysiological responsiveness to psychological stress in early schizophrenic reaction." *Psychosom. Med.*, 15 (1953): 456–63.

WOLF, S. *The Stomach.* New York: Oxford University Press, 1965.

WOLFF, HAROLD G. "Changes in vulnerability of tissue: An aspect of man's response to threat." *The National Institute of Health Annual Lectures*, U.S. Dept. of Health, Education and Welfare, Publication No. 388, 1953, pp. 38–71.

———. *Headache and Other Head Pain.* New York: Oxford University Press, 1963.

———. *Stress and Disease.* 2nd ed. Revised and edited by Stewart Wolf and Helen Goodell. Springfield, Ill.: Charles C. Thomas, 1968.

WOLPE, J. *Psychotherapy by Reciprocal Inhibition.* Stanford, Calif.: Stanford of University Press, 1958.

——— and A. A. LAZARUS. *Behavior Therapy Techniques.* New York: Permagon Press, 1966.

YOUNG, ARTHUR M. *The Reflexive Universe.* New York: Delacorte Press, 1976.

Zen Meditation. Mount Shasta, Calif.: Shasta Abbey, n.d.

ZIMBARDO, P. G. *The Cognitive Control of Motivation.* Glenview, Ill.: Scott, Foresman, 1969.

———. "The human choice: Reason and order versus impulse and chaos." *Nebraska Symposium on Motivation*, March, 1969.

Index

THE AUTHOR

KENNETH R. PELLETIER, Ph.D. is an Assistant Clinical Professor at the Langley Porter Neuropsychiatric Institute and the Department of Psychiatry, University of California School of Medicine, San Francisco. He is Director of the Psychosomatic Medicine Center of Gladman Memorial Hospital, Berkeley, and a clinical psychologist in private practice. During graduate school at the University of California, Berkeley, he was a Woodrow Wilson Fellow, studied at the C. G. Jung Institute in Zurich, Switzerland, and became Director of the Institute for the Study of Consciousness, Berkeley. He has published numerous articles on clinical biofeedback, psychosomatic medicine, and altered-states research. Dr. Pelletier is the co-author of *Consciousness: East and West*.